ACTA UNIVERSITATIS UPSALIENSIS
Studia Doctrinae Christianae Upsaliensia
20

Ingemar Holmstrand

Karl Heim on Philosophy, Science and the Transcendence of God

UPPSALA 1980

Distributed by
Almqvist & Wiksell International,
Stockholm — Sweden

Doctoral dissertation at Uppsala University 1980

© Ingemar Holmstrand 1980

Holmstrand, I.: Karl Heim on Philosophy, science and the Transcendence of God. *Studia Doctrinae Christianae Upsaliensia* 20, 177 pp.
ISBN 91—554—1026—X, ISSN 0585—508X.

Abstract
This dissertation is an investigation of the doctrine of the transcendence of God in the thought of the German protestant theologian Karl Heim (1874—1958). The investigation is set out as follows: In chapter 1, after a short biographical account, we give some remarks on the place of Heim within contemporary theological debate and a brief summary of his theory. Chapter 2 presents some analytical concepts, of which the main ones are those of "total view of reality" and of "basic assumption". A basic assumption, i.e. a rule for ordering facts, can e.g. be a metaphysical belief, a scientific theory or a religious belief, and which determines a total view of reality. Chapter 3 deals with some criteria for an acceptable total view of reality, according to Heim, in terms of basic assumptions. These concern philosophical theories (e.g. the law of polarity), considerations on basic concepts within scientific theory (e.g. on the notions of time and space and causality and determinism) and an interpretation of human existence against the background of philosophy and science. Chapter 4 presents some main definitions of the concept of transcendence/transcendent in order to describe Heim's treatment of the problem of the transcendence of God. Chapter 5 presents Heim's solution of this problem as developed by means of the concept of "space", based on the notion of basic assumption. The chapter concludes with some remarks on Heim's view on the relation between polar and supra-polar space (the latter signifying the metaphysical transcendence of God). Chapter 6, finally, mentions some similarities between Heim's approach to religion and recent discussions of religion, exemplified by Kuhn's theory of paradigm, as applied to religion, and Torrance's theory of multilevelled knowledge. The investigation concludes with some remarks on the role of nonobjectifiable space within Heim's theory and by a discussion whether Heim can be called a theological rationalist or not.

I Holmstrand, Faculty of Theology,Box 2006 S-750 02 Uppsala, SWEDEN

Printed in Sweden by
LiberTryck, Stockholm 1980   053934

Contents

I wish to thank Professor Anders Jeffner and Professor Urban Forell for their advice and encouragement during different stages of the present work. In addition, I am grateful to the Higher Seminar for Theological and Ideological Studies for providing the stimulus of constructive criticism.

Most of all I wish to thank my wife Catharina for her constant support and interest, which has been invaluable.

Uppsala in April, 1980

Ingemar Holmstrand

"Ich sehe niemand, der das Grenzgebiet zwischen Philosophie, Naturwissenschaft und Christentum mit Ernst in Angriff nähme und zugleich Fühlung genug mit der lebendigen Gemeinde hätte".*

Karl Heim

Chapter 1

Introduction

1.1. Biographical remarks

The German Protestant theologian Karl Heim—whose doctrine on the transcendence of God is the main subject of this investigation—was born in Frauenzimmern on the twentieth of January, 1874. He received his first theological education at the famous seminary Tübinger Stift. After being ordained in 1897 he was for a time minister in a little town, Giengen, and then chaplain at a teachers seminary. In 1899 he was offered an appointment as secretary in "Deutsche Christliche Studentvereinigung", a task which he after some hesitation accepted. As a delegate for DCSV he visited Paris in 1900. Afterwards he was employed as principal for a seminary for candidates for holy orders at Halle a.d. Saale. This allowed him to denote himself to his writing. In 1914 he was called to the professorship in dogmatics at the newly founded protestant theological faculty at Münster. However, his activity there became rather slight: During the first World War he was chaplain at a camp for wounded soldiers in Denmark. In 1920 he was appointed to the professorship at the university in his native province in Tübingen. He remained there until his retirement in 1939. During this period his main works were published; in 1923 "Glaubensgewissheit" (3rd ed.) and "Der evangelische Glaube und das Denken der Gegenwart", 1931f. It was then that he also made three longer journeys: In 1922 he went to Peking as a delegate at the congress of Christian Students World convent.[1] During this journey he became acquainted with the native religions, especially Zenbuddhism. He returned via Japan and USA. In 1928 he visited Jerusalem during the congress of International Mission Council. Finally in 1933 he made a journey to the USA to give a series of lectures. It was during this journey that he met Einstein.[2] Heim was a strong critic of Nazism. He published a brochure against the "Deutsche Christen" and the Aryan-paragraph, his sermons were banned from publication and he was warned for his out-spoken lectures. In spite of this, one get a general impression that he tried to avoid an open conflict with the Nazi authorities.[3] He sympathized during this period with the Confessional Church, but he never joined it on the grounds that his own spiritual background was too different. He was also very critical to the Barthian theology, which dominated the Confessional Church. On the other hand, he was a German patriot. Thus, e.g. in 1937 he declined an invitation from Princeton to be a member of an international scientific institute together with i.a. Einstein. His argument was that he was convinced that he ought to stay in Germany during its hard circumstances. He retired in 1939 and died on 30th August 1958.

1.2. On the literature on Heim

The literature on Heim cannot be said to be very great. There are a few monographs and a number of shorter presentations and reviews of his main books. We shall mention the most important of them here. In the first place, there are two minor papers from the twenties and thirties: *Ruttenbeck*, Die apologetisch-theologische Methode Karl Heims, 1925, and *Eisenhuth*, Das Problem der Glaubensgewissheit bei Karl Heim, 1925. These papers are probably the best presentations of Heim's thinking from that period. Ruttenbeck presents the development of Heim's view on Christian apologetics in his early writings, and Eisenhuth gives a very detailed analysis of the problem of certainty in religious belief. This later problem is also treated by *Schott* in the paper Das Problem der Glaubensgewissheit, 1931. These papers correctly present Heim's thinking, but since their authors are inclined to share Heim's general philosophical assumptions, their criticism is peripheral rather than fundamental. This is to some extent also true of *Cullberg's* brief presentation in Das Du und die Wirklichkeit, 1931. But it should also be mentioned that Schott gives a confessionally determined criticism from the theology of Luther. However, the most interesting criticism of Heim from this period can be found in *Bonhoeffer's* review article on GD, 1932, and in the articles of *Traub*, Erkenntnistheoretische Fragen zu Karl Heims Glaube und Denken, 1933 and Die neue Fassung von Karl Heims Glaube und Denken, 1934. Apart from these, there are also some brief presentations as *Thust*, Das Perspektivische Weltbild Karl Heims, 1925, *Adam*, Heim und das Wesen der Katholizismus, 1936 and *Vollrath*, Zum Verständnis der Theologie Karl Heims, 1920 and Religionsphilosophie und Gewissenstheologie, 1921. Of the more recent literature on Heim there is first of all the presentation in *Schwarz*, Das Verständnis des Wunders bei Heim und Bultmann, 1966. Perhaps this is the best presentation of those which seek to give a brief and clear account. Interesting, and sometimes also critical remarks on different parts of Heim's thinking can be found in e.g. *Michalson*, The Task of Apologetics in the Future, 1953, *Barbour*, Karl Heim on Christian Faith and natural Science, 1956, *Holmer*, Karl Heim and the Sacrifice of Intellect, 1954 and *Forell*, Gud och rummet, 1964. A more comprehensive and basic criticism can be found in *Schneider*, Erkenntnistheorie and Theologie, 1951. In *Timm*, Glaube und Naturwissenschaft in der Theologie Karl Heims, 1968, which is partly biographical, a good account of the background of Heim's thinking is given, but the analysis of the central theme is not very detailed. Finally, the little book by *Allen*, Jesus our Leader, 1949, should also to be mentioned. Recently a biography has appeared, *Köberle*, Karl Heim, Leben und Denken, 1979.

8

1.3 Heim's background and its influence on his ideas

Heim's background in Württemberg Pietism. As a theologian Heim has to be understood against the background of that South German spiritual tradition, which used to be called Württemberg Pietism.[1] It is obvious that this tradition had a decisive influence on his theological thinking.[2] Heim himself, whose family was deeply imbued with its spirit, was quite aware of this dependence, and he always expressed his thankfulness to it and his intention to remain a good representative of it.[3] This spiritual tradition contains at least two strands, which are of interest here. It contains a biblical line, presented inter alia by J A Bengel (1687–1752), M F Roos (1727–1803) and J T Beck (1804–1878) and a theosophic-speculative line represented by Fr Chr Oetinger (1702–1782) and Ph M Hahn (1758–1819), the latter dependent on Böhme.[4] They can also be found in the thinking of Heim, and it was his desire to join them.[5] Now, an important feature in the biblical version of Württemberg Pietism is that the only basic concepts which are necessary and permitted in theology, are the biblical ones. The proper task of theology then is to develop and interpret those basic concepts.[6] There is a similar idea in Heim: one of the most important tasks of theology is to construct basic philosophical concepts which can fit the New Testament's belief in Christ.[7] Furthermore, when reading Heim, e.g. JH, JW or WB one gets an impression of an almost classic piece of biblical theology. And in the speculative variant of the Württemberg Pietism it is an important feature to express a coherent and total view of reality[8]—a view that also says that the reality is essentially dynamic.[9] These features are important for Heim: A total view of reality should be coherent and it should also be possible to summarize it in an "Weltformel" or an ultimate "Urdatum".[10] And that reality is essentially dynamic can easily be demonstrated.[11]

Other influences. It is hard to say what other factors besides Württemberg Pietism have influenced Heim. But men such as Hudson Taylor, Elias Schrenk and John Mott, whom the young Heim met, had surely an importance for stimulating Heim's interest in questions concerning mission and evangelisation.[12] There are many papers of Heim dealing with these questions.[13] Perhaps one also ought to mention the general influence from the work in DCSV. DCSV had a methodistic colour at that time.[14]

On Heim's position within contemporary theological debate. Of course Heim took part in the contemporary theological debate, but he seemed not to have been greatly influenced by contemporary theologians. Much more important in his development were such philosophers as Spengler, Buber, Heidegger and Rickert[15] and scientists such as Einstein and Driesch.[16] However, since we are not principally concerned with the origins of Heim's thought we shall not discuss this matter in more detail.

Now, Heim seems to have occupied a rather isolated position in the contemporary debate.[17] He was commonly seen as an outsider, although respected for his honesty, originality and profoundity. The reason for this is mainly his program for the theology. And he was rather alone in this position. We shall illustrate this with a brief sketch of Heim's criticism of two very important matters: the dialectical theology during the twenties and thirties, and the demythologization program during the fourties and fifities.

Heim and dialectical theology. There are some features in Heim's theology, which link him with the dialectical theology.[18] His reaction against liberal theology and against a theory of religion based on Schleiermacher and Ritschl is such a feature. Both for theological[19] and personal reasons[20] he rejects such an interpretation of Christianity. Another similarity is that the majesty and absolute transcendence of God are very strongly accentuated.[21] Every analogy between the absolute transcendent God and creation is invalid,[22] and there is no path from creature to God[23] except through the revelation in Christ.

However, Heim sets himself apart from dialectical theology, and his criticism can be summed up in the following points:

1. A consequence of the dialectical interpretation of religion is that a great part of human culture and knowledge falls outside theology, in the respect that e.g. philosophy and science become irrelevant and uninteresting for theology, save as expressions for man's alienation from God. This consequence Heim judges as dangerous for Christian theology and faith. It brings about, at least in the long run, the intellectual and cultural isolation of theology. Theology should not be built on its own presuppositions and verification only. On the contrary, it is its duty to continue a dialogue with philosophy and science and to deal also with the questions arising in these disciplines.[24] If theology does not do so, it will become exposed to the wellfounded suspision that it is not fully convinced of the truth of its own confession and faith.

2. Dialectical theology cannot satisfy the needs of the Christian practise.[25] A believer, who has to decide between different courses of action, can, according to Heim, if the dialectical theological presuppositions are correct, not know with complete certainty, which alternative is God's will, and thus could be chosen with total commitment. And according to Heim, it is a necessary condition for an acceptable religious belief that there is, or at least can be, such a certainty.[26] But the insistence of dialectical theology on the infinite distance and the qualitative difference between God and man has no room for the thought of a direct guidance by the Holy Ghost.[27] Therefore, according to Heim the christology of Barth falls outside the dialectical scheme. Heim on his side tries to develop a theory about the transcendence of God that does not come into a conflict with the religious demand for direct guidance. Dialectical theology then, does not satisfy the last of the criteria for an acceptable religious belief.[28]

Neither can the insistance of dialectical theology on dogmatics as an activity of the church satisfy the needs of Christian practice, if the demand for authority cannot be justified in a way that can convince unbelievers. But dialectal theology does not try to do this.[29] On the contrary, it is one of its features not to do so.

3. The third criticism of the dialectical theology is a historical criticism. This criticism is somewhat astonishing. Heim says that the dialectical theology has not freed itself from the tradition of Schleiermacher and Ritschl.[30] He maintains on the contrary that there is a continous development from Schleiermacher via Ritschl, Harnack and Herrmann to Barth and Bultmann. The very point of this approach is that the sharp separation of dialectical theology between time and eternity after all is a continuation of the platonic-idealistic distinction between an eternal flow of time and an immutable eternity.[31] The consequence then becomes a platonizing of the biblical message.[32] The biblical dualism, then, is between this aion and the coming one. Barth on the other hand accuses Heim of wanting to create new kind of natural theology. Perhaps he has in mind on Heim's intention of justifying some important features in a religious belief. But Heim himself says that he does not want to reconstruct a traditional natural theology or to construct new proofs for a religious belief.[33] And he clearly rejects an interpretation of his thoughts, which maintains that he is a representative for a traditional apologetic. We shall return to Heim's apologetics below. But his own opinion on this question is quite clear: "We must nevermore fall back into a natural theology".[34] However, the question remains if nevertheless Barth's criticism is justified at least to some extent. We shall make some remarks about this in the concluding chapter.[35]

Heim and the question of the demythologization of the biblical message. We shall also pay some attention to Heim's position on the question of demythologising of the biblical message. It should be mentioned at once that Heim was a critic of that program. Köberle says about Heim that "Er hat sehr gelitten unter Bultmann".[36] But at a very general level, there are some similarities between them. They both realized that there was some apparent problems in the confrontation of Christian belief and message with modern man and his view of the world. They saw that this view of the world and modern man's interpretation of life was deeply and irrevocably shaped by natural science. They both also stress the importance of the kerygma of Christ and they share the opinion, derived from existentialism, that religious belief essentially belongs to a non-objectifiable realm of personal encounter. But the request for a justification of Christian belief in the modern world was differently met by them. One of Bultmann's major intentions was to free Christian belief from any dependence on objective knowledge, and thus the biblical message must be freed from its objective-mythological form. This program was both accepted and rejected by Heim. It was accepted in so far as it meant the libera-

11

tion from objective knowledge, but Bultmann's solution was rejected. The problem is not in the first hand a hermeneutical or anthropological problem or a problem of finding a correct translation of the biblical message from mythological forms into modern speech. The real problem is, according to Heim, if it is still justified to accept certain basic metaphysical views concerning the nature of reality, which are the very foundations of the biblical view of the universe and of man and his place within it. This involves the problems of divine transcendence and of a revelation in history. Thus, the problem cannot be reduced to the problem of understanding man's existence.[37] And this is an insight also of the early Heim.[38] Now, an important point in the demythologising program is that the historical anchorage of Christian faith is unimportant. According to Bultmann history, including salvation history and its apex the history of Jesus, in its ordinary meaning, plays no principal role for the faith.[39] His argument is that the objective truth of a historical fact cannot, and must not, be a condition for a belief in Christ. If so, faith becomes dependent on historical facts, and this dependence must in the long run corrupt the faith as faith, and transform it to a form of knowledge. Here is the decisive point of controversy. Heim objects that the facts of salvation, containing the events which are the revelation of God, must also be historical and have some anchorage in the actual history, described in the Bible, and that not only for traditional theological reasons, but for metaphysical reasons.[40] The existence of man takes place within time and space. And consequently, the salvation history must also take place within time and space. And to state this is of course not the same as to state that the biblical history must be literally true. Heim is not stating that objective facts in themselves are sufficient to bring about a belief. But a true belief must have an anchorage in historical events. The Christian message must be demythologized, in the sense that it must not be based on opinions which are actually false, but faith must not be dehistorized. If so, it cannot correspond to an actual condition of human existence.

Heim's apologetics. At this point it is convenient to deal with Heim's program in apologetics. On a general level it can be said that Heim's authorship as a whole is an apologetic authorship. We shall here only briefly present Heim's view on the method of apologetics.[41] It is mainly based on his older writings, but his principal view has not changed in any major respect.[42]

Heim first distinguishes between old and new apologetics. The first is defensive and the latter offensive in its nature.[43]

Now, defensive apologetics can be developed along two main lines.

Firstly, it can be based on a theory of religion, which states that religion constitutes a genuine and unique area of experience, which also has its own proper methods of verification. Such a position has, according to Heim, been defended by Schleiermacher and Ritschl.[44] It can be criticized in two ways: First of all, it is religiously unsatisfying: It cannot, according to Heim, be interpretated as a total view of reality, but an acceptable religion must express such a total view.[45] It is an "unerträgliche Abnormität" if the church gives up its conviction also to possess the truth about "den tieffsten Sinn der Naturgeschehen".[46] Secondly, according to Heim, it can be objected that the theory does not say that the believer really believes in God, as an opposed merely to believing in a more powerful or "higher" being relative to man. This seems to be an unfair interpretation of Schleiermacher and Ritschl. But we shall not enlarge on this.

The second version of defensive apologetics has also two variants. According to the first, scientific results are used in a manner which resembles traditional proofs of the existence of God: there are really scientific results which entails the existence of God. The second variant of defensive apologetics uses real or supposed gaps or inconsistencies within current scientific theory. And as long as these gaps or inconsistencies exist, a religious belief is compatible with a scientific view of the world.[47] According to Heim, such an apologetic contains an obvious danger:[48] The scientific theory can be developed or improved. Then the possibility of a religious belief also vanishes.[49]

How then should a sound apologetic be constructed? It must in the first hand be offensive, and he briefly sketches the offensive apologetic as follows: On a general level, science has hitherto operated with two basic assumptions: A causal-mechanical schema of explanation and with a materialistic philosophy.[50] Now Heim states that these foundations of science are going to be broken down from within[51] and there is no longer any need to attack them with the weapons of Christianity.[52] This means that new possibilities appear for apologetics. Instead of being continously on the defensive, the apologetic ought to

"... auf die Gedankengänge der atheistischen Gegner eingehen und zeigen, dass diese, sobald man sie in ihre eigenen Konsequenzen verfolgt, über den Atheismus hinausführen ... Diese Methode ist in der gennanten Schrift auf die wichstigsten Beweisgründe angewandt".[53]

Heim here says that it is not jusitified to infer a theism only from scientific theories and results. And this can further mean different things depending on the interpretation of the words "... über den Atheismus. . .". They can mean (1) the stronger position that science is, after all, incompatible with atheism. This then means that atheism must be refuted on scientific grounds. But they can also mean (2) the weaker position that science is, after all, compatible with a religious belief, in the sense that science operates with theoretical presuppositions, which are compatible with theism. Then science does not entail atheism. And to infer from science to atheism is to make science absolute in a manner which is not any longer scientific. But, as we shall see later,[54] Heim also intends to say that recent developments within science indicate that materialism and determinism simply are wrong or at least very doubtful, also from the scientific point of view, quite independent of its consequences for a religious belief. The very point of the apologetic program of Heim is the demonstration that recent scientific theory, after all, uses some ultimate and basic assumptions which are not contrary to, but rather completely compatible with a religious belief.

We shall finally pay some attention to Heim's view on the position of theology within the realm of sciences. Heim does not doubt that theology really belongs to the realm of science and he does not consider the objection that theology may not be a real science at all. Now Heim intends to reestablish the medieval position of theology as the highest science or the apex of science.[55] The proper task for theology is to construct an integrated and coherent total view of reality.[56] But it is not clear how Heim exactly means this shall be done. The talk about theology as "Wissenschaft vom Letzten" or as "Wissenschaft vom Ganzen"[57] can be interpreted as meaning that every kind of reflection on the ultimate therefore also is theology. But this makes theology identical with metaphysics, and that does not seem to be Heim's opinion. Thus it is more reasonable to interpret these words as referring to the task of theology of presenting a total view of reality. For this task to be carried out, theology must take into account theories and results of all other sciences and then present a total view of reality, from its own standpoint, which also can contain, or consummate, all other sciences.

1.4. On the continuity of Heim's thought

When an authorship extends over more than 50 years there are of course bound to be many changes. It is therefore an important question if they are so profound that they call into question the basic continuity of Heim's thought. We shall maintain that there is such a continuity as regards certain central themes, and further that these points together justify us in claiming that there is a continuity in the thinking of Heim.

The phenomenological reduction. The first of these points concerns a subject within Heim's philosophy. It concerns what we shall call "the phenomenological reduction".[1] It comprises the following opinions: 1) It is impossible (except in abstracts) to separate the subject and the object. They must be treated as realiter coexistent; 2) The question if there exists a mind-independent external world to the extent that it is regarded as soluble is left aside. Heim maintains this position which here only is briefly sketched, in all his books. In PA and WZ it is formulated thus: to ask for the existence of an independent object outside the limit of the mind is nonsense. It is not possible to transcend this limit.[3] In L1 and G the position is this. The relation between the subject and the object is a basic and unexplainable "Urfaktum", and both contribute to the appearence of a picture of reality, and the question of the independent external world is insoluble.[4] In WW the position is similar. The subject and the object can only be separated in abstracto[5] and the question of the existence of an independent external world is left aside.

The coherent view of reality. The next invariant feature in Heim's thought[6] is his idea of constructing a coherent and non-contradictory total view of reality. He does this by trying to unveil the basic structure of reality. In PA and WZ is this thought appearent: Reality is conceived as a complex but coherent system of relations.[7] And in GN the basic feature of reality is that of polarity. The law of polarity signifies the universe. It is "das Grundgesetz" or "das Urverhältnis".[8]

The following points are some material features in Heims view of reality.

The dynamic interpretation of reality. By the dynamic interpretation of reality is meant is that it presents a continous flow of events and that this flow of events is in some sense acausal and unpredictable.[9] This is a main point in PA and WZ: "Die ganze Welt webt sich aus schöpferischen Entscheidungen zusammen" and the future outlook of this process cannot be predicted.[10] There are no logical reasons for stating that it will be similar to that which we are used to.[11] In G this thought is expressed as follows: (a) First Heim argues that one has to assume that there is a non-objectifiable space within reality. (b) From the fact that this space is non-objectifiable he infers that it also stands outside causality. (c) The subject now is non-objectifiable and it contributes to the construction of a total view of reality.[12] A causal view of reality then arises by an invalid abstraction and cannot claim to embrace reality as a whole. (d) Consequently, an acausal view of reality is correct if reality as a whole is to be considered.[13] In GD the theory of the non-objectifiable ego as a partaker in the construction of a total view of reality returns.[14] In favour of this dynamic interpretation of reality Heim further uses several subsidiary arguments.[15]

The relativistic interpretation of human existence. The next feature is what we shall call the relativistic feature.[16] This refers to Heim's interpretation of human existence. This interpretation is in outline as follows. From a philosophical point of view it is not possible to give a satisfactory answer to the question why an individual exists at its actual place within the temporal and spatial continuum. This location is from a philosophical point of view arbitrary: he may as well have existed as someone other at another time and place. This thought is present already in PA and WZ. There is no satisfactory answer to the question why exactly those relational possibilities have been realized, which signifies a certain individual.[17] In G the thought is explicit: This situation is a "Willkür".[18] And in GD it is important. The impossibility of explaining the temporal and spatial place of an individual is something which signifies "the basic forms of experience",[19] and the thought of the arbitrariness of that place remains: Within polar space, there is no resting point, because every point is inserted in a polar relation, and no part of a polar relation is prior to another.[20]

The Christocentric structure of theology. The last significant feature in the thinking of Heim is the Christological structure in his theology. In his earliest writing perhaps this feature is not so important, but in L the Christocentricity is clearly stated.[21] In G the central question in the interpretation of Christianity is the question of accepting or rejecting Christ.[22] The Christocentric structure of GDG is perhaps somewhat more difficult to recognize. Briefly it is as follows: First Heim argues that there is a necessary relativity inherent in the existence of man. This relativity can only be removed in the encounter with the transcendent and personal God. And Christian belief states that this takes place in an encounter with the person of Jesus. He is the centre within universal and human history and the centre of Christian interpretation of reality.[23]

1.5. An outline of Heim's theory

We shall as an introduction present a brief outline of Heim's doctrine of the transcendence of God.

Now, we said that a main characteristic of Heim's thinking is his intention to integrate theological reflection and a Christian belief with a reasonable philosophical position and generally accepted scientific theories and results. This program presupposes of course an attitude of openness (which of course does not imply that it is uncritical) to contemporary thought in all its aspects,[1] and consequently to a search for points of connections between theology and contemporary thought. His intention is to create, or re-create a theological total view of reality which is both rationally possible but also which does not violate or remove the traditional content of Christian theology and belief.[2]

Throughout, Heim maintains that there really is such a point. It is philosophically justified and plays an important role within contemporary scientific theory. This point of connection is the concept of "space" ("Raum").[3] Therefore, when Heim develops his doctrine of the transcendence of God, he uses this concept, after a generalization of it.

But what is a space, according to Heim? The best way of presenting his view of it is perhaps to give some examples. Let us look at the concept of temperature. This concept can be considered as offering an one-dimensional space. The degree of heat can be exactly described by mentioning one coordinate (t_1), and it excludes all other temperatures (non-t_1). Therefore, a space is always a relational concept: The degree of heat is (t_1) only in relation to some other degree (t_2). But not all spaces are one-dimensional: The euclidian plane provides a two-dimensional space which, for an exact description, requires two coordinates, and modern physics assumes a four-dimensional space, and it is

16

also possible to conceive multi-dimensional spaces. But all these spaces, and indeed every possible space within this world have all a common feature: They are all relational.

Now Heim suggests (1) that the concept of space can be generalized in a way that all aspects of reality can be described in the category of space and (2) that this generalized concept of space also provides a suitable tool in expressing a doctrine of the transcendence of God.

When Heim develops this doctrine, he starts from an ontology, based on the generalized concept of space. He says that there are a number of spaces, and they are related to eachother in the following way: (The arguments for the real existence of these spaces and their internal relations are here omitted.)

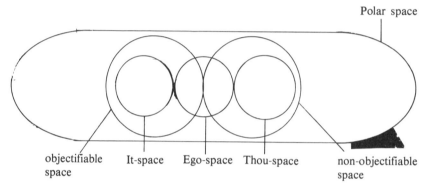

We shall return to the concept of space in chapter 5. However, the concept of polarity must be briefly explained. Heim says that all entities within the universe are related to eachother. And this relation is always what he calls a polar relation, which defines the entities within the relation. A polar relation has two characteristics: (1) The entities exclude eachother. This means that they occupy different positions, "coordinates", within a space. (2) They are essentially and necessarily connected. This means that one entity within a polar relation cannot be conceived without the other entity within the relation also being implicitly conceived. Examples of polar relations are the relations day-night, positive-negative and parent-child. Indeed, we can everywhere and always without exceptions find such polar relations within this world. The world of polar relations then constitute polar space.

The figure should be read: Polar space contains[4] objectifiable and non-objectifiable spaces, i.e. entities within these spaces are always polar-related to each other.

Objectifiable space contains It-space and some aspects of Ego(-space). Non-objectifiable space contains Thou-space and some other aspects of Ego(-space).

But it also says: It-space is characterized as being objectifiable and polar, Ego(-space) is characterized as being objectifiable/non-objectifiable and polar, and Thou-space is characterized as being non-objectifiable and polar.

Now, Heim suggests that the transcendence of God also can be conceived as constituting a space of its own, namely supra-polar space ("überpolares Raum"). This is the very point of his proposal. However, it offers some difficulties to express it graphically within the figure because supra-polar space, according to Heim, has a twofold relation to polar-space, (and thus also to all other spaces contained within it), namely the relation of continuity and discontinuity. The relation of continuity here means that polar space is in some way contained in supra-polar space, and the relation of discontinuity means that polar space is not contained but removed ("aufgehoben") in it.

The object of this investigation is to examine Heim's doctrine of the transcendence of God.

We shall proceed in the investigation as follows. First, after having introduced some basic analytical concepts in chapter 2, we shall in chapter 3 present some criteria, which according to Heim, ought to be applied to a religious belief in order to decide if it is acceptable. This part also presents the aspect of being a total view of reality of Heim's theology. In reading this chapter it may be useful to refer back to the brief presentation of the concept of space, given above. Chapter 4 then concerns the notion of transcendence and the problem of the transcendence of God in the thinking of Heim, and chapter 5 presents his solution of the problem. The last chapter contains some concluding remarks on Heim's theology.

Chapter 2
Analytical concepts

In this chapter we shall (2.1.) present some basic analytical concepts, and then (2.2.) apply them to two central passages from the writings of Heim.

2.1. Basic concepts within the analysis

First we shall present some basic concepts within our analysis of Heim's doctrine of the transcendence of God. We shall do it in a way that also will be useful when we present the criteria of an acceptable religious belief according to Heim.

Total view of reality. Our first basic concept is the concept of total view of reality. As an introduction it can be convenient to mention some world-views, which reasonably can be said to express total views of reality or an overall picture of reality. It is certainly the case that some philosophies present a kind of total view of reality. The philosophies of Platon and Hegel belong to this group. They contain interalia metaphysical doctrines on the ultimate structure and nature of reality and a theory about what is true or valid knowledge. They also present an interpretation of the existence of man within the universe and a theory on what is good or right.

But it can also be claimed that a political ideology can be a total view of reality, e.g. some versions of marxism.[1]

And, of course, a religious belief belongs to this group.[2]

Now, a common feature among the examples above is that they contain answers, and different answers, to some fundamental questions. Examples of such questions are e.g. metaphysical questions about the ultimate nature or the ultimate structure of reality, or on the existence or non-existence of God, or questions about what is good or right, and questions about the place and goal of man within the universe.

Answers to such questions can of course be differently related to eachother, and they can possess different degrees of internal logical consistence. We shall say that a total view or reality can be more or less theoretically elaborated. However, we shall not enter in a discussion about the degree of wagueness here, and discuss the limit where the vagueness becomes so great that the view ceases to be a total view of reality.[3] (But it is, at least prima facie, probable that most people have an implicit total view of reality.)

Now, a total view of reality can further be analysed from a meta-theoretical point of view. A metatheory on total views of reality then contains criteria, e.g. logical, for acceptable total views of reality, and also criteria for the relations between the contents of the answers to the questions exemplified above.

Of course, total views of reality can differ for several reasons. The main reasons are: (1) Differences depend on the demands of the metatheory for acceptable total views of reality. Different metatheories allow different total views of reality to be accepted. (2) Differences depend on the content of the answers to the questions. And different answers result in different total views or reality. (3) The relations between the answers can be differently conceived.

Now we can define a total view of reality as a view of reality which contains (1) doctrines on these subjects: (a) the ultimtate nature of reality (metaphysical doctrine), *and* (b) the content of true knowledge (epistemological doctrine), *and* (c) the good and the right (ethical doctrine), *and* (d) the place of man within the universe (philosophical anthropology). Of course these doctrines sometimes are closely connected. So is e.g. an ethical doctrine or an philosophical anthropology often based on a metaphysical doctrine. But it is not necessary to discuss here how these relations are conceived. But it is also necessary to state that a total view of reality must contain (2) a theory on the relation or connection between the doctrines. Unrelated doctrines cannot reasonably be said to present a total view of reality.

If a view is claimed to be a total view of reality but lacks one or more of the doctrines (a—d) or a theory on the internal relation between them we shall say that the total view of reality is incomplete. We shall in the following call a view of reality for a total view of reality only if it contains (1) and (2).

It is obvious that a religious belief is a total view of reality. It contains theories on the four subjects above, and also on their internal relations.

We can proceed to the next important concept within the analysis:

Basic assumption. It is the concept of basic assumption. Let us say that a total view of reality depends on a number of assumptions, which we shall call basic assumptions. It is a basic assumption, or a set of them, which gives a total view of reality its characteristic shape or structure. They generally determine a total view of reality in a certain way, namely in the way that if a basic assumption within a total view of reality is changed, then the total view is also changed. And if a basic assumption within a total view of reality is replaced by another, then this results in a new and different total view of reality. A problem here may be the question if a basic assumption can be said to be deduced from another assumption. It may be said that the ordering or structuring ability of a basic assumption is not dependent on its being deduced. Thus a deduced statement can also be a basic assumption. But if this is the case, then there is another assumption which is more basic than the first. Therefore a basic assumption must be said to be non-deducible from other assumptions.

Now it can be appropriate to mention here some examples of basic assumptions. The content of the dialectical laws can be said to be basic assumptions within marxism. They determine classical marxism, and without them marxism can reasonably be said to lose its essential content. And within Christian belief, the assumptions of the real existence of a transcendent God, that the world is created and that Jesus is the perfect relevation of God and the only Saviour of mankind are basic assumptions. They determine the Christian view of reality.

Here two important questions arise. The first question is: Can other assumptions than basic be replaced within a total view of reality without altering it essentially? And the natural answer to this question seems to be affirmative, depending on the ordinary use of the word "essentially" here. (We shall mention another position below.) But this affirmative answer is trivial. Let us take an example and suppose that the Nicene Creed basically determines the Christian view of reality. Therefore everyone, which accepts the Nicene Creed by definition accepts a Christian total view of reality (provided that he does not also accept other assumptions, contradicting the content of this Creed). But now a Christian total view of reality also contains other assumptions on subjects, not mentioned in the Nicene Creed, e.g. on the questions on infant baptism or on war. Now our definition says that a total view containing, except the Nicene Creed, both an acceptance or a rejection of infant baptism or a pacifist and a non-pacifist view on war is a Christian total view of reality. Statements about baptism or war therefore can be replaced without the total view of reality, based on the Nicene Creed essentially ceasing to be a Christian total view of reality. But statements within the Nicene Creed cannot be replaced by contradictory ones.

The second question is: How exactly does a basic assumption determine a total view of reality? This is a central question and we shall therefore mention some possible ways of determination.

The first possibility is to say that basic assumptions are axiomes within a deductive system. Then the determination consists in logical entailment, according to correct logical reasonings and applications of the logical laws. In this way it can be said that a basic assumption determines a total view of reality. In this case, of course, no statement, entailed by the axioms, can be replaced without the total view of reality being altered.

The second possibility is to say that a basic assumption is a necessary condition for other statements within the system. And without such a condition other statements within the system would lose their meaning or truth, but basic assumptions themselves are unconditioned.

The third possibility is to say that a basic assumption has the function of being a rule of construction of facts to a total view of reality. Then the notion of fact ought to be somewhat clarified before we go further. Now the notion of fact is somewhat unclear. It shall here be used in these two meanings: (1) The first meaning we shall call the ordinary meaning. Then in this case statements describing a fact describe things such as events, emotions or objects. These facts are single facts, and such facts are expressed in statements as "The event E has happened", "P is angry" and statements asserting that an object O exists. Here we can always say "It is a fact that. . .". But there are (2) other facts, which consist in relations between single facts, expressed in statements like "A is caused by B", "C is to the right of D" and "E is better than F". Here we also can say "It is a fact that. . .". And it is not necessary to here discuss the question how to justify the claim "It is a fact that. . .". Facts of both kinds then are ordered according to basic assumptions. We here use the notion of fact in a rather broad sense.

We shall here adopt the third possibility and say that a basic assumption is a rule of construction.

Now, different kind of reasonings can be used as arguments for a basic assumption within a total view of reality. We shall mention some:

The first kind of reasoning we shall consider as a possible argument for a basic assumption is the argument from a scientific theory, and thus ultimately from empirical evidence. Apart from the fact that scientific theories in fact are basic assumptions for a great many people (the most popular example is perhaps a kind of generalized theory of evolution), there is for obvious reasons no justification for excluding a scientific theory from being an argument for a basic assumption. And of course the arguments here are references to commonly accepted scientific theories and results of scientific investigations and experiments. And they are intersubjectively testable. And we can state this without entering into a discussion about philosophy of science here.

Now, if this position is accepted, then it also has an important consequence. There can be scientific results which exclude some basic assumptions (as well as other non-basic assumptions within a total view of reality) from being acceptable basic assumptions. Then facts, or at least some of them, in an indirect way become very important and central within a total view of reality. They determine directly basic assumptions and indirectly the total view of reality.

The next kind of reasoning which is a possible argument for a basic assumption consists in philosophical thinking. Once again we do not need to enter into a discussion about what constitutes a correct philosophy. But the point is that philosophical arguments for a basic assumption also are open for a rational investigation, and they are, at least to some extent,[4] intersubjectively testable.

Basic assumptions, based on these reasonings, are of course interrelated. But it is not necessary to discuss this matter here.

Finally, we shall accept a third kind of reasoning as a possible argument for a basic assumption, namely arguments from personal experience, which are not strictly scientific or philosophical. However, it is a prejudice to refuse them for this reason. It may very well be the case that personal experience can be a good reason for accepting a basic assumption within a total view of reality. But basic assumptions accepted on this ground are not intersubjectively testable in the same manner as the other ones, which is not the same as saying that they are not testable at all. But it is not necessary to investigate here which experiences are experiences of something really existing, i.e. of a real fact, and which are not.

We said that a basic assumption is a rule of construction for facts. But can a basic assumption be a statement describing a fact? The most natural answer here seems also to be affirmative. It is quite possible that a fact, which not is a single fact, for some reasons can be given an importance and universal significance, which makes it to a basic assumption. An example of this is e.g. a causal total view of reality. The notion of causality can refer both to the ordinary fact that some single events are causally connected, but it can also serve as a rule for ordering all facts to a total view of reality. And trivially, every basic assumption can be seen as also stating that something is a fact, e.g. the religious basic assumption that there is a transcendent God.

Hitherto our discussion of the notion of a total view of reality and basic assumptions has been mainly theoretical. How we shall move to a more empircal level and make some remarks on the question of the occurance of a total view of reality for an individual.

On this level we have to deal with two connected questions. The first one is (1) How is a basic assumption accepted?, and the second one is (2) How is a basic assumption properly applied?

Concerning the first question we have already mentioned some aspects which are relevant also on this level. We said that basic assumptions can be based on scientific theory, philosophical thinking and personal experience, i.e. that they are at least to some extent rationally founded. But it can also be argued that basic assumptions are intuitively apprehended. The insight into the truth of a basic assumption is not reached by a rational reflection on the basis mentioned above, but rather by an intuitive act of apprehending. This position is perhaps most frequently connected with the use of personal experience as an argument for a basic assumption. And naturally, if a total view of reality accepted on the ground of personal experience is ascribed a cognitive content, then the claim of a cognitive content for a basic assumption must be justified by an appeal to a theory of knowledge, which says that such intuitive knowledge is valid.

Concerning the second question similar remarks can be made: A correct application of basic assumptions to facts is made by rational reflection from scientific, philosophical or personal basic assumptions. Then the facts are (critically) examined, and then rationally composed to form a total view of reality according to the basic assumptions. And of course intuitively apprehended basic assumptions can be rationally applied to facts.

But also here the intuitive position is possible: It is then said that the insight regarding the proper application of a basic assumption is intuitively given. This can also mean different things. It can mean a kind of irrationalism, but it can also mean that the process of construction of a total view of reality is, for some reasons, at least partly an exception from the realm of rationality. This latter position does of course not exclude that rational criteria are applicable to total views of reality, but they are so only afterwards. This intuitive process of construction is impossible to completely describe and predict. There is always an irrational or unpredictable moment within it. This position is often connected with a rejection of the attempt to exactly determine the facts which can be valid foundation for a basic assumption. And of course, if a total view of reality is ascribed a cognitive content, then this claim must be justified by an appeal to a theory of knowledge, which says that such an intuitive knowledge is valid.

Complementary total views of reality. The third important analytical concept is that of complementary total views of reality. It may sometimes be the case that the same set of facts is equally compatible with different basic assumptions, i.e. different rules of construction, and thus also with different total views of reality.[5] This possibility has been much discussed,[6] but we shall not enter in that discussion here. It is an open question if it really is the case that there can be different total views of reality in this meaning. It seems to be minor problems when this possibility is applied to a limited part of reality. Then there always is a wider context, and when the part in question is inserted in this wider context, then perhaps its proper rules of construction can be determined. But the problem appears when this idea is applied to reality as a whole. Here there is by definition no wider context.

However, we shall hypothetically say that it is possible to conceive reality as a whole in this way. We shall refer to such total views of reality as complementary total views of reality.

Some popular examples of total views of reality are, concerning a limited part of reality, the discrepancy between the particle and the wave theory of light within physics,[7] and concerning total views of reality the contradiction between the religious doctrines of an almighty God and of a God fighting against a devil.[8] Some philosophers are inclined to interpret theism and atheism as complementary total views of reality.[9]

Supplementary basic assumption. Our next important concept is that of supplementary basic assumption. Our considerations here starts from the wellknown circumstance that the number of facts is not limited, but constantly increasing: New philosophical insights are established, scientific hypothesis are verified and new personal experiences occur. Some, perhaps most, of such new facts can without difficulty be integrated within an already accepted total view of reality, i.e. they can be ordered according to familiar basic assumptions. But sometimes facts occur, which cannot be ordered with the help of an accepted basic assumption. The facts which really are impossible to order are of course depending on earlier accepted basic assumptions. The same fact can be ordered according to one basic assumption, but not according to another. But when a real fact contradicts a basic assumption of a total view of reality, then it is necessary to revise one or more basic assumptions, or perhaps to accept a new basic assumption, otherwise an incoherent total view of reality appears. And an incoherent total view of reality demands a transformation to a coherent one. This can be done by accepting a new basic assumption, which can order the new fact. Such a basic assumption we shall call a supplementary basic assumption. However, a condition for accepting a new basic assumption is that it must not contradict other basic assumptions, and it must not alter the total view of reality in a way that it cannot any longer order earlier facts.

An example of this, taken from the history of science, is the transformation of the classical newtonian view of reality into the contemporary relativistic.[10] Another example is the conversion from theism to atheism or the reverse.[11]

Religious total view of reality. We also need a description of a religious total view of reality. But in order to avoid the wellknown difficulties connected with the definition of religion (it is e.g. quite possible that there are basic assumptions which are "religious" for one person, but not for another), we shall with the expression religious total view of reality mean a total view of reality which contains two basic assumptions: (1) There is a transcendent and personal God, and (2) This God can in some sense intervene in the world. In addition to these basic assumptions, a religious total view of reality can of course also contain other basic assumptions. When this is the case, the relations between the religious basic assumptions and the other ones must be in accordance to the accepted metatheory on total views of reality.

On the choice between different total views of reality. Our last important point concerns the question: Is a (rational) choice between different total views of reality possible? This question can be interpreted as a question relating to the (rational) criteria for the choice. Let us then distinguish the possible criteria in (1) internal and (2) external criteria.

(1) Internal criteria are simplicity, i.e. the demand for few basic assumptions, and absence of inconsistencies.[12] These criteria can be differently interpreted: as absolute criteria or as preference criteria. The criterion of simplicity, then, may most conveniently be interpreted as a preference criterion.[13] But the criterion of consistency must be regarded as an absolute criterion. Otherwise everything is provable within the total view of reality.

(2) External criteria are coherence with facts, including personal facts. And this criterion must be an absolute criterion. To not accept it would mean to allow every kind of speculation or irrationalism.

Concerning these criteria two positions are possible. If arguments from personal experience are judged as invalid here, then it is also possible to make a rational and intersubjectively testable choice between different total views of reality. But if personal arguments are not excluded, then this seems to be possible only to some extent.

And the question of the role of reason within such a choice is of course different from the question of evalution of total views of reality. Even if a total view of reality is intuitively accepted, at least to some extent on the basis of arguments from personal experience, this circumstance alone does not exclude it from being (critically) examined afterwards. And it is also a priori not the case that a choice based on personal experience means a less reasonable total view of reality. The question of the validity or truth of a total view of reality is different from that about the genesis of the view. Also a personally accepted total view of reality can be confirmed or refuted afterwards, as well as other accepted total views of reality.

Now it is important to state that a religious total view of reality is not excluded from the application of these criteria.[14]

Concluding remarks. What is now the point of our proposal about basic assumptions and total views of reality? We hope that it will have the following advantages: With the help of these concepts it will be possible to reveal some important features in Heim's thinking on religion, e.g. his emphasis that a religious belief ought to present a total view of reality and on the importance of the transcendence of God. It also enables one to discuss the relation between the religious basic assumptions and other basic assumptions.

A suitable starting point will then be to read some central passages from the writings of Heim. In addition to making us familiar with Heim's essay-like style, they will also illustrate some main points of his general approach to the problem of the transcendence of God. We shall in the next section apply our analytical concepts to the introductory passages.

2.2. What do the analytical concepts reveal when applied to Heim?

We shall begin and quote two important passages from the writings of Heim. The first one tells us what happens when the transcendence of God is revealed to an individual. (The roman numbers within brackets refer to the following comments. All italics are ours):

"Wenn das Wunder geschiet, dass *unter dem Eindrück irgendeines bestimmten Ereignisses* (I), *das eine Wendung in unserem Leben hervorruft* (II), wie unter einer erdbebenartigen Erschütterung die Türen des Gefängnisses aufbrechen und uns wie dem Knaben Elisas in der Erzählung 2. Kön. 6 ‚die Augen geöffnet werden' für den Raum der Ewigkeit, der uns unsichtbar wie die Luft von allen Seiten umgibt, dann geht uns dabei sofort auf, dass es mit dem Raum, den wir hier entdeckt haben, eine völlig andere Bewandtnis hat als mit allen Räumen, von denen bisher die Rede war. Auch wenn ich irgendeinen der andern Räume, zum Beispiel den Ich-Raum, neu entdecke, nachdem er mir bisher verborgen geblieben war, hat das zwar weittragende Folgen für mein ganzes Weltverständnis: ich erhalte eine neue Schau, die Wirklichkeit zeigt sich mir von einer neuen Seite; aber das alles ist doch *nur eine Erweiterung meines intellektuellen Horizontes. Es bedeutet noch keine Umwälzung meines ganzen Daseins* (III).

Völlig anders ist es, wenn mir die Augen für die Allgegenwart der ewigen Welt geöffnet werden. *Dann ist mir nicht bloss eine neue Seite der rätselvollen und unerschöpflich reichen Wirklichkeit aufgegangen, in der wir leben. Die Verwandlung, die damit eingetreten ist, geht vielmehr aufs Ganze* (IV). Alle Gebiete des Daseins, alle Seiten, die diese Welt hat, treten plötzlich in ein ganz neues Licht. Denn *der Grundzug der Zeitlichkeit, der jedem Sektor der Gesamtwirklichkeit seinen charakteristischen Stempel aufdrückt* (V), ist dann nicht bloss an einer einzelnen Stelle ausgeschaltet, sondern er ist auf der ganzen Linie überwunden.

Wenn es einen überpolaren Raum gibt, so erhält dadurch das Weltganze ein ewiges Gegengewicht. Das muss sich *auf allen Gebieten gleichzeitig bemerkbar machen* (VI). Es ist, wie wenn über einer Landschaft, die ganz in Nacht gehüllt war, ein Blitz aufflammt. Dadurch werden alle Berggipfel, alle Täler, alle Schluchten, alle Höhen und alle Tiefen mit einem Schlag in ein überirdisches Licht getaucht. So leuchten in dem Augenblick, da das Gefängnis der Zeitlichkeit an einer Stelle aufgebrochen ist, alle Lebensgebiete, vom grössten bis zum kleinsten, vom innerlichsten und zentralsten bis zum äusserlichsten, in einem ewigen Glanz auf. Jeder Mensch, der den Weg vom Säkularismus zum Glauben gefunden hat, *erlebt eine erstaunliche Verwandlung seines ganzen Wirklichskeitsbilds* (VII). Und umgekehrt: *Wem unter einem schweren Schicksalsschlag* (VIII) der Glaube zerbrochen ist, über dem verfinstert sich mit einemmal der ganze Himmel, und die Wirklichkeit erscheint ihm wie eine Landschaft, die in Dunkel gehüllt ist. Sowohl die Erleuchtung, die im ersten Fall erfolgt ist, wie die Verdunklung, die im zweiten Fall eintritt, geht von der zentralen Stelle des Wirklichkeitsbildes aus und verbreitet sich von dort aus sofort *auf das Ganze* (IX)[1].

The next passage contains some remarks on a world-view which Heim calls a "clarified secularism" ("abgeklärte Säkularismus"):

"Der ausgereifte Säkularist lebt in der Ueberzeugung, dass er allein auf den Boden der Wirklichkeit zurückgekehrt ist, während die anderen noch Phantomen nachjagen, die längst überholt sind. Der echte Weltmensch hat auch nicht das Gefühl, dass Dunkel über dem Horizont seines Lebens liegt. Es ist ihm, wie wenn ein frischer Morgenwind die Nebelgebilde weggewischt hat, die aus dem Fluss aufgestiegen waren und Berge und Wälder in grauen Dunst gehüllt hatten. Nun wird auf einmal die Landschaft hell, und die Konturen treten klar und deutlich heraus. Und nun entsteht *ein neues, in sich geschlossenes Gesamtbild der Wirklichkeit* (X).

Wir sehen: Das Weltgeschehen ist trotz der verschwenderischen Fülle von Formen, die es in sich schliesst, trotz des erstaunlichen Reichtums von mannigfalten Gestalten, die es hervorbringt, doch *zuletzt von einem einheitlichen Grundgesetz beherrscht* (XI). Wir mögen die Rotationsperioden berechnen, nach denen die Milchstrassensysteme in Milliarden von Jahren kreisen, oder die Bewegungen, die die Elektronen um den Atomkern herum ausführen, wir mögen eine Lawine beobachten, die durch einen Flintenschuss ausgelöst ins Tal rollt, oder wir mögen in die Pflanzenwelt hineinschauen und den lautlosen Krieg auf uns wirken lassen, der im Urwald ausgefochten wird; oder wir mögen zusehen, wie die winzigen Raupen, die Kinder der

‚Nonne', die diese in kürzester Zeit millionenweise hervorbringt, am Stamm der Kiefernbäume in die Höhe kriechen und die Nadeln fressen, so dass bald meilenweit nur noch ein kahler, abgestorbener Gespensterwald übrigbleibt; oder wir mögen mit Schrecken miterleben wie in einer einzigen eiskalten Mainacht die ganze Baumblüte eines Frühlings erfriert, oder mitleidig mit ansehen, wenn ein ganzer Ameisenhaufen mit allen kunstvollen Bauten, die in emsiger Kleinarbeit aufgeführt worden sind, durch den Huf eines Ochsen, der zufällig darübergeht, in einem Augenblick zertrampelt wird, oder wie in einem heissen Sommer Millionen von Fliegen an den Leimtüten, die der Mensch zu ihrer Vernichtung aufgestellt hat, trotz verzweifelter Befreiungsversuche elend verenden; oder wir mögen es miterleben, wie Menschenvölker ihre Weltkriege miteinander führen, in denen ganze Reiche samt allen ihren Kulturdenkmälern unter der Uebermacht einer stärkeren Koalition trotz verzweifelter Gegenwehr zusammen- brechen, — *das alles sind doch immer nur Variationen über ein einziges Thema, das trotz der unendlichen Mannigfaltigkeit der Formen und Gestalten in immer neuen Abwandlungen wiederkehrt* (XII). Ueberall in der Welt, im Reich der astronomischen Zahlen und im kleinsten Bereich der Protonen und Elektronen, im physikalischen und im biologischen Gebiet, in der anorganischen und in der organischen Natur, überall haben wir dasselbe Kräftespiel: Das Schwächere unterliegt dem Stärkeren, wenn es ihm auch einen langen und zähen Widerstand entgegengesetzt hat. So war es immer, und so wird es immer sein. *Dieses Urgesetz herrscht in allen Räumen und geht durch alle Zeiten* (XIII).

Das ist das helle durchsichtige *Gesamtbild der Wirklichkeit, aus dem heraus der echte Säkularist lebt und denkt* (XIV). *Auf dieses Grundgesetz ist auch seine Deutung aller Religionen und seine ganze Moral aufgebaut*... (XV).

Damit haben wir uns in kurzen Zügen die Grundhaltung des ausgereiften Säkularismus vor Augen gestellt, der der Ueberzeugung ist, *auf der unerschütterlichen Grundlage des Weltbildes der heutigen Naturwissenschaft* (XVI), vor allem der Ergeb- nisse der Astronomie, der Physik und der Biologie zu stehen.

Wir haben kein Recht, gegen die Umdeutung aller religiösen und ethischen Grundbegriffe, die der Säkularismus unternimmt, einen flammenden Protest zu erheben und sie als einen Aufruhr gegen Gott und eine Selbstvergötterung des Menschen zu bekämpfen, so lange wir nicht in der Lage sind, dem *Gesamtbild der Wirklichkeit, aus dem sich diese Umdeutung notwendig ergibt, ein anderes Weltbild entgegenzusetzen, in dem Natur und Mensch in einem anderen Lichte erscheinen* (XVII)".[2]

Heim on total views of reality. It is obvious that Heim in these texts says that there are different total views of reality. Secularism and theism (IV, VI, X, XII, XVII) and also atheism (VIII, IX) are such total views of reality. A total view contains i.a. metaphysical doctrine (e.g. on the existence or non-existence of God). It seems also to be the case that questions of ethics are differently stated within different total views of reality (XIV, XV, XVII). The same is also true of the interpretation of man's place within the universe (XVII, XVIII). The passages contain nothing about a theory of knowledge. But we will later on see that there are different epistemological positions connected with different total views of reality.

But Heim also says something more important, namely that a total view of reality is ultimately determined by one universal basic assumption (V, VI, XI, XIII), or that all events in some way reflect this universal basic assumption

(XII). (Here the basic assumption is an inductive generalization of facts.)

This calls for some critical remarks. It seems to be an oversimplification to say that there ultimately are only two total views of reality. Of course this can be trivially interpreted: If the basic assumption P determines a total view of reality, then the opposite non-P also determines a contradictory total view of reality. But the problematical point is if it really is true that a total view of reality is ultimately determined by only one basic assumption, or can be interpreted in this way. And if it is not so, then it is also possible to conceive different total views of reality based on the basic assumptions P and Q and P and non-Q respectively (provided that both possibilities are consistent). And this is a situation, other than that Heim describes.

Heim on basic assumptions. But the quotations above also tell us something about the thoughts, which according to Heim, in fact are basic assumptions. We shall here interpret the terms "Grundgesetz" (basic law) and "Urgesetz" (ultimate law) as basic assumptions. They certainly are a mixed collection. It contains e.g. principles within scientific theory such as all events are caused (XVI),[3] or a position which perhaps can be described as a generalization of such a theory, evolutionism, which, in connection with a certain philosophical position, results in evolutionism as a world-view, based on the basic assumption of the survival of the fittest (XIII).[4] But it also contains philosophical doctrines, e.g. different interpretation of the relation between a subject and an object,[5] or some main thoughts in the philosophy of Heidegger.[6] Perhaps it should also be mentioned that Heim does not accept all these examples of basic assumptions as valid.

Heim on the argumentation for basic assumptions. Concerning the non-religious basic assumptions, it is obvious that Heim maintains that there is room for argument. And he seems to accept that all types of reasoning can be accepted as arguments here, e.g. scientific generalization (XII, XVI), philosophical arguments[7] or arguments from personal experience (I, VIII). Such arguments then are reasonable with the partial exception of that from personal experiences, and there ought not at least in principle, to be any difficulties in reaching a consensus about which basic assumptions ought to be accepted. That there is in fact no such consensus depends, according to Heim, on the circumstance that certain commonly accepted assumptions are wrongly accepted as basic assumptions. Examples of such mistakes are the total views of reality of idealism and materialism.[8]

But there are also other basic assumptions, which Heim says are not accepted on the basis of rational argument. Their validity rather depends on intuitive insight (I, VII).[9] There is an intuitive knowledge about these. And Heim also says that this type of knowledge is valid.

This is a complicated question within the thought of Heim and it is difficult to give a conclusive answer. But we shall briefly mention his position here, and discuss it more in detail later.[10] As an introduction we shall quote some passages:

"Das geheimnisvolle Durcheinanderbedingtsein von Subjekt und Objekt, aus dem wir nie heraustreten können, besteht nicht etwa darin, dass Subjekt und Objekt bei der Gestaltung des Gesamtbildes wie zwei Ursachen zur Entstehung einer Wirkung zusammenwirken... Subjekt und Objekt sind nicht in diesem Sinn Kausalkoeffizienten eines Naturprozesses, bei dem man unterscheiden kann, welchen Anteil der eine und welchen der andere zum Gesamteffekt beiträgt".[11]

There is no sense in asking for a kind of preference for the subject or the object in the construction process of a total view of reality.[12] But in spite of this, the subject nevertheless is ascribed a certain role in this process:

"Wir können 1) in unsagbarer Weise erleben, erfahren oder ‚Urimpressionen' haben; und wir können 2) das Erlebte katalogisieren, also in letzte, nicht mehr beschreibliche Elemente zerlegen".[13]

And this constructive process always takes place according to certain rules, and these rules are contained in the mind. Heim calls them a "dimensional scheme" or a "system of coordinates":

"Das Schema der Dimensionen bestimmt die Art, wie wir sehen und das Gesehene in unser Weltbild einordnen. Jeder von uns trägt... ein Quadratnetz mit sich herum, mit dessen Hilfe er das Chaos der Welteindrücke sortiert. Dieses Quadratnetz ist vielmehr ... ein Teil eines Drahtgestells oder eines Koordinatensystems, auf dessen unsichtbare Wände alle Urimpressionen aufgetragen werden".[14]

We shall interpret the passages in this manner. It is the basic assumptions, which are statements about the dimensional scheme or system of coordinates. A basic assumption then, or a set of them, expresses the rule, according to which the content of the mind is ordered or structured. The problem is however how to exactly interpret Heim as regards this important point. The passages indicate that the rules of construction are located in the mind, and perhaps also are inventions of the mind, but there are also passages which indicate the opposite ("Raum", space, here means the same as a dimensional scheme):

Wir wissen ... wenn es sich um einen Raum handelt, nur so viel, dass ein unabschliessbares Kontinuum vorliegt, in dem Inhalte nach irgendeinem im Wesen dieser Mannigfaltigkeit enthaltenen Ordnungsprinzip ihre Stelle finden können".[15]

Here Heim maintains that the rule of construction, the principle of ordering, is not dependent on the mind, but rather essentially inherent in the entities of the space under consideration. But we shall return to this problem later.

How does a basic assumption determine a total view of reality? We shall now proceed to the next question: How does a basic assumption determine a total view of reality, i.e. how are the rules of construction applied, according to Heim? Here we can distinguish two positions of Heim.

We earlier said that a total view of reality can be constructed in a rational manner according to certain basic assumptions. There is in Heim's thought passages, which seem to suggest this. This seems to be the case concerning the scientific basic assumption, which says that every event has a cause.[16] Heim seems to accept that this basic assumption is correct. But then at once he makes an important restriction: This is certainly a basic assumption, which for pragmatic reasons can be accepted within science, but it is not universal.[17] And to ascribe it universality is then to make an invalid extension of it.[18]

Let us then investigate the other possibility. We said that a basic assumption also can be intuitively applied. This seems to be the case when Heims says:

"Die Einsicht in die Struktur der Dimension beruht also auf einem Innewerden, dem gegenüber Sinneswahrnehmung und Denken erst etwas Zweites sind. Was über die Dimension gesagt wird, kann also nicht mehr bewiesen werden, weder induktiv aus der Erfahrung, noch deduktiv aus denknotwendigen Axiomen".[19]

Here Heim says that the acceptance and the application of a basic assumption is not a result of rational reflection or sense-experience. This statement is quite compatible with assertions like (I, IV, VII, VIII). We shall continue this discussion later,[20] and only say that they are accepted on the basis of certain experiences. But we shall also mention one important problem concerning this subject. This also deals with the question of complementary total views of reality. Heim says in another important passage:

"In zwei Räumen kann ... eine und dieselbe Wirklichkeit gleichzeitig nach zwei verschiedenen Strukturgesetzen angeordnet sein. Ein und dasselbe Weltgeschehen kann sich uns zwei verschiedenen Aspekten darstellen".[21]

Complementary total views of reality. This seems to be an accurate description of what we called complementary total views of reality. And a position like this can perhaps also be underlying assertion (XVII), which says that theism and secularism can be seen as complementary total views of reality.

Supplementary basic assumption. Now, the escape from this position, which for Heim is absurd,[22] is to make a supplementary basic assumption. We shall investigate this matter some more.

Heim makes a clear distinction between supplementary basic assumptions and non-supplementary. The distinction is reflected in assertions such as (III, IV) and (V, VII, IX). There are experiences and insights of facts which are compatible with already accepted basic assumptions, and thus with a total view of reality, and experiences and insights of facts which demand a revision of a basic assumption or the acceptance of a new one. Now the crucial question becomes: Are there some general characteristics of such experiences and insights, according to Heim?

His answer to this question seems to be negative. He does not try to mention such characteristics. On the contrary, he seems to accept that every possible experience and insight can be relevant here (cf. I, XIII). And he does not say what experiences must bring about a new total view of reality. One possibility is to say that the difference is of a psychological nature, that impressive and profound experiences must naturally have such consequences (IV, V, VIII). But it is easy to imagine experiences, which for one person bring about the acceptance of the new basic assumption B, for another person the new basic assumption non-B, and for a third person no new basic assumption at all. And Heim seems to admit this. And further, if this difference is interpreted as psychological difference, then it is obviously not possible to decide which basic assumptions are valid and which are not. It depends on the set of previously accepted basic assumptions.

Heim on a religious total view of reality. We said that a religious belief is a total view of reality and so does Heim (IV, V, XVII). How then is a religious basic assumption applied? Concerning this question Heim denies that the religious basic assumption is applied in a rational way. The properties and actions which, according to the religious basic assumptions, are ascribed to God, are not of a kind that they can be rationally applicable.[23] He therefore accepts the intuitive position on this question.[24] (cf. VII)

Now, a characteristic of the religious basic assumptions is that there are no reasons for accepting them on the basis of the facts which they order. These facts can be given a quite different ordering according to other and non-religious basic assumptions. Therefore, Heim says that religious basic assumptions presents a "higher order" of facts. The reason for, in spite of this, accepting the religious basic assumption we shall return to in the following.[25] But a necessary condition for accepting them is of course that they are rationally possible and not only psychologically natural.[26] And Heim's theory as a whole can be interpreted as a theory, according to which it really is (rationally) possible to accept the religious basic assumptions. From a rational point of view there are existential reasons, which makes it natural to infer the religious basic assumptions, in order to arrive at an explanation of reality as a whole and of my own place within it.[27]

Heim on the choice between total views of reality. We shall now treat the question of a (rational) choice between different total views of reality. Here we can find some, at least implicitly stated, criterias within the writings of Heim. The first of these criterias is internal. We can state it like this:

1. One ought to prefer a total view of reality which contains as few basic assumptions as possible (XI, XII).[28] This is a basic feature in the thinking of Heim. He tries to establish a total view of reality, which is ultimately based on only one basic assumption, namely the law of polarity.[29]

The next criterion is also internal and says that

2. One ought to prefer a total view of reality which contains as few con-

tradictions as possible. And of course it is desirable to establish a non-contradictory total view of reality if it is possible.

Heim's defence of a religious total view of reality is an attempt to establish a non-contradictory total view of reality.[30]

The third criterion is a coherence criterion, and it says

3. If a religious basic assumption contradicts another religious assumption, then both cannot simultaneously exist or be applied within the same religious total view of reality.

This criterion focuses on a different problem. Is it the case that there are special logical rules for statements expressing religious basic assumptions? And according to Heim the answer is: no. Theological discourse cannot escape from the general criteria of knowledge:

"Sind somit die Versuche misslungen, die Religion künstlich zu isolieren, so müssen alle ihre Glaubensaussagen vor dasselbe unerbittliche Forum der Erkenntniskritik gezogen werden, vor dem die mathematischen, naturwissenschaftlichen und geschichtlichen Behauptungen erscheinen müssen".[31]

and he refuses a position which says that one

"... reserviert den Glaubensaussagen ein Sondergebiet, auf dem eine Art des Behauptens und Schliessens zu Recht besteht, die man auf jedem anderen Gebiet keinem wissenschaflichen Forscher verziehen würde. Um der Religion ihre Sonderstellung zu sichern, die ihr das Privilegium auf eine eigene Logik verschafft, haben die Theologen verschiedene Methoden befolgt".[32]

Therefore, this holds not only within the realm of a religious total view of reality, but also concerning the relation between religious basic assumptions and non-religious basic assumptions. Then we can describe the last criterion:

4. If a religious basic assumption contradicts a non-religious basic assumption, then both cannot take place within a religious total view of reality.

We shall more closely deal with this matter in the following chapter. However, we shall here make two remarks on possible contradictions.

a. A religious basic assumption contradicts a non-religious basic assumption. In this case it is of course also possible to criticize the non-religious basic assumption. Such a criticism is, as we saw, the main point in the apologetic program of Heim.

b. But there are also some non-religious basic assumptions, which are so well established that they cannot reasonably be doubted. In the case of a contradiction therefore it is inevitable that the religious basic assumption ought to be altered or replaced by a new one.

5. Of Course Heim also accepts what we have called external criteria. We devote the next chapter to this subject.

Heim on the choice of a religious total view of reality. Finally, what can be said concerning the choice between a religious and a non-religious total view of reality?

When Heim treats this question he somewhat astonishingly seems to neglect these criteria: Their main importance seems to be criteria, according to which one can afterwards, and only afterwards, justify an already accepted total view of reality. The reason for this is that the religious basic assumptions, and thus a religious total view of reality, is accepted in an intuitive way. And therefore, the pure and objective decision-situation is an abstraction.

This decision Heim describes as "the ultimate question" ("die Letzte Frage") or "the ultimate either-or" ("das letzte Entweder-Oder").[33] It is important to state that the alternatives are, from the theoretical point of view, from the pure-spectator-position,[34] equal but eachother excluding total views of reality. The condition for putting the question in this way is that the alternatives can be interpreted as presenting complementary total views of reality, and that one alternative is a religious total view of reality.[35] This seems to be Heim's intention when he writes:

"Denn der Glaube gibt uns nur dann die Kraft, die wir im Alltag brauchen, wenn er nicht von Wunderereignissen lebt, die den Naturzusammenhang durchbrechen ... sondern wenn ein und dasselbe Ereignis, dessen natürliche Ursachen wir vollständig durchschauen, zum Beispiel ein Krankheitsprozess, der zum sicheren Tode führt, oder ein Bombeneinschlag, der ein Haus zerstört, für uns als solches zugleich ein Handeln Gottes ist, das wir unmittelbar aus seiner Hand nehmen. Dieses Verhältnis, bei dem ein und dieselbe Wirklichkeit unter zwei verschiedenen Aspekten erscheint, ist aber nicht zwischen Inhalten, sondern nur zwischen zwei Räumen möglich, in denen derselbe Inhalt verschieden angeordnet ist...

Die Kraft des Glaubens ... beruht darauf, dass er sich nicht an übernaturliche Ereignisse klammert, sondern dass ein und dasselbe Geschehnis, dessen natürliche Herkunft offen vor Augen liegt, als solches zugleich ein Handeln Gottes ist ... Dieser Glaube ist nur dann möglich, wenn dasselbe Geschehen, das im polaren Raum im zeitlichen Kausalzusammenhang steht, gleichzeitig im überpolaren Raum völlig anders angeordnet ist."[36]

And further, to accept a religious total view of reality is ultimately a personal and existential decision. It cannot be made on philosophical or scientific grounds alone:

"Die Entscheidung des letzten Entweder-Oder hängt also von einer Stellungnahme ab, die vor aller Wissenschaft vollzogen worden ist. Hier muss der Denker seine eigene Persönlichkeit in die Wagschale werfen. Er muss aus der Reserve des kritischen Zuschauers heraustreten und sich selbst einsetzen ... Sobald wir aber unser eigenes Ich mit seiner leidenschaftlichen Sorge um sich selbst als entscheidenden Faktor in die Rechnung eingesetzt haben, sind wir beim Christentum angekommen".[37]

As a Christian thinker Heim says that there is no other possibility from the religious point of view, than to interpret an acceptance of a religious total view of reality as ultimately caused by God. The events and experiences, which brought about such an acceptance, are not themselves brought about by man. They are imposed on us from outside. Heim says:

"Wir stehen entweder verzweifelnd im Dunkeln oder dankend vor einer unermesslichen Gabe...

34

Es liegt offenbar nicht in unserer Gewalt, aus dem einen Zustand in den anderen überzugehen. Solange wir blindgeboren sind, können wir uns nicht aus eigener Kraft die Augen öffnen. Das muss ein anderer tun".[38]

But if theism and atheism are complementary total views of reality, why not be satisfied with this? The answer lies in the inadequacy of the pure-spectator-position. This position is namely an abstraction and this can, according to Heim, be rationally demonstrated, and therefore a personal decision is justified. From the personal point of view the possibilities are not complementary if the fact of the abstractness of the pure-spectator-position is also taken account of. According to Heim there are facts, which can only be interpreted reasonably according to religious basic assumptions. We shall return to this in 3.4.

Chapter 3
Four criteria concerning an acceptable religious belief

Introduction. In this chapter we shall deal with some criteria of an acceptable religious belief. As we have stated before it is not our opinion that Heim explicitly uses them, but we want to show that they are hidden presuppositions underlying his reasoning. We shall give a brief presentation of them. They are:

1. The criterion of universality. This criterion states that an acceptable religious belief must present a total view of reality.
2. The criterion of philosophy. This criterion states that an acceptable religious belief must not contain basic assumptions which are in conflict with basic philosophical assumptions.
3. The criterion of science. This criterion states that an acceptable religious belief must not be in conflict with commonly accepted scientific theories and results. (In this context science is taken in a rather broad sense. It includes not only natural science but also the humanities e.g. history and psychology.)

Our further examination will show that the criterion of philosophy and the criterion of science are not—in Heim's thinking—independent of eachother. We will show that Heim, when dealing with scientific matters, implicitly presupposes some basic philosophical assumptions, and that they determine the interpretation of scientific theories and results. We shall examine this relation later, in connection with the criterion of science.

The last criterion is:

4. The existential criterion. This criterion states that an acceptable religious belief has to fit, or give an explanation to, a set of profound human experiences. These experiences are common to all men, in the sense that every reasonable man, when reflecting on the conditions of human existence, must arrive at an irrefutable existential insight into certain problems, which—according to Heim—are deeply embodied in the conditions of human existence.

We will also see concerning this criterion that Heim here presupposes some basic philosophical assumptions, in the way that they determine exactly what features in the conditions of human existence are problematic.

It is also important to state that the criteria are belief-independent, or more correctly: The arguments in favour of the basic assumptions (except the religious basic assumptions) are belief-independent. This means that it is not necessary to have a certain belief in God or a special gift of knowledge from him in order to see the truth of those assumptions. It is sufficient—according to Heim—to undertake correct philosophical and scientific investigations of relevant aspects of reality and the human knowledge relating to it. Reality is equally accessible to all rational men. We shall in the following try to formulate the criteria in terms of the concept "basic assumption".

3.1. The criterion of universality: An acceptable religious belief must present a total view of reality

We shall begin by developing one of those themes in Heim's thinking, which occupied an important place in the preceeding chapter. We saw that Heim maintained that a religious belief ought to grasp the whole of reality. It must in the first place be a total view of reality, a "Gesamtbild der Wirklichkeit".[1] But it is difficult to give a positive presentation of Heim's view. He often speaks in a general manner about a religious belief as being a total view of reality.[2] But he does not often draw positive consequences from it.

Now, the formulation of the criterion of universality is somewhat vague, depending on the meaning of the expression "total view of reality". We shall try to clarify it below. But first it is convenient to mention a feature in the thinking of Heim, which perhaps can clarify it.

Heim's criticism of incomplete theories of religion. This feature is Heim's criticism of what we shall call incomplete religious theories. There are, according to Heim, theories of religion which for different reasons ought to be refuted. The reason for this is that they express what we shall call incomplete religious theories. By an incomplete religious theory we shall mean a theory of religion which says that there is at least one non-religious basic assumption, whose content and consequences are irrelevant for the content of an acceptable religious belief.[3] It do not satisfy (2) in our description of a total view of reality in 2.1.

This position means that a religious belief does not express a total view of reality. A consequence of such a theory of religion will then be that there are areas which cannot be theoretically integrated with a religious total view of reality or are irrelevant for the construction of such a view.

Such areas are e.g. scientific theories or a certain class of experiences. Some proponents of incomplete religious theories say, for different reasons, that these areas cannot, or should not, be integrated in a religious total view of reality. If we want to translate this position into terms of basic assumptions, we can say that they mean that (1) it is not necessary to relate the religious basic assumptions to other basic assumptions, or (2) they are in certain respects so different that it is impossible to relate them to each other. As examples of such incomplete religious theories Heim mentions Schleiermacher and Ritschl.[4] They say that other basic assumptions than those which belong to the vague areas which are characterized as "Gefühl" (Schleiermacher) and "Werturteile" (Ritschl) can not be integrated in a religious view of reality. Another example Heim finds in a feature in Barth's theology. A consequence of some of Barth's thoughts is, according to Heim, that some experiences, which are important for a believer, after all cannot be integrated into a religious total view. A believing man's experience of the immediate guidance of the Holy Ghost is, in Heim's opinion, inconsistent with Barth's doctrine of the transcendence of God. The reason for this is that Barth does not accept certain non-religious philosophical basic assumptions.[5]

Presentation of the criterion. Let us now turn to a positive presentation of this criterion. It can be developed in two, or perhaps three, directions. In the preceding chapter we saw that Heim is searching for a consistent religious total view of reality.

The first possibility is to interpret this criterion as a criterion of consistency and coherence. It then means that no logical conflicts between religious and non-religious basic assumptions are allowed. In this interpretation it coincides with the use of criteria of philosophy, science and the existential criterion. Here we can make a remark on Heim's view on incomplete religious theories. He seems not to see that there is an important distinction between (1) facts which are not theoretically possible to integrate in a religious total view of reality. They demand a non-religious basic assumption, and (2) facts which, for some reason, it is not necessary to integrate because religion, by its very nature, cannot take account of them. If (1) is the case, then a contradiction cannot be avoided, and the result is a non-consistent total view of reality. But if (2) is the case then the matter is different. Irrelevant facts (and their basic assumptions) can be consistent with a religious basic assumption, but this possibility is uninteresting for religion. This offers no problems for incomplete theories, because it is their very point to be incomplete. Then Heim's criticism of those theories must be regarded as a criticism of (2): There are no irrelevant facts within a religious total view of reality.

But on the other hand, there is not an entailment relation between them. Heim's position is somewhere between irrelevance and entailment in the sense that religious and non-religious basic assumptions are independent of each other. This means here that a religious basic assumption must not entail a non-religious basic assumption. To not say this is to say that God can be integrated in e.g. a scientific theory. But Heim explicitly rejects this position. To accept a religious basic assumption must e.g. not mean that it changes a scientific theory. If a scientific theory is to be changed, then the reason for changing it must be other than a logical conflict with a religious basic assumption.

The next possibility is to interpret it as a criterion of reference. We shall present this below.

The last possibility is more complicated. It has to do with Heim's opinion that religious assertions, or at least some of them, refer to reality as a whole in a special sense. We shall conclude this chapter by dealing with this matter.

As a criterion of reference. Let us now turn to the reference-interpretation. Heim says that a religious belief implies, or ought to, a special interpretation of physical nature as a whole, or a special view of it. The following passage indicates this:

"Die Auseinandersetzung mit diesem Gesamtbild (i.e. the secularistic view of nature) kann nur darin bestehen, dass wir ihm ein anderes Gesamtbild entgegensetzen, das genau so wie das Weltbild des Säkularismus die ganze Wirklichkeit der Welt, wie wir sie heute sehen, von den Spiralnebeln an bis zu den Elektronen, in sich schliesst".[6]

It is obvious that one of the main reasons that Heim insists on the totality of a religious view is his apologetic intentions. But we shall not continue this theme here.

Instead we shall read the passage like this: Heim seems to be of the opinion that statements expressing a religious total view of reality must in some way refer to the same reality as non-religious statements, e.g. scientific ones.[7] A possible interpretation of this may then be expressed in terms of basic assumptions:

They must have what we shall call a common point of reference. This thesis needs some comment. It means that, if a religious belief really expresses a total view of reality, then it also deals with facts which are accessible to all rational men, e.g. philosophical or scientific facts. This is e.g. a consequence of the doctrine that there is a divine revelation, within the limits of time and space, and accessible to man: If God reveals himself—in some manner—through e.g. the course of history, then these historical events also are objects for a historical investigation. The historical facts of revelation is the point of common reference between theology and history. Or if it is claimed that the revelation is given through some kind of mental events, or through the metaphysical or physical structure of the universe, then these things are the points of common reference for theology and a psychological theory, a metaphysical belief and a physical theory respectively. It is also always possible to speak of such facts in a non-religious way. But there is one exception: Talk about the transcendent God. The transcendent God cannot properly be discussed in a non-religious way.

Does then a religious basic assumption refer to a commonsense-"fact" or to what in an unreflected manner is taken as an unproblematical "state of affairs"? Our position above seems to mean that. But this is not Heim's opinion. We shall later see that, according to Heim, the notion of some important "facts" is indeed very problematic. And a correct philosophical analysis of them will reveal that the notions of such "facts" are mixed up with serious logical inconsistencies. Examples of such notions are the concept of "time" and a "self". But there are of course other unproblematic notions of facts which are confirmed by ordinary or scientific experience. In such cases it must be demonstrated that they are in accordance with correct non-religious basic assumptions and that they do not affect religious basic assumptions.

But to quote another passage:

"Die zweite Möglichkeit ist das Weltbild des Glaubens, in dem der persönliche Gott die allbeherrschende Mitte bildet ... In dieses zweite Gesamtbild werden wir nicht hineingeboren; es kann uns nur durch eine ‚zweite Geburt' als Geschenk in den Schoss fallen".[8]

This passage seems to introduce another set of facts which religious basic assumptions can refer to: A specific set of experiences. We shall treat different aspects of them later,[9] and only make some general remarks here. This seems to be a possible interpretation of the quotation:

1. There are some experiences of which a theistic interpretation is the most convenient, i.e. they can be a reasonable but not a decisive argument in favour of a religious basic assumption and thus for a religious total view of reality, in such a way that a theistic interpretation of them is the most preferable. This expresses the middle-way between irrelevance and implication.
2. But such experiences are of course also open to other types of investigation, e.g psychological or philosophical. This feature is the point of common reference between them.

As a criterion of universality. We shall now pay some attention to another feature in Heim's thinking. It is an important feature, but it is difficult to find a proper and suitable place within a presentation of Heim's criteria for an acceptable religious belief. However, this feature may enlighten Heim's opinion that a religious belief must present a total view of reality. The following quotations have some connections with the preceeding investigation, but they also introduce some quite new ideas: (As before, the italics and the roman numbers within brackets are ours.)

"*Alle Glaubensaussagen,* von der einfachsten ethischen Ueberzeugung, die einem Vertrauensverhältnis zugrunde liegt, bis zum vollendetsten Dogmensystem einer orthodoxen Kirchenlehre, *bilden eine einheitliche Klasse von Erkenntnissen* (I). Sie stimmen alle in zwei wesentlichen Eigentümlichkeiten miteinander überein. 1. Sie bleiben alle *nicht bei begrenzten Aussagen über Teile der Wirklichkeit stehen, sondern wagen Aussagen über das Ganze der Welt* (II), über das, was *immer und überall und für alle Wirklichkeit ist* (III). *Sie sind universale Aussagen* (IV). 2. Sie beschränken sich aber bei ihren universalen Aussagen nicht auf hypothetische Sätze ... Sie reden von einem *wirklichen Tatbestand* (V)".[10]

"Denn die Glaubensüberzeugung enthält immer eine Aussage über das, was *zu allen Zeiten und für alle Subjekte gilt* (VI)".[11]

And when a religious basic assumption is accepted the following happens:

"Wir sind vom Festland des *unmittelbar Gegebenen* (VII) und daraus Erschlossenen abgestossen und sind aufs hohe Meer der *allumfassenden Glaubensaussagen* hinausgefahren (VIII) . . . Es gibt also kein Uebergangsgebiet, wo wir uns zunächst in kleinerem Umfang und an einem leichteren Gegenstand im Glauben an etwas Unsichtbares üben könnten, ehe wir zu den schweren, *weltumspannenden Sätzen der Religion* (IX) übergehen. Wenn wir uns überhaupt auf den Boden des Vertrauens begeben, so müssen wir sofort vollwertige *Glaubensaussagen machen, die das Ganze der Wirklichkeit umfassen* (X)".[12]

The following quotation says that Christianity contains two different interpretations of reality

"Das eine *Gesamtbild* leuchtet vor uns auf, wenn wir im Schoss des Vaters ruhen und uns der 'Zentralblick' (Jakob Böhme) geschenkt wird, für den *das ganze Weltgeschehen* (XI) transparent wird, und wir sehen: Es kommt alles von Gott, *Gott ist in allem zuletzt der allein Wirkende* . . . Aber niemand kann diese hohe Schau in diesem Leben wirklich allein festhalten. Denn wir sind alle in die Empörung gegen Gott hineingezogen. Darum drängt sich uns notwendig immer wieder aus unserer eigenen Erfahrung heraus das entgegengesetzte Gesamtbild auf. Wir müssen *das Gesamtgeschehen als einen Kampf zwischen Gott und den dämonischen Gewalten sehen* (XII) . . .".[13]

Here Heim states inter alia:

1. All belief-statements belong to a certain class of statements (I—IV, VI, VIII—XII).
2. All belief-statements must be universal (II—IV, VI, VIIII—XII).
3. All belief-statements must be true in the meaning that they must refer to a real fact ("Wirkliches Tatbestand") (V, XI—XII).

These statements certainly need some clarification. Let us begin with the first point.

Heim's position here seems to be somewhat peculiar. It is certainly not the case that all belief-statements belong to the same class of statements, not even in Heim's sense. On the contrary, belief-statements are of different kinds, e.g. metaphysical assumptions, statements about historical events, moral commands etc. And it is a wellknown fact that it is a controversial thing to ascribe to all these different kinds of statements, truth or falsity. However, we can avoid this difficulty by limiting the expression "all belief-statements" to contain only the religious basic assumption and not discuss the truth or universality of other kinds of belief statements. It is sufficient for our purposes here. But what then is the meaning of ascribing to basic religious assumptions both truth and universality and to say that they refer to a real fact?

Let us now investigate the second point, where Heim says that the religious basic assumptions must be universal.

Now, the property of being universal, when ascribed to assertions can mean different things. We shall first present some of those meanings and then try to discover Heim's position.

(1) The first meaning of universal is that an universal statement is an "all-statement", i.e. a statement of the kind "all X are Y". It means that the property Y is ascribed to every entity X, or that Y signifies all X.

(2) The second meaning is that a statement is universal if it is true for all individuals within this world. This means that statement "X is Y" is true for every subject within this world. The same can also in some cases be expressed by saying that a statement is universal if it is in principle possible for every individual within this world to verify it at all times and space.

(3) The third meaning of universal is that a statement is universal if it refers to some property of the universe as a whole in a collective meaning.[14]

Now, which meaning of universality have the religious basic assumptions according to Heim?

Let us consider the alternatives.

The first possibility is not very suitable. The religious basic assumptions are not "all-statements" of this kind. But perhaps there is a complication. All basic assumptions may not belong to the same class of universal statements. It can be argued that Heim says that there are some other basic assumptions which are "all-statements" of this kind, e.g. the law of polarity and the religious basic assumption that there exists a transcendent God, i.e. supra-polar space, means the denial of the law of polarity. But both a statement and its negation of course belong to the same class of statement.

The second possibility seems not to be more suitable. We shall see that Heim probably not had this kind of universality in mind. There are certainly some statements which are universal in this meaning, namely those which express philosophical basic assumptions. A philosophical reflexion must, according to Heim reveal that they are true or valid for every individual within this world. But concerning the religious basic assumptions this possibility must be rejected as a possible interpretation of what Heim actually says on this question. It is possible that God does not exist.[14b] He also says that every possible event can be if not an instance of strict verification in favour of the religious basic assumption at least a kind of confirmation of them. And Heim's description of a religious assertion as "eine Aussage über jede mögliche Zukunft"[15] must mean that no future event can really falsify the religious basic assumption. This means that it must be possible to order every future fact according to the religious basic assumptions.

But the problem of the universality of the religions basic assumptions is not exhausted with these considerations. It is of course related to the question of the verification of statements according to Heim. This brings us, as we shall see, to the last possibility.

Heim's theory of verification. Let us begin here with some general remarks on Heim's treatment of the subject of verification. He identifies truth with universality and then, consequently, the criterion of truth also becomes the criterion of universality. And of course, if a statement is true, then it is also universal in the meaning (2). But this is trivial.

What is then the criterion of truth according to Heim? He first briefly examines the usual possibilities, statements of logic and empirical statements, as follows:

Statements of logic are always true if they do not contradict the laws of logic. These statements are of course universal also in the meaning (1), but they tell us nothing about reality or about the real state of affairs. They only tell us what is a fact if something else also is a fact. But what really is a fact cannot be decided through logical investigation only.

Empirical statements, on the other hand, are either statements about isolated events or they are inductive generalizations. In the former case they are of course not universal, and in the latter case they can perhaps have a very high degree of probability, but they can never be absolutely certain.

What is then, according to Heim, the criterion of absolute certainty? And Heim's answer is: "The immediately given".

However, we shall not investigate all the aspects of this answer. And it is also not essential for our aim here. We shall therefore restrict ourselves to mentioning the basic features of his theory in a way that also reveals the problematic point of the argument in support of ascribing universality to the religious basic assumptions.

Now, the basic and only criterion of certainty is that only what is immediately given ("unmittelbar Gegeben") is absolutely certain. Let us quote some important passages:

"Dem erkennenden Subjekt ist immer nur der Inhalt seines *eigenen* Bewusstseins *unmittelbar* gegeben ... Dem erkennenden Subjekt ist nur derjenige Teil der Erfahrungswelt *unmittelbar* gegeben, der gerade im Umkreis seines jeweiligen raumzeitlichen Gesichtsfeldes liegt".[16]

"... nur das absolut sicher ist, was im strengsten Sinn des Worts *unmittelbar* gegeben ist. Unmittelbar gegeben ist aber nur das, was *mir jetzt* gegeben ist".[17]

Here Heim states that (1) Only what is immediately given is absolutely certain and therefore also absolutely true, and (2) The immediately given is so given only to individuals at a certain time and place, and that it therefore is limited.

But then, what is exactly the immediately given? It is difficult to answer this question satisfactorily. But it is not essential for our reasoning to do so. However, the most convenient interpretation seems to be to see it as a kind of "sense-datum". Heim says:

"Unser Bewusstsein enthält einerseits Gedanken, Vorstellungen, Phantasiebilder, andererseits Tatsachen, Wirklichkeiten, also Inhalte, die wir nicht bloss denken und vorstellen, sondern sehen, hören, greifen, also sinnlich wahrnehmen ... Tatsachen, die wir beobachten, sind Bewusstseinsinhalte erster Hand. Gedanken und Vorstellungen Beuwusstseinsinhalte zweiter Hand ... Die Sinneswahrnehmung ist also die primäre Quelle aller inhaltlichen Erlebnisse, die im Bewusstsein auftreten".[18]

They are a kind of

"... letzten Sinnesqualitäten, in die wir die farbige und tönende Erlebniswelt zerlegen können, den Farben des Regenbogens, den Tönen und den Tastqualitäten".[19]

These sense-data are some kind of ultimate units within experience. But they are, Heim says further, only apprehended as having a relation to eachother. And the property of the mind to relate them to eachother is simply a basic property. Now, the way of apprehending these sense-data Heim describes with the term "erleben" (experience) in contrast to "beobachten" or "wissenschaftlich Erkennen" (scientific knowledge).[20] And what is immediately given, experienced, cannot properly be described, it can only be directly apprehended.

However, and this is important, Heim states not only (1) that sense-data are immediately given and apprehended with absolute certainty and are therefore true, but he takes a second step and says (2) that also the relations between the sense-data are immediately given and apprehended with an equal degree of certainty. According to Heim, it is the case that

"Wir können 1) unbeschreibliche Eindrücke haben, an die wir uns nur durch Ideogramme und verabredete Zeichen gegenseitig erinnern können. Und wir können 2) das Chaos der Wirklichkeit sortieren, klassifizieren, rubrizieren und katalogisieren".[21]

Here Heim says that relations between sense-data are also apprehended with equal certainty. The mind has namely a basic capacity to intuitively make such distinctions. This corresponds to a "nichtgegenständliches Innewerden".[22]

Now, this second step in Heim's reasoning is connected with some problems, but it is not necessary to examine them all. We shall omit the problems connected with (1). But it is important to mention this: It is not the case that the correctness of (1) entails the correctness of (2). This is a problem, because to apprehend sense-data and to apprehend relations between them are two different things. Even if sense-data are correctly apprehended, their relation to eachother can be mistaken. And further, how can one decide between different possible apprehended relations? And here it will not do simply to state that there are immediately apprehended relations, made by a number of individuals.

The universality of the religious basic assumptions. We are now in the position to determine Heim's theory of the universality of the religious basic assumptions. It is obvious, for different reasons, that the most reasonable interpretation is to say that he ascribes to the religious basic assumptions the third kind of universality. They then express a theistically conceived universe. This is the meaning of expressions like "Durchblick durch das Ganze" or "Zentralblick".

But there remains a serious problem within Heim's position. Even if there really are such immediately given truths concerning the universe as a whole, universality in the meaning (3), they are still given to individuals which means that they are universal in the meaning (2). How can they then be absolutely true, i.e. not related to individuals?[23] This problem forces Heim to the theory that there is within reality a space, which makes it possible for an individual to make universal statements in the meaning (3). This space is non-objectifiable space. Due to this it is also possible to give the religious basic assumptions an universal significance:

"Die räumliche Objektivität kann nur in ihre Schranken gewiesen werden, wenn der ganze Raum der Gegenständlichkeit einschliesslich aller Lokalisierungsmöglichkeiten, die er in sich schliesst, als der Raum des Gewordenseins erkannt ist. Dann kann vom gegenständlichen Weltzustand, ohne seine Bedeutung für unsere Welterkenntnis im geringsten anzutasten, ein anderer Gesamtzustand unterschieden werden, der noch diesseits aller Objektivation und Lokalisierungsmöglichkeit steht. Damit ist die Alleinherrschaft der Objektivität und des Körperraums gebrochen und Raum für ein neues Wirklichkeitsverständnis gemacht, in dem wenigstens die Möglichkeit besteht, eine Aussage, die ein Ich über die Welt macht, ernst zu nehmen".[24]

We shall return to non-objectifiable space and to the arguments in favour of its existence in the following part.

3.2. The criterion of philosophy: An acceptable religious belief must not contradict basic philosophical assumptions

Introductory remarks. We shall now examine the next criterion concerning how to decide if a religious belief is acceptable or not. This criterion is perhaps the most important of them all. But before we do this, we shall make an introductory remark: With the notion of philosophy here, we do not mean every type of philosophy or all philosophical schools, but only the philosophical tradition for which Heim is representative.[1] We are not going to discuss the genetic questions in Heim's philosophy. But it is not even this philosophical tradition, the Neokantian-Existentialist tradition, as a whole which concerns us here, but only some of its basic assumptions. And the origin of its thoughts are of minor interest for Heim, as well as for us here.

Presentation of the criterion. Now, we said that this criterion stated that an acceptable religious belief must not contradict basic philosophical assumptions. This means that the religious basic assumptions must not contradict the philosophical basic assumptions. This can further mean different positions. We shall mention some cases which satisfy the criterion.

1. The first one is obviously this one: The philosophical basic assumptions do logically entail the religious basic assumptions. This was e.g. the case within traditional Thomism: The Aristotelian notion of cause entails that there is a transcendent God.

2. The second one is a weaker version of the first. It says: the philosophical basic assumptions are such that it is possible to accept the religious basic assumptions. This is equivalent to saying that it is not the case that the philosophical basic assumptions entail the negation of the religious basic assumptions.

3. The third possibility is the reverse of the first: It says that the religious basic assumptions entail the philosophical ones.

This position needs some consideration. If the philosophical basic assumptions can be accepted for other reasons than their being entailed by the religious basic assumptions, then in this case it can be argued that the religious basic assumptions have some indirect support.

4. The last position is that the religious basic assumptions are such that they also make philosophical basic assumptions possible. But if this case is not to lose its interest from the beginning, then it must be argued that the philosophical basic assumptions can also for other reasons be accepted. And then we come back to the previously mentioned possibilities.

Survey of the following investigation. Our following tasks will then be to answer these questions: 1. What are the philosophical basic assumptions according to Heim? and 2. How does he argue in favour of them? After having done this, we can make some remarks concerning the importance and role of the philosophical basic assumptions within a religious total view of reality. Finally we shall determine Heim's position in relation to the various versions of this criterion.

We can so proceed to the first philosophical basic assumption according to Heim.

The first basic assumption: the law of polarity. Earlier we said that it—according to Heim—was sufficient to accept only one philosophical basic assumption in order to create or to establish a coherent and consistent total view of reality. We also saw that it was important for him to reduce the number of other basic assumptions as much as possible. It is this one basic assumption we shall treat now. What then is this assumption? We shall at once call it "the law of polarity". Let us quote a couple of important passages concerning the law of polarity and then comment on them:

The law of polarity is first of all universal:

"Wir können das... auf ein ganz allgemeines Gesetz zurückführen, das die ganze Struktur der Ich-Du-Es-Welt umfasst, in die wir hineingestellt sind. Es ist das Gesetz der Polarität, dem alle Unterscheidungen unterliegen, die wir innerhalb dieser Welt vornehmen müssen...".[2]

"Wir können darum alle Erfahrungsräume, ... so verschiedenartig ihre Struktur im einzelnen sein mag, in einem Raum zusammenfassen und diesen als den Raum der Polarität oder den polaren Raum bezichnen".[3]

It is a problem in Heim's thinking that he never gives a definition of this important law of polarity. He seems to be satisfied with giving a long sequence of examples of entities, which have this polar relation to each other.[4] But this relation has a special nature:

"Das polare Verhältnis ... bedeutet also nicht, dass die beiden Gegebenheiten, die in diesem Verhältnis stehen, im Kausalzusammenhang, etwa in Wechselwirkung miteinander stehen. Es bedeutet auch nicht, dass sie sich logisch bedingen wie Grund und Folge. Die Polarität steht noch diesseits aller kausalen und logischen Beziehungen. Sie ist das Urverhältnis, an dem alle innerweltlichen Verhältnisse gleichermassen teilhaben. Es ist darum aus keinem dieser besonderen Verhältnisse ableitbar oder aus ihm zu erklären. Es ist sui generis."[5]

This law is shortly "a basic law", "ein Grundgesetz".[6] It seems to be constitutive both for the reality and for our reception of it. It states shortly that every entity has necessarily a relation to some other entity. Such a necessary relation is now characterized like this:

(1) These entities are exclusive. This is valid both for temporal and spatial relations: An event at time t_1 cannot happen simultaneous at t_2. The time t_1 excludes all other times. The same reasoning can without difficulty be applied to spatial relations. But the law of polarity is not only valid in objectifiable space. It is also valid in non-objectifiable space:[7] My experental world is not identical with yours. Thus, both entities within an experental world and such worlds themselves have a polar relation to eachother.[8] But the law of polarity states not only this exclusivity, but also that

(2) These entities are correlative. There is a kind of necessary correlation between those exclusive entities. One can find several, and very different, examples of this:

"Sowohl das Nacheinander der Ereignisse innerhalb der Zeitstrecke als das Nebeneinander der Gegenstände im Körperraum wie auch das völlig andere Gegenüber von Ich und Du im unobjektivierbaren Raum der Begegnungen ist von einem Grundgesetz beherrscht, das in allen diesen Verhältnissen in immer neuen Variationen wiederkehrt. Es ist immer eine Beziehung da, bei der die beiden Glieder, die aufeinander bezogen sind, einander gegenseitig ausschliessen und einander doch gegenseitig bedingen. A verdrängt B, und A kann doch nicht ohne B sein. A kann nur dadurch im Gleichgewicht gehalten werden, dass B als sein Gegengewicht gegeben ist ... Wir erleben dieses Gesetz am unmittelbarsten im täglichen Wechsel von Tag und Nacht, die einander ausschliessen und bedingen, im Verhältnis zwischen Eltern und Kindern, vor allem im Gegensatz zwischen dem männlichen und weiblichen Geschlecht, die nicht ohneeinander sein können. In allen irdischen Verhältnissen finden wir es in immer neuen Variationen."[9]

A problem in the interpretation of the law of polarity. It is obvious that the exact meaning of the law of polarity is not clear in the philosophy of Heim. It is possible to give it two different interpretations.

1. The first interpretation would be that the law of polarity is an epistemological law or principle. It tell us something about the conditions of knowledge or something about the way in which knowledge is acquired. It is plausible to interpret Heim in this way when he says that the law of polarity is "... das Grundgesetz unseres Wahrnehmens und Vorstellens..."[10] or "Das entspricht dem polaren Charakter unserer Erfahrung und unseres gesamten Denkens, aus dem wir nicht heraustreten können".[11] But if the law of polarity is an epistemological law, then it can be given a psychological or an aprioristic interpretation. But it seems to be the most convenient interpretation of Heim to see him as an apriorist on this point. At least he explicitly rejects psychologism.[12]

2. The second interpretation of the law of polarity says that it is not only an epistemological law but also a metaphysical law. As such it states something about how reality ultimately is constructed and about the way in which all existing entities are related to eachother. All those different examples of the law of polarity that Heim gives us, cannot reasonably be otherwise interpreted.

It is clear that if Heim is right in his claim that the law of polarity is a metaphysical law, then it also is correct to say that it also is an epistemological law in its aprioristic version. But the reverse seems not to be valid. It is doubtful if the correctness of the epistemological interpretation of the law of polarity entails the metaphysical interpretation. But this latter position Heim seems to accept.

Argumentation in favour of the law of polarity. Let us then go on to treat Heim's arguments in favour of the law of polarity. But when we come to this we are at once confronted with a great difficulty: He gives no explicit argument for it. The reason for this is of course that he is satisfied with pointing out some examples of it. Maybe he had in mind an inductive argument of this type. It applies to the metaphysical version of the law of polarity.

(1) The law of polarity is valid for the circumstances a. . . .n

- - -

(2) The law of polarity is valid for all circumstances.

The argument, related to the epistemological version of the law of polarity, would then look like this:

(1) The law of polarity is valid for the knowledge a. . . .n

- - -

(2) The law of polarity is valid for all knowledge.

The mixture of the epistemological and metaphysical aspects of the law of polarity is summed up by Heim in the following words:

"Wir können das nicht erklären (= ein Anfangsglied einer Reihe vorzustellen), aber wir können die Tatsache, vor der wir hier stehen, auf ein ganz allgemeines Gesetz zurückführen, das die ganze Struktur der Ich-Du-Es-Welt umfasst, in die wir hineingestellt sind. Es ist das Gesetz der Polarität, dem alle Unterscheidungen unterliegen, die wir innerhalb dieser Welt vornehmen müssen. . ."[13]

Two consequences of the law of polarity. We now notice two consequences of the law of polarity, i.e. two themes, which Heim in some way sees as consequences of it.

The first of them is Heim's theory of the (possible) existence of an "indifferent state". This theory has some connections with the theory of "suprapolar space". Now, the point of this theory is that Heim sometimes seems to argue that one has to infer such an indifferent state as a "background" or "contrast" to the polar reality. Heim illustrates this theory with some considerations on the polar concepts "rest" and "movement":

"Die Polarität weist auf den Indifferenzzustand zurück, in dem die Gegensätze eine Einheit bildeten. Betrachten wir den Uebergang aus dem Indifferenzzustand in den Gegensatz, so sehen wir, dass dabei zwei polare Verhältnisse entstehen, die untereinander zusammenhängen, die aber deutlich unterschieden werden müssen: 1) Ruhe und Bewegung konstituiren sich gegenseitig, der Ruhezustand ist nur da, wenn auch der Bewegungszustand da ist, und umgekehrt. 2) Das ganze Verhältnis zwischen Ruhe und Bewegung ist als polares Verhältnis nur da, weil der ursprüngliche Indifferenzzustand als Ausgangspunkt im Hintergrund steht. Dieser Indifferenzzustand braucht nicht als ein Zustand angesehen zu werden, der irgend einmal wirklich da war. Es genügt, dass es denkbar ist".[14]

To describe this indifferent state Heim choses the term "ens".[15] It is this "object" which is differentiated through the mind into a polar world, or to view of reality, based on this concept. Naturally, such a differentiation can be elaborated in several different ways:

"In jeder Philosophie und Theologie stossen wir irgendwie auf dieses letzte Undefinierbare und dann auf ein Schema, ein System von Schubfächern, in welches das rätselhafte X eingeordnet wird, um es zu bewältigen."[16]

This idea of an indifferent reality has some similarity with the concept of a supra-polar space. But there is an important difference: Heim never says that this undifferentiated reality is metaphysically transcendent. It is perhaps beyond the limits of knowledge, but this does not mean that it is metaphysically transcendent.

The other consequence of the law of polarity, is this: A polar order cannot be concluded or ended:

"Diese Polarität aller unserer Unterscheidungen, die wir vollziehen, ist der Grund, warum alle Beziehungen, in denen wir stehen, unabschliessbare Reihen sind, innerhalb deren wir unaufhaltsam vorwärts oder rückwärts schreiten müssen ... Wir haben nicht die Möglichkeit, die Zeitstrecke oder die Reihe der Ursachen und Wirkungen an irgendeiner Stelle anzuschliessen und einen Anfangspunkt oder Endpunkt zu setzen." [17]

This aspect of Heim's thinking plays an important role in what we shall call the scientific and the existential criteria. We shall therefore continue our examination of this theme when we deal with these.

The importance of the law of polarity within a religious total view of reality. The polarity of the world is its basic characteristic. This fact cannot be overestimated and this makes it inescapable within a religious total view of reality. But how does Heim integrate it in such a religious view? What is the nature of the relation of the religious basic assumption that there exists a supra-polar space (i.e. a metaphysically transcendent God) to the philosophical basic assumption of the polarity of the world? This is the main theme of our investigation and we cannot fully deal with it here. But let us at least say this:

1. It is not the case that the existence of the polar world implies the existence of supra-polar reality. We are not logically forced to such a conclusion.
2. But if we are true to a profound and correct analysis of man's existence in the polar world, then the results of such an analysis is a good argument in favour of the acceptance of the religious basic assumptions.

There exists a non-objectifiable space within reality. We can now proceed and treat the next one of the philosophical basic assumptions. This basic assumption is Heim's doctrine about the existence of non-objectifable space ("das Nichtgegenständliches"). This doctrine is a central point in this thinking, and it has a decisive importance. [18]

Now, this doctrine states that besides objectifiable space, there also exists another space, which is non-objectifiable. And this non-objectifiable space is as real as the objectifiable. It may even sometimes be called "the primary reality". Let us quote:

"... die gegenständliche Welt der Linien und Farben, der Töne und Tastgebilde, die sich anschaulich vor uns ausbreitet, ist nicht das erste und ursprüngliche Datum, das zunächst für sich allein da wäre und in das wir uns selbst und die übrigen Bewusstseinswesen erst hinterher einordnen müssten. Diese objektive Welt ist vielmehr ein sekundäres Gebilde. Es ist die Welt des Gewesenen. Die primäre Wirklichkeit ist die unanschauliche Gegenwart, die wir uns noch gar nicht gegenüberstellen können". [19]

"Die gegebene Welt, in der wir uns vorfinden, setzt sich aus zwei Daten zusammen, die einander so entgegengesetzt sind, dass das eine immer nur durch Negation des andern ausgedrückt werden kann, und doch so eng miteinander verbunden, dass keines ohne das andere gedacht werden kann, die Region des Nichtgegenständlichen und die gegenständliche Welt. Das Nichtgegenständliche ist das, was uns allzu nahe steht, als dass wir es objektivieren könnten ... In dieser nichtgegenständlichen Region des allzu

Nahen, allzu unmittelbar Gegebenen wurzelt nun die gegenständliche Welt. Alles objektiv Gegebene ist nur da, wenn das nicht mehr Objektivierbare gegeben ist." [20]

"Es soll der Nachweis geführt werden, dass die Region des nichtgegenständlichen Gegebenseins wirklich da ist, dass es keine Erfahrung und kein Denken gibt, bei dem diese Region nicht immer als gegeben vorausgesetzt ist." [21]

Here Heim says that non-objectifiable space is something absolutely near. There is no kind of distance (temporal and spatial) to it. It is in the present. But having stated this, these problems arise: 1) How is it possible to have a knowledge of non-objectifiable space under such conditions? and 2) How can we even say that there is such a space?

Concerning the first question Heim says that there are two different kinds of knowledge. First we have a knowledge which ultimately can be derived from sense experience. This knowledge presupposes a temporal and spatial distance between the subject and the object. This knowledge is objectifiable thanks to the distance which makes it appear as a distinct entity from the temporal and spatial position of the subject. But Heim says that this is only the one kind of knowledge, and it is not according to the law of polarity to make absolute this kind of knowledge (i.e. to confuse the abstract distinction with a factual separation). This kind of objective knowledge has its limits:

"Das gegenständliche Erkennen, also das Empfinden, Vorstellen und Denken, in dem sich unser ganzes wissenschaftliches Arbeiten bewegt, vermag nicht das Ganze zu erfassen, das uns gegeben ist. Es ist nur *eine* Art, sich des Gegebenen zu bemächtigen. Es gibt noch eine zweite Art und Weise, eines Gegebenen inne zu werden. Das Wesen dieser zweiten Art, etwas zu ermitteln, können wir vom Standpunkt des gegenständlichen Erkennens aus nur negativ ausdrücken. Der Grenzbegriff des Nicht-mehr-Objektivierbaren, ... ist also nicht die Grenze des Gegebenen überhaupt, dessen, was überhaupt erfasst werden kann. Nein er ist nur die Grenze des *gegenständlich* Gegebenen." [22]

Now, an obvious objection to this is that a knowledge of the non-objectifiable is a contradictio in adiecto. But Heim is of the opinion that this is no decisive argument. It may very well be the case that there is a kind of knowledge which cannot be expressed in positive statements. We can know more than we can tell:

"... objektivierende Sprechen über mich selbst und mein Wollen ist immer von dem Bewusstsein begleitet: Ich rede hier uneigentlich und deute in gegenständlichen Bildern auf etwas hin, was noch diesseits der Objektivität steht. Ich bin mit dem, wovon ich hier objektiv rede, auf eine so unmittelbare Weise vertraut, dass ich überhaupt keinen Abstand davon bekommen kann, um es zu objektivieren, weil ich unmittelbar darin lebe." [23]

We have thus an immediate insight in non-objectifiable space, according to Heim.

Let us now turn to the second of the questions above. There are, Heim says, two possible ways of demonstrating that there is a non-objectifiable space. The first he calls the direct and the second the indirect way.[24] The direct way, of which empiricism, critical and speculative idealism are representatives, must be rejected.[25] With the help of these philosophies it is not possible to demonstrate the existence of a non-objectifiable space. But it is not because of that failure that they ought to be rejected, but because they are exponents of different kinds of incorrect interpretations of the law of polarity.

Let us then try the other way. It has two versions:

"Es soll also zunächst ... (I) gezeigt werden: Die gegenständliche Erfahrungswelt enthält Antinomien, die sich alle auf *einen* letzten Urwiederstreit zurückführen lassen. Dieser Urwiderspruch würde logisch betrachtet das Zustandekommen der Erfahrung unmöglich machen. Dass die Erfahrung trotzdem zustande kommt, beweist also das Gegebensein eines nichtgegenständlichen Datums, in dem der Urwiderstreit gelöst ist. Dann soll ... (II) gezeigt werden: Die gegenständliche Erfahrungswelt enthält Unterschiede, ... die doch im gegenständlichen Erfahrungsinhalt selbst keinen Anhaltspunkt haben. Diese Unterschiede lassen sich alle auf *eine* Urunterscheidung zurückführen, nämlich die perspektivische Gruppierung des Gegebenen. Diese Unterscheidung lässt sich aber nur aus dem Dasein eines nichtgegenständlichen Datums erklären." [26]

Let us now follow Heim's reasoning concerning the two indirect ways. He illustrates the first of them with the wellknown paradoxes of Zeno (The beginning of time, The flying arrow and Achilles and the tortoise), Kants Antitheses of Pure Reason and the concept of infinity within matemathics.

Let us restrict ourselves to the paradoxes of Zeno. The reasoning can, mutatis mutandis, be applied also on the other two.

First of all, Heim reduces the matter to be a question of the nature of time.[27] It is possible to divide time into not-overlapping instants or parts, e.g. days or minutes. Of course, it does not matter how long these instants are. That is the very point in the Achilles-and-the-tortoise-paradox. Now, between those instants there always is an "either-or-relation".[28] This makes it impossible to experience two instants of time simultaneously. An experience must have taken place either at time-instant t_1 or at some not-t_1, but at both is impossible.

But it is also obvious that such an analysis is according to Heim contrary to experience. We *know* that Achilles sooner or later will reach the tortoise and that the arrow really flies. It is only possible to justify this knowledge if we suppose that there is also a "both-and-relation" between the instants of time i.e. the instants of time are overlapping. Now, this statement about time, that it presents both an "either-or-relation" and a "both-and-relation" is a contradiction. That we do not in our daily life notice this depends, according to Heim, on, that we are so used to it, that we do not really reflect on it. But it is a mistake to say that experience is contrary to the either-or-interpretation. And no solution is possible as long as we have an objective understanding of time. The only way to solve the problem is, according to Heim, to accept the existence of a non-objectifiable space. In that space the contradiction is removed. Only this acceptance can make sense of our daily experience:

"Dieses Urverhältnis ist aber ein unvereinbarer Widerspruch, solange wir die Erfahrungswelt als einen an sich seienden Gegenstand, als ein rein gegenständliches Nacheinander und Nebeneinander von Elementen auffassen. Dass die Erfahrungswelt trotz dieses Widerspruchs da ist, ist also ein indirekter Beweis für das Gegebensein eines Nichtgegenständlichen, in welchem der Widerspruch auf eine nicht mehr objektivierbare Weise aufgehoben ist".[29]

The other variant of the indirect demonstration of non-objectifiable space has some connections with the existential criterion. We shall therefore present the argument there in detail. Here we shall only give a brief outline of Heim's reasoning (presupposing the following presentation of a perspective centre).[30] Heim says that it is not possible to satisfactorily explain, except within the framework of objectifiable space, why a certain individual perspective centre within the temporal and spatial continuum has the place that it actually has. In order to do this it is necessary to accept the basic assumption that there is a non-objectifiable space within reality.

To give my "here-and-now" any special importance within the spatio-temporal continuum would require the existence of non-objectifiable space:

"Vom Standpunkt der Gegenständlichkeit aus betrachtet hatte ja jeder Zeitpunkt genau soviel Recht, wie der andere, Jetzt zu werden. Wenn irgend ein Zeitpunkt Jetzt werden muss, um eine Zeitstrecke zustandezubringen, so sollte es darum unendlich leicht sein, den Jetzpunkt innerhalb der Zeitreihe beliebig hin und her zu rücken. Statt dessen ist er nun aber unverrückbar festgelegt ... Diese Festlegung kann nur kraft des Nichtgegenständlichen erfolgt sein."[31]

The metaphysical significance of non-objectifiable space. Concerning this point it is not difficult to discover Heim's position. He is very anxious to show that non-objectifiable space really exists:

"Das nichtgegenständliche Gegebensein des einen Elements ist aber genau so wirklich und wahr und wissenschaftlich ernst zu nehmen wie das gegenständliche Gegebensein der andern."[32]

And concerning the law of polarity he rejects a psychological or a physiological interpretation of it. It cannot be derived from

"die Unvollkommenheit unserer Sinnesorgane ... In jenem physiologischen Tatbestand kommt vielmehr etwas zum Ausdruck, was von der besonderen Einrichtung der menschlichen Empfindungsorgane unabhängig ist und in der Natur der Sache liegt."[33]

The relation between non-objectifiable and objectifiable space. Objectifiable and non-objectifiable spaces have a polar relation to each other. They mutually exclude each other. The non-objectifiable "now" excludes the past and the future, but the very concept of a "now" presupposes a time sequence. The same reasoning is also valid for the concept "here". But objectifiable and non-objectifiable space are also correlative:

"Die gegebene Welt, in der wir uns vorfinden, setzt sich aus zwei Daten zusammen, die einander so entgegengesetzt sind, dass das eine immer nur durch Negation des andern ausgedrückt werden kann, und doch so eng miteinander verbunden, dass keines ohne das andere gedacht werden kann, die Region des Nichtgegenständlichen und die gegenständliche Welt." [34]

A consequence of the existence of non-objectifiable space. There is one consequence of the existence of non-objectifiable space, or more correct, the existence of non-objectifiable space is of decisive importance for the understanding of the ego ("das Ich").

On the one hand Heim's basic thesis is that the ego is non-objectifiable. Of course there are many characteristics which we usually say belong to the ego, namely those characteristics which can be objects of medical and psychological investigations or objects of memory and introspection. But these things do not belong to the essence of the ego.

The reason for stating this is that, for the very notion of all these things, one must presuppose that there is a distance between them and the subject. But the ego itself cannot be an object of such a notion. Thus it is non-objectifiable.

"Der Versuch, mich meiner selbst denkend zu bemächtigen, gleicht also der Bewegung des dürstenden Tantalus, vor dem die Frucht, nach der er greifen will, immer im selben Augenblick zurückweicht, da er sie fassen zu können glaubt." [35]

But the ego is on the other hand not wholly non-objectifiable. It has its place on the border between objectifiable and non-objectifiable space. The ego has the power to make a synthesis of these two spaces. And this power is a natural power of ego, a kind of basic property, in favour of which no arguments can be given. It is not possible to go behind this property and detect the reason for it. This power simply signifies the existence of the ego:

"Aber das Ich fasst in einer übergreifenden Schau die Ereignisse zusammen, die sonst als Teilstücke auseinanderfallen müssten. Es stellt das ‚Und' her, durch das die Oder-Verhältnisse zusammengehalten werden. Es schafft eine Gleichzeitigkeit zwischen zwei ungleichzeitigen Ereignissen. Es ist ein Punkt, von dem aus beide mit einem Blick zusammen gesehen werden und als Einheit erlebt werden können. Nur dadurch ist Erfahrung möglich. . .". [36]

The reality can therefore only in an abstract way be separated into these two spaces. Really they are inseparable. But the ego has not, in spite of its non-objectifiable character, an existence outside time and space. The existence of the ego within the temporal and spatial continuum Heim calls "destiny" ("Schicksal"). But we shall return to the problems of the individual destiny in the chapter on the existential criterion.

There are of course other important consequences of the doctrine about the non-objectifiable space concerning the notions of time and space. But, since these also involve considerations on scientific theory, it is more convenient to treat them in connection with the criterion of science.

The significance of non-objectifiable space within a religious total view of reality. Let us now look at the importance of non-objectifiable space within a religious total view of reality. We have seen that the basic assumption about the existence of non-objectifiable space is in accordance with the law of polarity. But what about its relation to a religious total view of reality? We shall mention some points:

1. The first, and wholly decisive point, is Heim's assertion that the existence of non-objectifiable space is a necessary condition for an acceptance of the religious basic assumption about the transcendence of God. Heim says:

"Wenn wir aber das Gegenständliche mit dem Gewordenen in eins setzen müssen, was folgt daraus für das Wesen des nicht gegenständlichen Ich, dem die Gegenstandswelt gegenübertritt? Die Antwort auf diese Frage entscheidet über das ganze Verständnis unserer Existenz. Wir werden . . . sehen, dass von ihr das Verhältnis abhängt, in dem das Ich zur absoluten oder zur transzendenten Wirklichkeit Gottes steht."[37]

"Dieser Nachweis (i.e. of the real existence of non-objectifiable space) ist, . . . die Bedingung, unter der allein Glaubensgewissheit denkmöglich ist".[38]

This simply means that non-existence of non-objectifiable space would make the religious basic assumption impossible. We shall devote chapter 4.2 to this problem.

2. It is within non-objectifiable space that religious belief has its place. It is impossible to demonstrate the possibility of accepting the religious basic assumptions within objectifiable space. This space presents a totally closed system signified by causal relations. And such a system leaves according to Heim no room for a belief in God. A religious belief must then be, as Heim expresses it, rejected as a kind of mental illness.[39]

3. The basic assumption that there exists a non-objectifiable space does not entail the religious basic assumption. The existence of non-objectifiable space does not entail either the existence or the transcendence of God. Non-objectifiable space certainly has a kind of transcendence, but it is not a metaphysical transcendence (see further chap. 4). It is still quite possible to accept the existence of non-objectifiable space, but deny the existence of a transcendent God. But the importance of the demonstration that non-objectifiable space really exists, has once and for all broken the total sovereignity of a causal-mechanical view of nature, by demonstrating that there really exists a realm within reality, and a realm to which a causal framework cannot be applied. Such a causal interpretation of reality can therefore not cover reality as a whole or reveal the depths of human existence. How Heim treats these matters we shall see in the following chapters on the scientific and existential criteria.

The law of perspective. We shall finally turn to the third philosophical basic assumption. Let us call this basic assumption the "law of perspective". It states that every total view of reality is arranged around an individual subject. This subject is the perspective centre of the view of reality, the point from which the view of reality is conceived. We shall also see that Heim develops the law of perspective in a way that makes it dependent on the assumption that there is a non-objectifiable space.[40] But let us quote some passages:

"Es gehört zum Wesen jedes raumzeitlichen Erlebnisses, dass es von einem bestimmten Punkt aus erlebt wird, der den perspektivischen Mittelpunkt desselben bildet. Wenn wir z.B. ein rein zeitliches Erlebnis haben, also etwa ein Violinsolo oder ein Domgeläute hören, so können wir ja die Fülle von Tönen, die wie ein breiter Strom an uns vorüberrauscht, nie als Ganzes auf einmal in uns aufnehmen, sondern nur in stetiger Aufeinanderfolge der Teile, d.h. so, dass uns immer nur Ein Augenblick der zeitlichen Erlebnisreihe wirklich gegenwärtig ist, . . . der Eine Ton, der gerade erklingt, bildet sozusagen den perspektivischen Mittelpunkt des Ganzen".[41]

"Zum Wesen des erlebten Raums gehört es aber, dass er ein perspektivisches Zentrum hat, das in einem bestimmten Augenblick nur ein Einer bestimmten Stelle liegen kann. Es kann jetzt an dieser Stelle liegen, dann an einer andern. Aber es kann nicht zugleich an zwei verschiedenen Stellen liegen, sondern nur nacheinander".[42]

"Es gehört zur Struktur jeder Gegenstandswelt, dass sie eine perspektivische Mitte hat, dass sie also von einem Standpunkt aus gesehen wird . . . Es gehört zum Wesen des Subjekt-Objekt-Schemas, das der Erfahrungswelt ihre Gestalt gibt, dass das Weltbild perspektivisch auf einen Punkt bezogen ist. Wir können von dieser perspektivischen Beziehung abstrahieren und versuchen, uns einen Begriff von der Welt zu machen, wie sie ohne Perspektive an sich wäre. Aber was wir dabei gewinnen, ist nur ein Abstraktum ohne Blut und Leben, das wir uns nicht mehr vorstellen können. Die konkrete Wirklichkeit, mit der wir es zu tun haben, ist immer die von einem bestimmten Standpunkt aus gesehene Welt".[43]

Here Heim says that it is impossible to conceive an "objective" non-perspective view of reality. The individual subject therefore becomes the central, middle point of reality. Around the subject the surrounding world is arranged. (It is of course not necessary to suppose a human mind as such a perspective centre.)[44] And he further says that the property of the subject to be a perspective centre is given with its existence. It cannot exist otherwise than in the form of a perspective centre:

"Jedem Subjekt ist ohne sein Zutun eine bestimmte Stelle der Gegenstandswelt schon mit dem Eintritt in seine Existenz als die perspektivische Mitte seines Weltbildes zugewiesen".[45]

And the perspective centre must be seen as the "I-here-and-now". It occupies a certain place within time, space and the plurality of (possible) minds:

"Die Gegenstandswelt, die sich uns darbietet, ist immer auf eine perspektivische Mitte bezogen, die wir mit dem Wort Ich bezeichnen, wenn wir sagen: es ist meine Welt, meine Erinnerung, meine Umwelt, meine Umgebung. Wir kennen nur einen Raum, der von einem Mittelpunkt aus gesehen wird, den wir als Hier bezeichnen. Wir kennen nur eine Zeitstrecke, die von einem Mittelpunkt aus erlebt wird, den wir Jetzt nennen".[46]

The perspective centre is non-objectifiable. Now, from this Heim makes the important conclusion that the perspective centre is non-objectifiable:

"Das Grundgesetz der Perspektive ist in dem Satz ausgedrückt . . .: Der sehende Punkt sieht sich selber nicht, allgemeiner gesprochen: Das Zentrum des perspektivischen Gebildes ist unsichtbar. Alles andere ist von dieser unsichtbaren Mitte aus sichtbar und greifbar . . . Alles andere is wenigstens soweit entfernt, dass es fassbar wird. Die Mitte selbst aber ist absolut nahe. Das, was im strengen Sinne des Worts hier ist, ist unendlich nahe. Es ist darum nicht mehr gegenständlich fassbar."[47]

Argument in favour of the law of perspective. Heim's arguments in favour of the law of perspective are not easy to detect. He seems to postulate that the law of perspective has an aprioristic status. This seems to be the most reasonable interpretation of words like "Zum Wesen des . . ." or ". . . zur Struktur des. . ." in the introductory quotations above. And he explicitly rejects a psychological or a physiological interpretation of the law of perspective. To argue from this interpretation of the law of perspective is simply wrong. He says:

"Haben wir uns einmal unter Einsteins Einfluss von der realistischen Verachtung der Perspektive freigemacht, dann wird das Gesetz der perspektivischen Gruppierung mit einemmal aus einem Gesetz der Psychologie der Sinnesorgane zu einem Weltgesetz. Die Perspektive wird zur Grundform der gesamten Erfahrungswelt. Was wir über die Besonderheiten des perspektivischen Sehens und Hörens beim Menschen psychologisch feststellen können, das ist nur ein Spezialfall eines viel allgemeineren Gesetzes, das als apriorische Form die ganze Wirklichkeit beherrscht".[48]

Thus, the law of perspective does not depend on the constitution of the human mind or of any other possible mind. It only reflects a necessary constitution of reality, a constitution in which we have an immediate insight. It is impossible to imagine a total view of reality, which is not according to the law of perspective.[49]

Three consequences of the law of perspective. We shall now briefly treat three consequences of the law of perspective. Heim seems to consider that they are important, and they are so in our investigation also.

1. The first one deals with the notion of "objectivity". Heim says that there is no objective perspective, because of the characterization of the perspective centre as something individual and present. The "I-here-and-now" is not a firm and resting point, from which we can remember our experiences and then order them to a total view of reality. On the contrary: The "I-here-and-now" is also involved in the continuous flow of events:

"Die perspektivische Mitte . . . ist nicht ein ruhender Punkt, sondern ein Punkt, der sich in Bewegung befindet. Und zwar bewegt er sich innerhalb der ununterbrochen weiter rückenden Zeit immer in einer bestimmten Richtung vorwärts . . . Auf das Geschehen, das die bewegte Mitte der Umwelt bildet, kann ich immer nur mit dem vielsagenden hinweisenden Fürwort ‚dieses' hindeuten als auf das Geschehen, das mich absolut nahe angeht. . ."[50]

Therefore, the pure spectator-position is an abstraction. It has nothing to do with the real conditions of human existence.

2. The next consequence has some connections with the first. Heim says that every individual perspective is relative and in a certain sense arbitrary, namely in that it is not possible to give a sufficient answer to the question why my perspective view of reality looks as it actually does. Of course, its content depends on the position of my "here-and-now" within the temporal and spatial continuum, but it is not possible to give my "here-and-now" a certain importance or precedence in relation to other perspective centres. There is no firm and resting point within polar space. Therefore every perspective centre also has an irrefutable character of arbitrariness and relativity.[51] This thought plays an important role in what we shall call the existential criterion, and we shall return to the matter in that connection.

3. The last consequence is a rather peculiar one. It follows from the law of perspective together with the postulate we shall mention below. Heim says that there is a kind of antagonism between different perspectives. The point of the reasoning is this. On the basis of our daily experience Heim says that there is a manifold of individual perspectives within reality. And we saw that he said that the individuality of the perspective centre was an essential property. Now, the manifold of perspectives is not compatible with its essential individuality. The result of this is that there appears a contradiction between the fact that there are a manifold of perspectives on the one hand and its essential individuality on the other. Now, Heim states that the individual perspective has a natural tendency to authorize itself as the only real and authentic perspective. This is a postulate for which he has no arguments. But the claim of authenticity and authority of the own perspective is impossible to justify because this claim contradicts the relativistic consequence of the law of perspective. This means that the existence of different individual perspectives is in itself an anomaly within reality, which essentially ought to have only one perspective centre.

The significance of the law of perspective in a religious total view of reality. Of course, the law of perspective is important when Heim treats the Christian view of reality. When he presents this view he must somehow relate it to the law of perspecive.

Here it could be natural to interpret a Christian belief as being one expression of a certain perspective among other possible perspectives. But this interpretation is precisely what Heim rejects. Not to do it would mean to abandon Christian belief to relativity:

"Jedes Urteil, das perspektivischen Charakter trägt, vor allem die Auffassung der Person Jesu als der Zentralpersönlichkeit der Menschheitsgeschichte, als der Mitte der Zeiten, erscheint von vornherein als eine bloss subjektive Weltdeutung, als ein blosses Bewusstseinsphänomen, über das der objektive Weltlauf zur Tagesordnung übergeht. Solange das perspektivische Gesamtbild der Innenwelt angehört, von der die Aussenwelt unabhängig ist, ist diese Anschauung unwiderleglich".[52]

Heim's reason for saying that a Christian perspective is not relative is the circumstance that the perspective centre of a Christian view of reality has a kind of anchorage, not in the continuous flow of events, but in a reality beyond it: supra-polar space. And the anchorage of a Christian perspective is immediately given from outside. It is in this connection, when Heim as a Christian thinker interprets the acceptance of the religious assumption concerning the transcendence of God, that he says that the Christian perspective centre expresses an "existence in Christ" and that it transcends all relative perspectives. It is a "higher-degree-perspective", or a perspective on a higher level, which consummates all other perspectives in itself:

"Alle diese räumlichen und zeitlichen Bindungen an Heimat und Familie, an die Jetztzeit und an ‚Bezugskörper' werden relativiert ... sobald sich die gegenständliche Reflexion auf sie richtet und der Gedanke entsteht: Könnte ich nicht an sich ebensogut an einem anderen Ort und zu einer anderen Zeit geboren sein und die Welt von einem anderen 'Standpunkt' aus betrachten? Die Eigenart der Gebundenheit an Christus liegt aber gerade darin, dass sie diese Feuerprobe der Reflexion besteht, dass sie vergegenständlicht werden kann, ohne irgend etwas von ihrer Unbedingtheit zu verlieren. Wenn ich an diesen ‚unsichtbaren Ort' Christus trete, also ‚in Christus' bin, so umfängt mich die Ruhe der Ewigkeit, in der die Drehkrankheit des Relativismus geheilt wird. Die Setzung, von der wir stehen, ist also der ganzen perspektivischen Erfahrungsform, aus der der Relativismus als notwendige Folge entsteht, absolut entgegensetzt. Wenn wir diese ewige Setzung fassen wollen, müssen wir eine neue Kategorie einführen. Wir sind auf etwas gestossen, das jenseits der ganzen perspektivischen Weltform steht. In Gott sind alle Perspektiven aufgehoben ... Es ist ein ‚transperspektivischer' Akt vollzogen. Es entsteht eine neue, allen irdischen Mannigfaltigkeiten diametral entgegengesetzte Perspektive höherer Ordnung, deren Mitte Christus ist".[53]

The thoughts in this long passage are of course of decisive importance in Heim's construction of Christian dogmatics: It becomes very christocentric.[54] And the center of this "higher-degree-perspective", the person of Christ, can only be revealed.[55] But we shall not continue this theme here, but in the investigation of the existential criterion.

3.3. The criterion of Science: An acceptable religious belief must not contradict commonly accepted scientific theories and results

Introduction. Before we examine this criterion, we shall begin by mentioning an aspect of Heim's thinking which is best dealt with here. It concerns one of his premises in the criteria of science. It also follows from the criterion of universality, interpreted as a criterion of reference. Heim says:

"Ueberall, wo in der Naturbeschreibung ein Absolutum auftaucht, wo also mit einer Grösse gerechnet wird, die keiner anderen Grösse bedarf, durch die sie existiert, die vielmehr nur durch sich selbst da ist, oder mit einer Daseinsform, die keiner anderen Daseinsform bedarf, zu der sie relativ in Geltung steht, sondern die lediglich durch sich selbst gilt, da ragt der Glaube in die Naturbeschreibung herein, auch wenn das Wort Gott oder Glaube dabei überhaupt nicht vorkommt. Denn die subjektive Funktion, die jedem Absolutum entspricht, ist das, was Luther im Grossen Katechismus meint, wenn er von dem spricht, worauf wir unbedingt vertrauen und uns ganz und gar verlassen können ... Ueberall da, wo in die Naturbeschreibung und Berechnung ein absoluter Faktor aufgenommen werden muss, ragt im Grunde der religiöse Glaube in die wissenschaftliche Berechnung herein".[1]

This passage needs some consideration. Heim here seems to state two things:

First, he says that the object of religious devotion and commitment must, in some sense, be absolute. And it seems to be convenient in this connection to interpret this absoluteness as meaning a metaphysical transcendent being, having aseity.[2] And it seems to be a reasonable demand, in regard to the psychological features of religious belief. It is certainly a fact that almost every religious man ascribes such a property (absoluteness) to God, and deprived of this property, God would cease to be an adequate object for religious devotion and commitment.

Heim's second condition seems to be more problematic. He tends to identify the quest for the absolute within science (we shall return to the content of it below) with the quest for God. But this identification seems to be arbitrary as far as it concerns the object of the quest. The absolute within science may in no way possess metaphysical transcendence, and even if it does, it makes no sense to ascribe to it personal properties. Heim's examples of such absolutes are the concepts of an absolute object, the notions of absolute time and space and the notion of causality.[3] It is no point in ascribing to these concepts some kind of metaphysical transcendence. It is not inconsistent to deny that identification. Besides, most scientists who are searching for an absolute concept of this kind within science would probably deny that they also are searching for God. It may even be the case that the psychological aspect mentioned above can serve as an argument against such an identification. We shall examine further this matter in the chapter on the existential criteria. Although it may be an existential problem for some people, the reference-interpretation of the criteria of universality cannot be theoretically justified in this way.

Presentation of the criterion. We shall now present the criterion of science. It says that the religious basic assumptions must not contradict scientific basic assumptions. One can distinguish four different versions of it.

1. The scientific basic assumptions logically entail the religious basic assumptions. This means that the scientific basic assumptions work as a premise in a rational proof of the truth of the religious basic assumptions. This is the position of e.g. some kinds of natural theology or of an empirical theist.[4]

2. The scientific basic assumptions logically entail the negation of the religious basic assumptions.

This is an interesting position. To hold it of course entails atheism. But in order to avoid a contradiction within a religious total view of reality, one can claim that it is of course a legitimate task to critizise the scientific basic assumptions on their own terms, e.g. by demonstrating that they entail logical contradictions. (This is exactly what Heim does in his apologetics.)[5] There are no a priori reasons for taking the scientific basic assumptions for granted and ascribing to them a kind of absolute status.

3. The third case is the reverse of the first: The religious basic assumptions entail the scientific basic assumptions. To accept this position means that religious basic assumptions (among other basic assumptions) determine science. But it is obvious that religious basic assumptions cannot be integrated in a scientific theory in this way, e.g. as a kind of ultimate explanatory factor. Science is, as well as philosophy, belief independent. And it is quite a different task to construct a total view of reality, which includes both science and religion.

4. The religious basic assumptions logically entail the negation of scientific basic assumptions. Here we can, mutatis mutandis, make the same remarks as we did on the second possibility, because they are equivalent.

What this criterion not states. We shall also say something about what this criterion does not state. In order to do this we shall distinguish two levels: the level of religious and scientific basic assumptions at one hand and the level of scientific results and religious doctrines at the other. A religious doctrine then is one (of many) possible interpretations of facts according to the religious basic assumptions, and a scientific result is one (of many) possible interpretations of facts according to scientific basic assumptions. And concerning these, there are of course cases, when the facts, from the scientific point of view, can have only one reasonable interpretation. The scientific result is commonly accepted and considered well-established (e.g.: It is unreasonable to interpret relevant facts within astronomy as presenting a geocentric universe). Now, it is on the level of scientific results and religious doctrines that the relation between sciences and religion is popularly discussed. The most famous example of this is of course the contradiction between a literal interpretation of the creation story of Genesis and the theory of evolution.

The criterion of science then says that it is not on this level that the relation between science and religion ought to be discussed. But we shall make some remarks on possible and general relations between religion and science on the level of results and doctrines.

5. A scientific result confirms a religious doctrine, and thus its underlying basic assumption.

If this is the case, then the relation between religion and science is unproblematical. But it is also a mistake to think that the religious doctrine and its underlying basic assumption is in some way verified. To speak about verification here is only possible if the underlying basic assumptions really are not contradictory. Otherwise this case can be interpreted as being merely an accidental coincidence between science and religion. (This is often the position of popular apologetics, where scientific results sometimes are interpreted in this way.)

6. A scientific result confirms the negation of a religious doctrine and its underlying basic assumption.

In this case two solutions are possible: The first one is of course to say that the religious doctrine is not possible. This is not the same as to generally deny a religious total view of reality. The other possibility is to argue that religion and science can present different total views of reality, and that it is possible to accept both under the condition that they are complementary and that the religious basic assumptions are rationally possible.

7. The next possibility is to say: A religious doctrine confirms a scientific result. This is a special case of 5. and we can make the same remarks as we did about it, with the observation that this possibility is uninteresting from the scientific point of view, if the religious basic assumption is not claimed to have also some other empirical evidence.

8. A religious doctrine confirms a scientific result. This case is equivalent with 6.

The relation between philosophical and scientific basic assumptions. Let us now turn to the question of the relation between philosophical and scientific basic assumptions. Heim says (concerning the conflicting wave and particle theories of light within physics):

"Die Physik ist an dieser Stelle durch ihre eigenen Ergebnisse in eine Zwangslage geraten. Entweder sie muss hier von einem unbegreiflichen Rätsel stehenbleiben, oder sie muss über ihren eigenen Bereich hinausgehen und sich dazu entschliessen, einen Umbau der Grundmauern vorzunehmen, auf denen unser ganzes abendländisches Denken bisher aufgebaut war. Damit ist sie in das Gebiet der Philosophie hinübergetreten ... Der Dualismus zwischen Korpuskel und Welle, Partikel und Feld stellt uns nicht bloss vor ein physikalisches Problem, das durch Experimente und Berechnungen gelöst werden könnte. Es geht vielmehr hier um eine letzte philosophische Frage".[6]

This passage seems may be best construed as a quest for those basic assumptions within scientific theory.

Heim seems here to argue that scientific basic assumptions coincide with philosophical basic assumptions. This seems to be a reasonable position. The basic concepts within scientific theory, such as time, space and causality, can of course be philosophically treated without regards to their function within scientific theory, and of course every scientific basic assumption can be investigated philosophically. A consequence of this is that science and philosophy cannot be treated as separate areas. It is important to state that Heim holds the opinion that philosophy not only is prior to science in the sense that science cannot operate with concepts, and rules for the application of those concepts, which are incompatible with philosophical basic assumptions, but also that science is forced to accept some philosophical basic assumptions. Heim is therefore anxious to show that basic assumptions within science are philosophical assumptions and that science does not need basic assumptions other than philosophical ones.

It is inadmissible to introduce within a scientic theory a concept, which cannot be given a philosophical justification.

In this sense, a correct scientific investigation can give further evidence to what already is known through a philosophical analysis. The distinction between the two types of basic assumptions is more dependent on the context in which the assumption is used than on its content. But basic philosophical assumptions are of course also important within a scientific theory.

We can thus proceed to examine some important scientific basic assumptions according to Heim. These basic assumptions are assumptions about (1) time and space and (2) about causality and determinism. Let us begin with the first couple.

A basic assumption on time: Time has two aspects. It may be convenient to start with some central passages. Heim here states that the concept of time can be interpreted in a twofold manner or that time presents itself in two ways. He says:

"Das Wort ‚Werden' erhält . . . einen doppelten Sinn. Es ist einesteils der Vorgang, den wir vor uns sehen, wenn im Erinnerungsraum die immer schon abgeschlossenen Bilder des Geschehens in stetiger Aufeinanderfolge auftreten. Das ist ein Werden im sekundären Sinn des Wortes, nähmlich das zeitliche Nacheinander von Gewordenem innerhalb des vorhandenen Zeitkontinuums. Andererseits bedeutet Werden, im primären Sinn genommen, den Uebergang, in dem das Werden im sekundären Sinn selbst entsteht. In dem Uebergang, der mit dem primären Werden gemeint ist, geht also die Wirklichkeit aus der Form des Ungewordenen erst in die Form des Gewordenen über".[7]

"Wenn wir also einen Werdeprozess, ‚unmittelbar beobachten', ‚miterleben', ‚mitansehen', . . . so bekommen wir in Wahrheit nicht den Werdevorgang selber zu Gesicht, sondern wir nehmen in stetiger Aufeinanderfolge bereits gewordene, abgeschlossene Tatbestände und unabänderliche Bilder in uns auf. Es ist genau wie bei einer Filmvorführung, in der ja auch lauter bereits fertige Einzelphotographien in schneller Aufeinanderfolge an uns vorüberziehen".[8]

According to Heim time thus presents itself in a twofold manner, as "becoming", "Werden" and as "passed", "Gewordensein", or as "presence", "Gegenwart" and as "past", "Vergangenheit".[9] It can at once be said that this view on time exactly corresponds to our second philosophical basic assumption about objectifiable and non-objectifiable space. The former space is identical with the past ("Vergangenheit") and the latter with the present ("Werden"). We shall now call the former interpretation of time the objective-linear notion of time. According to it time consists appearently of a sequence of time-instants $t_1, t_2, \ldots t_n$. The non-objectifiable notion of time may be interpreted in terms of becoming in the now-point. Now, Heim states that this interpretation in some sense is primary to the objective-linear interpretation. This is the very point of this theory. Now, the theory of the priority of the non-objectifiable notion of time may be made somewhat clearer if we present his arguments for it. It is possible to distinguish three such arguments, which are interrelated.

Arguments for the double interpretation of time. 1. The first argument starts from the law of polarity. It says that there is a polar relation between the past and the present. Some passages would indicate this:

"Neben der Urbeziehung Ich und Welt ... steht ein zweiter polarer Gegensatz, in dem wir uns bei allem, was wir empfinden und denken, ununterbrochen bewegen müssen ... Das ist der Gegensatz zwischen dem, was gegenwärtig ... ist, und dem, was vergangen ... ist ..."[10].

"Neben der dimensionalen Spaltung und dem paradoxen Verhältnis zeigte sich der polare Charakter der Unterscheidung der beiden Dimensionen. Es gibt keinen Erinnerungsraum ohne die Gegenwart, aus der er hervorströmt, von der aus er in zeitlicher Rückschau gesehen wird; und es gibt umgekehrt keine Gegenwart, die sich nicht vortwährend in Vergangenheit verwandelt, also kein Dasein, das nicht immer schon ein In-der-Welt-Sein ist. Beide Seiten der Sache lassen sich nur durch eine Abstraktion voneinander loslösen."[11]

This passage may be interpreted in two ways. First all time instants can be said to have a polar relation to eachother both in the objective-linear- and becoming-interpretation of time. Secondly, it can be said that the objective-linear and the becoming-interpretations of time have a polar relation to eachother.

2. The next argument is more explicit. Here the starting point is the basic assumption that the ego is non-objectifiable. Heim says:

"Es (i.e. das Jetzt) ist zwar von der einen Seite gesehen ein Punkt unter unendlich vielen andern Punkten, die sich innerhalb der Zeitstrecke aneinanderreihen. Von der andern Seite gesehen steht es aber ausserhalb des ganzen Zeitablaufs; es hat überhaupt keinen Ort innerhalb des gegenständlichen Zeitraums, sondern gehört dem nichtgegenständlichen Raum an. Es ist die Stelle wo das unobjektivierbare Ich mit der Zeitstrecke in eine geheimnisvolle Verbindung tritt".[12]

"Wenn wir vom Ich absehen, ist ... die Zeitstrecke nichts als eine Reihe aufeinanderfolgender Augenblicke, die ebensogut nach vorwärts wie nach rückwärts durchlaufen werden könnte und in der jeder Augenblick dasselbe Gewicht hat wie jeder andere. Auch der gegenwärtige Augenblick wird vom Zeitstrom fortgerissen, um zu versinken und dem nächsten Augenblick Platz zu machen. Völlig anders wird das Bild, wenn wir die Zeit vom Ich aus betrachten. Dann ist der gegenwärtige Augenblick nicht ein Zeitpunkt, der vom Zeitstrom fortgerissen wird. Auf das Jetzt fällt ein Akzent, der aus einer anderen Dimension kommt. Es ist, vom Ich aus gesehen, das nunc aeternum, das immer stillstehende Jetzt, durch das der Zeitstrom fortwährend hindurchfliesst. Wie das ‚Hier' gleichzeitig innerhalb und ausserhalb des Körperraums liegt, so liegt also auch das „Jetzt' immer gleichzeitig innerhalb und ausserhalb der Zeitstrecke".[13]

Here Heim says that the fact that the ego is non-objectifiable is a premise in the argument. The non-objectifiable nature of the ego implies that it cannot only be seen as occupying a place in a sequence of time-instants.

3. The third argument has some connection with the second. Heim argues that the notion of the perspective centre also makes it natural to infer that time is twofold. The perspective centre is non-objectifiable. Heim therefore says that:

"Die perspektivische Mitte ... hat also ein Doppelgesicht. Das eine Gesicht ist der Gegenwart zugewendet, das andere der Vergangenheit. Betrachten wir die Mitte von der Seite der Gegenwart aus, so ist sie ein Dasein, das keine Stelle im Zeitkontinuum einnimmt ... Betrachten wir sie aber von der anderen Seite her, von dem vorhandenen Zeitkontinuum der Vergangenheit aus, so nimmt sie eine Stelle in ihm ein".[14]

The natural power of the perspective centre to receive impressions and put them together, both from objectifiable and non-objectifiable space, to form a total view of reality, makes it reasonable to infer that time has this twofold nature.

Concluding remarks. We shall now mention some other considerations relating to some features in Heim's view of time. They are connected to his dual understanding of time.

1. The first one deals with what we shall call the "generation" of time. This generation is in some sense incomprehensible, and it consists in saying that the past "is born" from the present. This generation is said to be always taking place. This is an essential feature of reality, which cannot be reduced to another feature.[15] Therefore the objective-linear notion says that all time-instants on the line are equal (and polar), also the "now" (and the imagined future). The becoming-interpretation containing the non-objectifiable moment of time says that only the past is objectifiable, but the now is non-objectifiable. The non-objectifiable is the place of the becoming. And the priority of the latter means that it is the proper notion of time, because it is not based on an objectifying abstraction. Heim says:

"Die Gegenwart ist ja noch gar keine Stelle in einem ohne sie vorhandenen Kontinuum. Sie ist der allgegenwärtige Mutterschoss, aus dem dieses Kontinuum erst hervorgeht. Wenn wir also das, was im Uebergang, also im Werdezustand der Gegenwart fortwährend geschieht, richtig beschreiben wollen, so müssen wir sagen: der Nullpunkt, in dem es überhaupt noch keine Zeitstrecke gibt, verwandelt sich in ein Kontinuum; bei dieser Verwandlung aus dem ersten in das zweite Stadium wird der Nullpunkt, aus dem die Zeitstrecke erst geboren wird, zum Mittelpunkt und damit zu einem Punkt, der nun ... ein Punkt unter anderen Punkten ist, also als willkürlich ausgewählter Punkt erscheint."[16]

Time manifests itself as an eternal becoming ("Uebergang"). And now the concept of this becoming is contradictory. It reveals both the distance between the different time-instants *and* the necessary connection between them.[17]

2. *The ego and temporal existence.* The next important consequence concerns the question of the metaphysical status (or level) of the non-objectifiable ego. We saw that Heim was very anxious to maintain that the ego exists within non-objectifiable space, i.e. within the realm of becoming.

However, this fact does not entail that the ego has a kind of non-temporal existence. Some critics of Heim seems to have interpreted him in this way, according to an idealistic tradition, in saying that the ego is in some way an independent and creative instance in the construction of a total view of reality. This criticism of Heim is certainly wrong,[18] but there is another passage that may more appropriately be interpreted in this way:

"Wir haben noch ein Gefühl davon, dass dieser Punkt (i.e. Das Dasein des Ich als solchen und dem bestimmten Punkt in Raum und Zeit) immer etwas Zweites ist, in das wir erst hineintreten, das uns also erst angewiesen wird, dass wir also aus einer anderen Region kommen, die noch diesseits des vorhandenen Zeitraums steht".[19]

We shall in more detail treat this matter in the part on the existential criterion.

But Heim's position is in fact the opposite: Although the ego is non-objectifiable, this fact does not entail that it has a kind of existence above or outside time. On the contrary: its existence, or mode of existence, is essentially time-dependent.[20] Perhaps this feature in the existence of the ego is Heim's decisive argument against mysticism.[21]

"Ist die Gegenstandswelt präsenzlos, also im Zustand des Gewordenseins, so folgt daraus nicht, dass das nichtgegenständliche Ich ausserhalb der Zeit steht; sondern es folgt daraus immer nur das eine: Zum Wesen des Ich gehört die Präsenz, das Werden, das Noch-nicht-entschiedensein. Das Ich ist also ganz und gar zeitlich, sein Dasein ist Zeit sein".[22]

And such is the existence of the ego: To its essence belongs existence in time.

3. The last consequence is about the motion, or direction, of time. On the basis of the objective-linear notion of time, it is natural to say that time moves, and that it moves forward. In this respect it is correct to say that every event is connected with a certain time-instant within the objective sequence of time-instants. Then it is also natural to imagine that this time-line can be tightened or projected into the future. But as we shall see later, in the subsequent section on determinism, that this projection cannot, according to Heim, be justified. Further, given the objective-linear notion of time, it is also possible for the mind to make an (imaginative) journey on this line. In this context Heim develops a kind of criterion of objectivity, applicable to events in the past.[23] Such a fictive journey in time (e.g. in the form of dreams or fancies) can always be conceived as real as the ordinary reality. Such a journey presents also a closed and structured system of events within a certain time and space, namely

the dreamed time and space. But we have no material reason to judge them as fictive and unreal only because they are dreamed. But the decisive point is: they cannot be connected with the flow of events within the ordinary time and space without certain inexplicable interruptions. Heim says:

"Worauf beruht der Gegensatz der zwei Welten, den wir empfinden, wenn wir aus einem Traum erwachen oder aus tiefem Nachdenken wieder in die Wirklichkeit zurückkehren? Der Gegensatz beruht immer nur darauf, dass die Welt, in der wir uns im Traum oder bei lebhafter Vorstellungstätigkeit bewegen, in den raumzeitlichen Zusammenhang der wachen Empfindungswelt nicht hineinpassen will." [24]

According to the other concept of time, no such journey is possible. The ego is necessary bound to the present.

Heim's theory of space. Let us now turn to Heim's theory of space. It is important to say that his theory of space is a general theory and not only about the three-dimensional space, which we ordinarily experience. (In what follows, when we talk about the ordinary space, we shall refer to it as the "o-space".) We shall further see that Heim has no separate theory of space. Instead he develops this theory on the foundation of his theory of time. But here we meet a problem: Because Heim accepts a dual theory of time, this also results in a dual theory of space. Thus we have a corresponding basic assumption concerning space. We get one concept of space, corresponding to the objective-linear interpretation of time, and another concept of space, corresponding to the becoming-interpretation of time. These spaces we shall call objectifiable and non-objectifiable spaces. It may also prima facie seem natural to identify the objectifiable space with the o-space. This is correct, but only to some extent. There are also other and more limited objectifiable spaces, e.g. the time-sequence. Thus, time and space are not, as in the philosophy of Kant, two equal but different forms of perceiving. On the contrary: Heim's theory of space can be traced back to this theory of time. These theories are basically of the same nature. Our task is to investigate Heim's view on the relation between these theories.

Let us begin with objectifiable space. Heim says:

"Denn beide (i.e. die Zeitstrecke und die Raumlinie) haben, abgesehen vom ihren Besonderheiten, eine gemeinsame Grundform. Das gemeinsame Grundelement von beiden ist eine Linie, die in stetigem Fortschritt durchlaufen wird." [25]

"Diese (i.e. die Grundeigentümlichkeit der Raumanschauung) besteht darin, dass das Verhältnis, das beim reinen Zeiterlebnis zwischen den Gliedern einer Reihe besteht, übertragen wird auf die Beziehung zwischen verschiedenen Richtungen, in denen Erlebnisreihen durchlaufen werden können. Das Raumverhältnis ist also in gewissem Sinne ein Zeitverhältnis zweiten Grads". [26]

But there is of course something new in the concept of space: The dimension of depth:

"Die Raumwelt mit ihrem Nebeneinander und ihrem Abstand zwischen sehendem und gesehenem Punkt bringt kein neues Verhältnis in die Anschauungsformen ein, das nicht schon in der einfachen Zeitstrecke enthalten wäre ... Aber gibt es nicht noch eine besondere Eigentümlichkeit des Raumbilds ... nämlich die Tiefendimension?"[27]

How can then a transformation from a simple objective-linear concept of time to a concept of space take place? Heim seems to have two different theories as answers to this question. We shall call the first answer the logical theory and the second answer the psychological.

1. Let us begin with the second answer. According to this Heim says that the transformation of time to space is due to a kind of habit, and this habit is so well established and we are so used to it that we really do not reflect on it. He says:

"Wir Älteren haben gelernt, durch ein kompliziertes Schlussverfahren die Entfernung der Gegenstände von unserem Auge einigermassen zu schätzen, wenn wir dabei auch noch trotz täglicher Uebung fortwährend Täuschungnen ausgesetzt sind ... Aber alle diese Methoden, durch die aus dem ursprünglichen Flächenbild der perspektivische Eindruck der Körperlichkeit wird, sind nicht in dem unmittelbaren Erlebnis selbst enthalten, sondern erst hinterher zum unmittelbar Gegebenen hinzugekommen durch ein Schlussverfahren, das uns durch lange Uebung so zur Gewohnheit geworden ist, dass wir es vom unmittelbar Gegebenen kaum mehr unterschieden können."[28]

The addition of the dimension of depth is then not something which we are directly acquainted with or directly apprehend, like impressions of colours or sounds or the natural power of the mind to make distinctions between colours and sounds. What is it then? Heim says that it is the immediate experience of a distance between the perceiving eye and the object.[29] If this distance did not exist, then the experience of space would be identical with the experience of time. And it is the combination of different directed time-sequences which makes it possible to extend it to a notion of space.[30] But this extension is as incomprehensible as the transformation of a sequence of time instants to a continous time.[31] With this we have reached the logical theory which answers the question.

2. Here Heim's problem is: How is the theory of space to be logically interpreted in terms of the theory of time? And again: It seems reasonable to suppose that it is the objective-linear notion of time for following reason (apart from the consideration that to assume the becoming-interpretation of time would make this reasoning nonsensical): Now, how is the concept of space exactly related to the objective-linear concept of time? "Wie kommt es, dass auf diesem gemeinsamen Fundament zwei verschiedene Anschauungsformen aufgebaut sind?"[32] or "Was ist das Neue, das zum Zeiterlebnis hinzukommt, wenn es sich zum Raumerlebnis entfaltet?"[33] We said that the objective-linear notion of time is the exclusive either-or-relation: Either a certain event is connected with a certain timepoint, t_1, or it is not. Now, the point is that an experience of space can arise, because it is possible to combine several and different-directed objective-linear time-sequences with eachother:

"Das Raumverhältnis ist also in gewissem Sinne ein Zeitverhältnis zweiten Grads. Aus diesem Grundcharakter des Raumerlebnisses müssen nun noch die weiteren Eigentümlichkeiten der Raumanschauung verstanden werden, die Unterscheidung zwischen dem sehenden und dem gesehenen Punkt, das Nebeneinander, also die Gleichzeitigkeit der Raumteile, und endlich die Tiefendimension, aus deren Verbindung mit der Fläche die dreidimensionale Körperlichkeit entsteht." [34]

This certainly needs some explanation. A possible explanation is this: (We shall here use the concept "dimension" as follows: every event is connected with a time-instant within a time-sequence. A set of events, connected with different time-instants would then constitute a dimension (the dimension of time).) The same reasoning can, mutatis mutandis, be applied also on the o-space.

All temporal distinctions (i.e. the connection of a certain event with either t_1 or not-t_1) are only possible within the objective-linear concept of time. But now it also is possible to make a distinction between different dimensions [35] and this distinction is logically of the same nature as a distinction within a certain dimension. [36] This means that the relation between different dimensions is also an either-or-relation. Now, the experience of space can be said to arise from such a combination of simple dimensions in the sense that with such a new combination there is the possibility of a totally new and more complex mode of experience. [37] The temporal relation "after" can in this way be combined with the spatial relation "beside", which can be said to belong to a new and other-directed time-sequence. This latter is also temporal, because it takes a certain time to move from a position to another along this too. Then a more complex mode of conceiving is possible: Two events can be seen to have different places within one dimension but not within another.

But this logical analysis gives no answer to the psychological question of how this addition of a new dimension actually take place. The psychological process is from the logical point of view wholly incomprehensible. [38]

Now, Heim based his theory of space on this theory of time. But, because he had a dual interpretation of it, it resulted in a corresponding theory of space. Then we have an objectifiable notion of space, depending on an abstraction from the subject, and a non-objectifiable notion of space, which takes account of the perspective centre. The "here" in the "I-here-and-now" is as non-objectifiable as the "now".

Let us now turn to Heim's treatment of the second pair of scientific basic assumptions: The complex problem of causality and determinism.

A basic assumption on causality: Only objectifiable space presents a causal system. By way of introduction, let us briefly sketch Heim's theory. It says that the following two statements are true: (1) There is certainly determinism and causality within reality, but determinism and causality can only properly be ascribed to events within objectifiable space. These events are once and for all

connected with different time-instants in the objective-linear timesequence.[39]
(2) But there is also certainly indeterminism and acausality within reality. Events within non-objectifiable space cannot properly be said to be caused or determined. And his main argument for this assertion is that the relation between objectifiable and non-objectifiable space is not a causal, but a polar one. The content of this theory raises at once some important questions:

1. Which view of causality and determinism is correct according to Heim?
2. What kind of relation is there between objectifiable and non-objectifiable spaces? Is there really nothing more to say about it than that it is polar? And this leads to the question
3. What is the content of the concept of becoming ("Werden")?

But before we proceed we must examine the concepts of causality and determinism, and then we can look at Heim's answers to these questions.

The relation between causality and determinism. It is reasonable to start with some remarks on the concepts of causality and determinism. They are of course very intimately connected.

We shall define determinism like this: Determinism is the view that holds it to be true that everything that happens in the world, even the thoughts and activities of men, has a cause. The opposite view, indeterminism, is then said to hold it to be true that not everything that happens in the world has a cause. So far we have said nothing about the way in which events actually follow each other.

A common view now says that events follow each other according to the laws of nature. With the concept "law of nature" we shall only mean laws within empirical science. It is further not necessary to discuss here the kind of argument for stating a regularity as a law of nature.

We shall not discuss whether such reasoning is inductive on the basis of empirical evidence or aprioristic or something else. The only things we require of a law of nature is that it must be universal, i.e. it must cover all members of a given class without exception, and that it must be predictive, i.e. it must be possible to make true predictions by applying them correctly.

We can now define a stronger version of determinism and indeterminism. Determinism is the view that holds it to be true that everything that happens in the world, even thoughts and activities of men, happens according to universal laws of nature. This view we shall call a causal-mechanical world-view. Indeterminism, then, holds it true that not everything in the world happens according to a universal law of nature.

The concept of causality. So far, we have related the concepts of determinism and indeterminism to the concept of cause. What is a cause then? Let us now try to give a brief outline of this concept and start from this consideration: Given two events, E_1 and E_2, of which E_1 is said to temporally precede E_2 and that E_2 is said to be caused by E_1, how are then these relations to be interpreted? What shall these relations be like to properly characterize E_1 as the cause of E_2?

Let us go directly to the main point and limit the discussion to the two alternatives: (a) a cause is a necessary condition, and (b) a cause is a sufficient condition.[40]

(a) According to this view, the meaning of the term cause is "simply the empirical fact that in the absence of E_1, E_2 never occurs. Thus, in the absence of oxygen, we never have fire." For the appearance of fire, there must also be some other circumstances present: The presence of sufficient heat, a piece of inflammable matter, and so on.

(b) According to this view, the meaning of the term cause is that "when ever E_1 occurs, then E_2 invariably occurs. If rain is falling on the street, the street will be wet". This is of course invariably true, but the street may have been wet for other reasons as well. It is not difficult to imagine other circumstances, resulting in the streets being wet.

Heim's view on determinism. Let us now turn to Heim and quote a passage, where he makes some remarks on this question. He says:

"Solange wir rein empiristisch, d.h. rein gegenständlich denken und die perspektivische Figur, in Klammer setzen', ensteht weder der Begriff der Kausalität noch der der Freiheit, weder die Idee des berechenbaren Weltganzen, der notwendigen Bedingtheit aller Ereignisse, noch der Glaube an einen freien Akt, der ausserhalb der Berechenbarkeit steht und unbedingt ist. Der Empirismus kann immer nur ein Nacheinander von Ereignissen feststellen".[41]

And after some remarks, in which Heim accepts Hume's analysis of causality, provided that abstraction from the essential connection between the subject and the object is made,[42] he continues:

"Dass diese Aufeinanderfolgen nicht bloss regelmässig, sondern notwendig sind, dass sie Umsätze eines konstanten Energiequantums ... sind, dieser Gedanke ist vom reinen Empirismus aus unerreichbar. Erst wenn ein Lebensakt aus dem Nichtgegenständlichen heraus in die Weltmitte tritt und sich als Glied eines Gesamtgeschehens vorfindet, sind mit einem Schlag beide Eindrücke zugleich da, der Eindruck der Schicksalsnotwendigkeit, die die Aufeinanderfolgen des Weltgeschehens zu einem lückenlosen Kausalzusammenhang zusammenschliesst, und das Bewusstsein der Freiheit, durch das sich der noch nicht zur Tat gewordene Lebensakt vom Kausalzusammenhang der gegenständlichen Welt unterscheidet".[43]

And thus Heim concludes that determinism and indeterminism are polar concepts, corresponding to the polarity of objectifiable and non-objectifiable spaces. Now, according to Heim, the assumption that determinism is true entails an antinomy: For this statement to be true, it is necessary to make an exception from the realm of determinancy, namely the individual who makes that statement:

"Der Determinismus und der Indeterminismus sind, richtig verstanden, die zwei Seiten eines und desselben perspektivischen Gesamtbildes, von denen keine ohne die andere gedacht werden kann. Dies lässt sich durch eine einfache Ueberlegung zeigen. Ich kann die deterministische Weltanschauung nur dann haben, wenn ich an Einer Stelle eine Ausnahme von ihr mache. Ich kann nur dann an die Allgemeingültigkeit des Kausalgesetzes für alle körperlichen, seelischen und geistigen Vorgänge glauben, wenn ich Ein Element von der Unterordnung unter das Kausalgesetz ausnehme. Dieses Eine Element ist der Bewusstseinsakt, durch den ich mir die deterministische Weltanschauung aneigne, das Urteil, durch das ich die Allgemeingültigkeit des Kausalgesetzes als wahr erkenne. Denn wenn ich auch diesen Erkenntnisakt selbst für ein Glied der Kausalkette ansehe, also für ein psychologisches Ereignis, das ein notwendiges Produkt der Einflüsse und Verhältnisse ist, die auf mein Bewusstsein eingewirkt haben, dann habe ich kein Recht mehr, von der Wahrheit meiner deterministischen Ueberzeugung zu sprechen ... Ja es hat überhaupt keinen Sinn mehr, von Wahrheit zu sprechen".[44]

This last passage contains a very interesting and doubtful assumption. It is really the case that a statement in order to be true, must not be caused? This is a very problematic assumption, in favour of which Heim, as far I can see, does not give any arguments. And to state this is to confuse the questions of the genesis and the validity of knowledge. Statements on determinism are not exceptions from general criterias of truth. Why cannot a caused statement on determinism be true as well as a caused statement on other subjects? Perhaps it is Heim's intention to say that meta-statements on determinism (as well as on other subjects) must not be caused. This may be a correct view, but Heim gives no arguments in favour of this either. But because a further examination of this problem not is relevant here, we shall leave it.

Now, the realm of causality is then, according to Heim limited to objectifiable space. Causal concepts do not apply outside that space:

"Alles, was abgeschlossen ist, auch meine eigenen Willensentscheidungen, sobald sie getroffen sind, auch meine eigenen Gedanken, sobald sie gedacht sind, reihe ich als Glieder in einen geschlossenen Kausalzusammenhang ein, betrachte sie als Verwirklichungen von Möglichkeiten, die schon vorhanden waren, als Umsätze eines konstantes Energiequantums in eine neue Form".[45]

"Die gegenständliche Erfahrungswelt muss also einen geschlossenen Kausalzusammenhang darstellen, es muss sich in ihr ein konstanter Energievorrat nach notwendigen Gesetzen in immer neue Formen umsetzen, wenn es möglich sein soll, auf Grund der gegebenen Sachlage einen Entschluss zu fassen ... Wenn aber der Willensakt nur entstehen kann auf Grund der Feststellung der im Kausalzusammenhang liegenden Möglichkeiten, geht damit nicht seine Freiheit wieder verloren? Wird er damit nicht zu einem blossen Ergebnis des bisherigen Kausalzusammenhangs? Nein. Denn wenn der Entschluss auch auf Grund einer Prüfung der vorhandenen Möglichkeiten gefasst wird, so ist er doch selbst von diesen Möglichkeiten deutlich unterschieden".[46]

Everything, that belongs to objectifiable space, has then afterwards always been found to have happened according to a causal law. And Heim seems further to be of the opinion that that causal laws are ultimately based on the principle of the constancy of energy. And these laws have no exceptions.[47] We can say that Heim accepts the stronger view of determinism we mentioned above.

What is a cause according to Heim? Now we can examine Heim's concept of cause. He says that to mention the cause of an event is to answer the question why some event happened or why a certain change occurred.[48] Besides the reference to man's natural curiosity as a motive for asking such why-questions and the psychological need for an answer, Heim also states something more important. The question is intimately connected with the natural power of the mind to distinguish one state of affairs from another state of affairs.[49] And states of affairs are different at different time-instants. Now, the answer to such a why-question consists in an explanation. What constitutes an explanation according to Heim? He says:

"... wir empfinden es schon als eine Antwort auf die Warumfrage, wenn der neuen Erscheinung, die uns auffällt, auf irgendeine Weise das Neue und Besondere genommen wird, wenn gezeigt wird, dass sie nur die spezielle Anwendung eines allgemeinen Begriffs ist, den wir auch in vielen anderen Fällen anwenden, oder ein Spezialfall einer Regel, die immer schon gegolten hat".[50]

The expression "ein allgemeines Begriff" obviously has the same meaning as the expression "eine Regel". But how do men arrive at such a rule? And under what conditions is the use of such a rule correct? Heim gives two answers to such questions, but we shall only treat one of them here (in the other one he says that the difference between different states of affairs, is in a certain sense an illusion, because every state of affairs and every change obeys this rule). And in this one answer he also says something about what a cause is. In this case

"... ensteht der Begriff des induktiv aus der Erfahrung abgeleiteten Naturgesetzes. Ein Naturgesetz ist eine Aufeinanderfolge von zwei Ereignissen a und b, von denen das zweite regelmässig eintritt, wenn das erste geschehen ist, z.B.: wenn Reibung da ist, entsteht Wärme ... Wir können dann auch sagen: das Ereignis a ist Bedingung für das Ereignis b, b ist die ‚notwendige' Folge von a. Wenn a geschehen ist, ‚muss' b eintreten. Die Worte ‚Notwendigkeit' und ‚Müssen' sind dabei nur der Ausdruck des Glaubens: die Regel, nach der b auf a folgt, ist das konstante Element im Wechsel der Ereignisse, die Einheit, der alle diese Ereignisse unterworfen sind."[51]

Here we have to discuss two things: the concept of rule and the concept of cause. Let us begin with the concept of rule. Our discussion involves two points: (a) What signifies a rule? And the answer is quite simply: It is a law of nature. (b) Under what conditions is an application of a rule correct? And also here the answer is a brief one: Under the necessary condition that the object for it belongs to objectifiable space.

Let us then proceed to the concept of cause. To which meaning of this concept does Heim's view correspond? What is the meaning of words like

"Bedingung" and "muss" in this context? Let us examine the alternatives: Can it be said that Heim when using the concept of cause here means

(a) a necessary condition? If this is so then as we have said in the absence of E_1, E_2 never occurs. But there is nothing in the quotation which indicates this interpretation. We shall therefore not interpret Heim in this way. Such an interpretation would further make Heim's concept of cause inconsistent with his theory of decision ("Entscheidung"), which we shall explain below.

Is the meaning of the concept of cause then

(b) a sufficient condition? When this is the case, we said that when E_1 occurs then E_2 invariably occurs. This seems to be a more reasonable interpretation of the quotation, and we shall therefore adopt it. And this interpretation is consistent with his theory of decision.

We have thus interpreted the concept of cause in Heim's thinking as meaning: An event is a cause, if it is a sufficient condition for another event and both events belong to objectifiable space.

This has consequences for his view on determinism. We have just said that only events within objectifiable space can properly be said to be determined. But there seems also to be a more interesting consequence (which Heim implicitly seems to accept): Given that a cause is a sufficient condition, it is possible to infer E_1 from E_2. An event may then happen without being causally necessary (this relation we shall explain below). Here a quotation from R. Taylor seems apposite to our discussion:

"Contemporary philosophers have for the most part tried to resolve the problems of logical determinism by distinguishing between modal concpets, such as necessary, impossible and so on, and the non-modal concepts of true and false and by refusing to make certain inferences from one kind of concept to the other. Thus, from the fact that something happens of necessity, it follows that it happens, and from the fact that it is impossible for something to happen, it follows that it does not happen. The reverse of these inferences cannot be made, however; something might happen without being necessary, and something might fail to happen without being impossible".[52]

What kind of relation is there between objectifiable and non-objectifiable space? We shall now turn to the question of the relation between objectifiable and non-objectifiable space. We also said that perhaps something more could be said about this relation, apart from saying that it is polar and that non-objectifiable space could only be described in negative terms of objectifiable space. We shall quote some passages on this matter, which contain the central concept of decision, "Entscheidung". Now, this concept covers a spectrum of meanings in Heim's thoughts. We are here only interested in one of them. Very often he uses it as synonymous with becoming, "Werden".

And this term describes the kind of connection between objectifiable and non-objectifiable space. Then the term decision signifies that something is happening now, at this very moment, and that a change from one state of affairs to another is taking place. Heim says:

"Die Gegenstandswelt ist die Welt im Zustand des Gewordenseins. Wir selbst, die Subjekte, die in der ersten Person von sich reden müssen, stehen im ersten Zustand der Welt. Wir stehen im Präsenzzustand der Entscheidung".[53]

"Das Gesamtgeschehen, dessen Glieder wir selbst sind, durchläuft zwei Räume und damit zwei total voneinander verschiedene Gesamtzustände. Raum A ist der Raum des Nichtgegenständlichen, der noch nicht zur Objektivierung gelangten Möglich-keiten, Potenzen, Kräfte und Wollungen. In diesem Raum ist alles noch gegenstands-los und quantitätslos, unmessbar und unanalysierbar. Die Beziehungen zwischen den Inhalten dieses Raumes sind also in gegenständlicher Sprache immer nur indirekt ausdrückbar, in Bildern, deren Uneigentlichkeit wir empfinden. Erst im Raum B nimmt das Geschehen gegenständliche, messbare, quantitativ abgrenzbare Gestalt an. Dabei müssen wir sofort etwas hinzufügen, das sich nicht begründen, sondern nur als Tat-sache aussprechen lässt: Alles, was im Raum A, also im Jetzt-Zustand, gewesen ist, das bleibt auch dann, wenn es in den Raum B getreten ist, also objektive Gestalt gewonnen hat, immer noch auf eine nicht mehr zu beschreibende Weise im Raum A erhalten. Man könnte es auch so ausdrücken: Was aus Raum A hervorgetreten ist und Tatsache wurde, das kehrt durch einen geheimniswollen Kreislauf wieder in den Zus-tand A zurück, nimmt dort wieder die Form einer gestaltlosen Potenz oder un-terbewussten Möglichkeit an, die aufs neue Möglichkeit werden will".[54]

Here the spaces A and B obviously are non-objectifiable and objectifiable space respectively. In this passage Heim says that there is, after all, a kind of relation between these two spaces. We can state his position as follows:

(1) Events within objectifiable space have at some earlier time-instant been within non-objectifiable space.

(2) Actual events within non-objectifiable space will in the future appear within objectifiable space.

(3) Every event within objectifiable space determines the following events within non-objectifiable space.

(4) Actual events within non-objectifiable space determine in some sense following events.

(5) All events within non-objectifiable space are in some way contained in ob-jectifiable space.

Here Heim says some things, which seem to contradict what he had said before. He says that the same event both remains and does not remain in the following. This seems to be the meaning of the end of the quotation. This is of course the same idea which we have met before namely in the contradictory connection of "either-or" and "both-and" concerning time. But it is somewhat unsatisfactory to leave the matter with this contradiction, so let us therefore try a new approach to the problem.

This approach starts from the question if there can be a logical necessary connection between different events. Of course there is something odd with the use of words here. Logical relations can only be said to hold between propositions. But this formulation of the concept of a logical relation between events will remove that problem:

"At the time of occurrence of E_1, there exists that which can only be completely described by propositions, P_1, which logically imply propositions P_2, that state that E_2 occurs subsequently".[55]

There is in this passage an interesting and perhaps problematical assumption, namely that there is only one complete description of E_1. But how can we be sure that this assumption is true? Maybe there can be two alternative ways of describing E_1, say P_{11} and P_{12}, of which P_{11} logically implies E_2, but P_{12} does not. But perhaps it is not necessary for us here to consider the arguments for this conditional assumption. But it seems to be the case that there is no a priori reason why it should be impossible to construct a way of describing events, which excludes alternative descriptions. Now, if we adopt the view that there is only one complete description of an event, then this, together with the assumptions that there are logical entailments, results in a deterministic world-view. It is of course possible to argue against it. This can then be done in two ways: One can argue that (1) It is in fact possible to give alternative descriptions of the same event, or (2) It is in fact impossible to give a complete description of an event. It can be impossible for (a) psychological reasons: The mind of the man can only cover a minor part of the universe, and so on. But it can also be said that this is impossible for (b) logical reasons. Then the claim that a description is complete entails a logical contradiction. It is a matter of fact that it is impossible to abstract from the natural connection between a subject and an object, and that therefore the subject in some way intervenes in the observation-process. An example of this argument is Heisenberg's principle of indeterminancy.[56]

Now we can express Heim's position by saying that he (a) accepts the existence of logical necessary relations between events within objectifiable space, but that he (b) denies that this holds within non-objectifiable space. And then the worlds as a whole cannot be said to be determined.

Let us consider his arguments. He seems to accept the arguments (1) and (2.b.) above. (1) is a consequence of the fact that it is impossible to completely describe non-objectifiable space. But his main arguments, from (2.b.), runs like this (we are already acquainted with it): The inescapable law of polarity implies that it is impossible to abstract from the connection between the subject and the object. And this seems, for Heim, to imply that it is impossible to give a complete description of an event, because the activity of the description is itself an event. Then this would require a higher level of description of these two events, and so on. He also uses the argument from Heisenberg. There is then no logical connection between events in objectifiable and non-objectifiable space.

Science presents a dynamic view of reality. But let us return to the last quotation from Heim. According to it, reality consists of two spaces, of which the priority belongs to non-objectifiable space, which is characterized as a process of eternal becoming. This basic assumption makes it then natural to infer to a dynamic view of reality:

"Damit ist dem statischen Weltbild, das der Alleinherrschaft der Gegenständlichkeit entsprach, eine dynamische Weltauffassung gegenübertreten, die die Wirklichkeit nicht als Sein, sondern als Akt erlebt. Was das Erkennen objektiv vor sich sieht, ist dann nicht der Akt selbst, sondern immer schon das abgeschlossene sekundäre Ergebnis desselben. Die primäre Wirklichkeit, in der wir selbst mit unserer ganzen Existenz stehen, ist ganz und gar Dynamik und lebendige Aktion".[57]

The scope and limits of scientific basic assumptions within a total view of reality. After the presentation of some scientific basic assuptions we can proceed to discuss their place within a total view of reality. For this purpose we shall distinguish between

(1) those total views of reality which accept the basic assumption that there exists a non-objectifiable space within reality, and

(2) those total views of reality which deny that there exists a non-objectifiable space within reality.

Let us begin with the last group. If this position is accepted then it also have an important consequence. The scientific basic assumptions concerning time, space and determinism then cover the whole of reality. They catch everything that exists in their net, according to the objective-linear concept of time and the causal relations. Such a position, according to which the scientific assumptions are given an ultimate and absolute position, does then naturally result in a kind of scientific total view of reality, which we have called a "causal-mechanical world-view".[58] This total view of reality has no place for independent religious basic assumptions. They must either be rejected as invalid and of no cognitive content or they must be re-interpreted in accordance with the scientific basic assumptions, which makes them uninteresting from a religious standpoint.

Let us then consider the first group of total views of reality, based on the assumption that there is a non-objectifiable space within reality. If this position is accepted, then it also must be admitted that there are entities within reality, which cannot be proper objects of scientific investigation. We have seen examples of such entities: The non-objectifiable nature of the ego, and the I-Thou-relation. It must also be admitted that the realm of the scientific basic assumptions is limited to objectifiable space, i.e. the past.

The scope and limits of scientific basic assumptions within a religious total view of reality. Now we shall make a further distinction among those total views of reality which accept that there is a non-objectifiable space, namely between those which in addition to this also accepts the religious basic assumptions and those who not do it.

What place have then the scientific basic assumptions within a total religious view of reality according to Heim?

Prima facie it seems to be possible to give his view two possible interpretations.

The first one says that the scientific basic assumptions are limited to objectifiable space. But because it is non-objectifiable space which is religiously significant its existence is a necessary condition for the truth of religion then it also seems to be natural to say that events within objectifiable space cannot have any real significance for a religious total view of reality. But however natural this interpretation may be, it can hardly be said to do Heim justice. We have earlier mentioned some points, which are incompatible with this interpretation: Heim's criticism of incomplete religious theories and our reflections upon the criterion of the universality of the religious and non-religious basic assumptions.

The second and more probable interpretation we illustrate with this quotation:

"Dasselbe Geschehen, das, wie die Frommen ganz gut wissen, ein Glied des raumzeitlichen Kausalzusammenhanges ist, also die Wirkung eines unabsehbaren Geflechts von Kausalreihen und Willensakten, wird als Ganzes in eine zweite Beziehung hineingestellt. Es wird ihm eine zweite Herkunft zugeschrieben, die sich an jeder Stelle bemerkbar macht. Was innerhalb des Kausalzusammenhangs auf natürlichem Wege entsteht, wird zugleich von Gott ‚geschaffen' und ‚erhalten' ".[59]

We have mentioned our view on this matter before:

Religious basic assumptions must be logically consistent with basic scientific assumptions, i.e. they must not entail the negations of them. But religious basic assumptions must also be logically independent of current scientific results, in the sense that they must not serve as conditions for these results. Conversely of course, the religious basic assumptions must not be implied by current scientific results.

3.4. The existential criterion: An acceptable religious belief must explain certain human insights/experiences

What this criterion states. We shall formulate this criterion as follows. An acceptable religious belief must explain certain insights and experiences of e.g. paradox and relativity which are deeply embodied in the conditions of human existence.

We shall make some remarks on this formulation of the criterion because it needs some clarifications, e.g. on the notion of explanation and on the notions on experience and insight in this connection.

On explanation: To explain is to integrate. What then is an explanation? In what does it consist? Some common views on explanation are e.g. (1) to explain a fact is to mention its cause, (2) to explain a fact is to subordinate it under a law (of nature). But we shall not enter into a discussion of these views.[1]. We shall instead accept another view of explanation which has some connections to the concept of "understanding" ("Verstehen"),[2] without coinciding with it. We shall say that a fact is explained if it can be integrated in a total view of reality, i.e. the fact can reasonably be ordered according to basic assumptions of the total view of reality under consideration. Conditions of integration then are that the fact does not (1) violate a wellconfirmed basic assumption, and (2) contribute to the explanatory power of the total view of reality, i.e. all facts, belonging to the same class, must be explicable in the same manner. This view on explanation differs of course from a causal explanation, although a causal explanation in some cases, as we shall see, can be in accordance with it. This view also admits that there are explanations which are not causal explanations or which belong to the other kinds of explanations mentioned above.

Now, we said that there are some fundamental questions or problems hidden in the conditions of human existence. Therefore it is natural to present this criterion in a question-and-answer-form.[3] The question-part of this criterion corresponds to an analysis of the conditions of the existence of man, which according to Heim, reveals some inescapable characteristics of that existence, characteristics which cannot be explained within the framework of the analysis itself. We shall below give some examples of such characteristics.

The answer-part of this criterion, then, must present an explanation, in our meaning above, of human existence.

Our task is then (1) to present some relevant points in the analysis of the conditions of human existence (under the head: basic assumptions concerning human existence), and (2) to present some main characteristics which an answer must possess in order to be a true explanation (under the head: basic assumptions concerning the answer).

A suitable starting-point is a set of important questions, which are quite frequent in the writings of Heim. Here are some examples:

"1. Warum bin ich in diese unabänderliche Lage hineingestellt? 2. Was soll ich aus meinem Leben machen, soweit es noch veränderlich ist?"[4]

Such questions also return in a general version as a question for the meaning of the individual existence as a whole. This question Heim also calls the religious version of it:

"Was ist der ewige Sinn meiner jetzigen Lage?"[5]

And the main content of this question seems for Heim to be:

"die Frage nach dem Warum der kausalen Welterklärung, und die Frage nach dem Woher der letzten Sanktion unseres Handelns".[6]

We shall make some remarks on this kind of questions, which we shall call "why-questions". According to Heim such questions have two aspects, one theoretical and one practical.[7] Heim here asks for two different, but, as we shall see, related things.

The first thing he asks for is a kind of explanatory answer to why-questions. This is the theoretical aspect of the question.

The second thing he asks for, has ethical significance. This is the practical aspect. This question can be interpretated in two ways: Either (1) as a quest for the reasons or conditions for preferring one action before another, or (2) as a quest for the characteristics of, or the justification of, good actions. On this point Heim further says that interpretation (1) has a kind of priority before the interpretation (2) in the sense that it is not possible to answer questions in the interpretation (2) if the question in interpretation (1) not has been answered before.[8]

Now, this first type of question, especially in its religious version, is indeed problematic.[9] It can e.g. be doubted if they are meaningful and genuine questions at all.[10] But we shall not enter into that discussion. We shall instead hypothetically say that they are genuine and meaningful questions, which in some sense can be answered. And this answer then consists in a kind of explanation.

The relation to the philosophical and scientific basic assumptions. When we continue to analyse these why-questions we find that we do not have to use basic assumptions other than those which we already are acquainted with, namely the philosophical basic assumptions of the law of perspective and the law of polarity and the scientific basic assumption of the twofold nature of time.[11] If these basic assumptions are applied to human existence, they will, according to Heim, reveal that there are inescapable problems connected with human existence. Thus the "why-questions" naturally appear when they are applied to human existence.

The most important, and perhaps also interesting, point here is the fact that, according to Heim, the conditions of human existence are not exceptions from the conditions of existence in general.[12] Heim's position is that the whole of reality is governed by the same set of basic assumptions. So that e.g. the fictitious placing of the perspective center at some other "place" than a human mind would only result in a minor and relative change in the total view of reality, but not in a total change in it.[13] Other living organisms do not experience a world principally differentiated from ours. Their experiental world is also polar. But, as we shall see that in order to give an explanatory answer, one has to make some additional basic assumptions, which cannot be deduced from the analysis of the question-part.[14]

We can now examine the question-part of the existential criterion. Here Heim's basic assumption is simply: Human existence is inherently and essentially paradoxical. Now the predicate "paradoxical" is vague. We shall distinguish two meanings:

The first one says that human existence cannot be expressed without using logical contradictions, or that every description of human existence, for some reason, must entail logical contradictions. Sometimes Heim seems to accept this view,[15] but sometimes his position can more reasonably be interpreted as stating that if a thing or an event cannot be explained, then the thing or the event is paradoxical in relation to a set of basic assumptions. Now what is paradoxical in relation to a limited set of basic assumptions, e.g. philosophical or scientific, may not be paradoxical in relation to a wider set of basic assumptions, which perhaps includes religious basic assumptions (in addition to scientific and philosophical). It is also important to say that a paradox is not the same as an illusion. Paradoxical things or facts are just as real as those which are not paradoxical.

Now, Heim's general thesis is that human existence, in all its aspects, both individual and general, cannot be wholly explained within the conceptual framework of philosophical and scientific basic assumptions.

Now we can present Heim's consideration on the questionpart in two steps:

1. First we shall give a brief sketch of his notion of human existence. This presentation starts from the notions of relativity, destiny and of decision as applied to human existence. These notions are partly interrelated and have undergone certain changes in the thinking of Heim.[16] However, they are not of a nature that will affect our argument.

2. Then we shall present some points in Heim's notion of the experience of human existence in the light of the notions of relativity, destiny and decision.

Let us begin with the notion of relativity as applied to human existence. We shall take as our startingpoint the law of perspective.

Human existence and relativity. Heim says that human existence is in some sense relative. It is relative in the sense that there is no "objective" and once-and-for-all unchangeable view of reality. Here he argues from the theory of relativity.[17] The fundamental concepts in the interpretation of reality are essential subject-dependent. Therefore he says that human existence is not an existence within a neutral universe where the subject plays no role, like the newtonian universe, but in a universe, where the measuring of time and space are dependent on the position of the measuring subject within the same universe.[18] (We have treated this matter before, in 3.3.). This is no accidental fact, but an inescapable fact in the universe, and it can be derived from to the law of polarity. Relativity determines the existence of man. Now, for Heim the relativization of time and space seems to imply that the view of the universe as a closed and causally determined universe can no longer be justified. And this further means that there are no answers to why-questions within the framework of relativity or that every answer is equally plausible. This we shall call the relativistic paradox. This fact Heim describes in terms of destiny ("Schicksal") or with the synonymous term arbitrariness ("Willkür"). Let us therefore turn to the notion of destiny, which sums up problem of relativity. The notion of destiny is derived from the notion of relativity.[19]

Human existence and destiny. Destiny as applied to human existence is shortly described as

"... die Setzung des perspektivischen Zentrums innerhalb der raumzeitlichen Welt".[20]

Here we have the concept of placing ("Setzung"). It is an important concept in the thinking of Heim. It has two meanings: It can be used, as here, to refer to human existence. But it can also be used to refer to the universe as a whole, which also can be said to be placed.[21] This dual use of the concept of placing corresponds to the dual use of the concept of decision. Here we shall only deal with the first use of the concept of placing, as applied to human existence.

Now, this placing of the individual existence has also a dual nature corresponding to the nature of the ego. Let us quote:

"Betrachten wir diese Setzung rein gegenständlich, setzen wir also z.B. die Zeitstrecke, die vom Jetzt aus erst möglich ist, als gegeben voraus, indem wir einen Augenblick vom Jetztpunkt absehen, dann erscheint die Setzung des Jetzt als der unverrückbaren Zeitmitte als Ergebnis einer Auswahl aus unendlich vielen Möglichkeiten. Diese Auswahl hat nicht den geringsten Anhaltspunkt im gegenständlichen Inhalt. Inhaltlich betrachtet hätte vielleicht jede andere Zeit eher verdient, Gegenwart zu werden, als gerade die jetzige. Die Auswahl hätte an sich genau ebenso gut anders ausfallen können, als sie tatsächlich ausgefallen ist. Sie ist also ‚Willkür' im strengsten Sinne des Worts. Betrachte ich nun aber umgekehrt die Setzung des Jetzt vom Standpunkt der nicht-gegenständlichen Region aus, in die der Jetztpunkt aufgenommen ist, also von mir aus, der ich in diesem Augenblick im Jetzt lebe, so sieht die Sache ganz anders aus. Dann beruht die Setzung des Jetzt überhaupt nicht auf Auswahl. Denn die Mannigfaltigkeit, aus der ausgewählt werden soll, ist ja nur da, wenn ich da bin, der ich im Jetzt lebe".[22]

"Offenbar liegt in dem Wort ‚Schicksal' und in allen andern Worten, die ihm entsprechen, immer das dunkle Gefühl für diese rätselhafte Doppelseitigkeit der Setzung, um die es sich hier handelt. Von der einen Seite gesehen Willkür und Zufall, von der entgegengesetzten Seite gesehen höchste Notwendigkeit, eine Notwendigkeit, kraft deren alles andere, was notwendig ist, seine Notwendigkeit erst erhält, eine Notwendigkeit, die aber gerade darum für unser Denken unnahbar ist. Nur wenn wir beides gleich stark empfinden, was im Wort Schicksal enthalten ist, die Willkür von der einen Seite, und die Notwendigkeit von der andern, wissen wir, was mit diesem Wort gemeint ist".[23]

Let us now make some remarks on these quotations. Heim is saying that the concept of destiny, as applied to individual human existence, can be interpreted in two ways:

1. The first interpretation starts from an abstraction from the non-objectifiable character of the ego, from its existence as a perspective centre

This results in a scientific approach to the ego.[24] It is then possible to give its place a causal explanation and to point out the causal chains which have determined its situation. This interpretation and its corresponding approach are of course justified in some cases. But Heim calls it theistically neutral because it abstracts from a realm of reality (i.e. non-objectifiable space) and thus it does not involve a quest for a total explanation,[25] and thus it cannot answer the religious version of a why-question. Thus this interpretation is only partly correct; it fails to do justice to Heim's intentions.[26] A causal explanation is not his main interest.[27] On the contrary, this abstraction is an escape from destiny[28] and it results in despair[29] or, to use an expression borrowed from Kierkegaard, "Krankheit zum Tode".[30] And the essence of that despair consists in the insight that there is and cannot be an ultimate explanation of the placing of the ego within a world, conceived as an objective and causal world.

2. The second interpretation, then, starts from the correct basic assumption of the non-objectifiable nature of the ego. Here we have arrived at the religious version of the question.[31] What is required here is a kind of non-causal explanation, indicated by the term "highest necessity" in the quotation. It corresponds to properties as supra-causal[32], "supra-temporal"[33] or "irrational",[34] ascribed to explanations.

The meaning of these terms are paradoxical in terms of the first interpretation. Granted that the causal assumption is correct they must be regarded as nonsense. A causal explanation entails a rejection of the reality of decision.[35] It is simply nonsense to try to explain a decision, because non-objectifiable time, the present, belongs to another dimension of reality than the past.

But if the possibility of a non-causal explanation is accepted, then it is also possible to explain the relativistic paradox. This paradox then vanishes and the actual location of man appears to be, not an accidental or arbitrary fact, but as necessary and meaningful. And the meaningfulness of the actual location does not contradict the fact that other locations are also possible. To accept ones actual placing is then to accept a religious belief.[36] We will return to this matter below.

Human existence and decision. We said before that the notion of decision had a double meaning which corresponded to the double meaning of placing.

On the one hand, the concept of decision can be applied to the universe as a whole. Then it signifies a change within the universe.

On the other hand, it can be related to human existence. It then signifies human actions.

Here we shall only deal with one aspect of this latter meaning, namely the part which contains the concept of choice or preference of e.g. an action or a total view of reality. Although there are differences between a decision between actions and between total views of reality, there also are similarities. From the logical point of view, all decisions are of the same nature, since all reality, including the existence of man, is subordinated to the same set of conditions. But because the decision between different total views of reality is of basic importance, we shall denote a separate section to it below. Let us then turn to the decision between different courses of actions which is best dealt with in terms of Heim's theory of ethics.

Heim says that it is not only theoretically true, but also an empirical fact that it is only against the background of answered why-questions, i.e. eliminated paradoxes, that it is possible to have a satisfactory theory of ethics and a connected morality. His argument runs like this: He starts by saying that men, living under the conditions of relativity and destiny have to act morally. But the relativity entails a paradox, and it is absurd to allow uneliminated paradoxes.[37] But when making morally significant decisions, man have no guidance from the (content of) non-objectifiable space alone.[38] The destiny of man makes every argument in favour of a theory of a natural moral law relative, because every such theory ultimately expresses the law of polarity.[39] Therefore, in this case moral decisions, and the resultant actions, are based on relativity. And this is an absurd position, because, according to Heim, morally justified actions must be accompanied by an evident certainty. This is a postulate, parallel to that of religious certainty. The only possibility is to base them on non-objectifiable space. Only men who believe themselves to be placed by God, can make a decision in a non-relativistic manner, and consequently be released from relativism and uncertainty.[40]

This is of course a position which can (and perhaps also ought to) be criticized. It can e.g. be objected that Heim confuses relativity with ethical relativism. But the former does not entail the latter.[41] But we shall not develop this criticism here, since it is not our main theme.

Now, it is somewhat unclear what Heim wants to say with his theory. Perhaps he wants to say that it is only against the background of eliminated paradoxes that human actions can have the feature of evident certainty which is a necessary feature of responsible actions. But if we interpret Heim in this way, the theory is empirically probably false: It is quite possible to admit relativity, but nevertheless have good reasons for preferring one action to another.

But perhaps Heim wants to say that it is only possible to construct a consistent and justified ethical theory when the paradoxes have been eliminated.[42] But Heim has not demonstrated that the opposite position involves contradictions or that it cannot be defended in some other way. When we in the following investigation sometimes refer to the notions of relativity, destiny and decision together, we shall, for the sake of simplicity, refer to them as "human destiny" only.

Demanded basic assumptions of the answer. Our next assumption concerns the answer to the inherent questions of human existence. And the answer must

84

be an explanation to those questions. Now this answer is a compound assumption, containing these parts:

1. Only the acceptance of a transcendent and personal reality[43] can be a satisfactory explanatory answer and eliminate the paradox of human destiny and

2. This transcendent and personal reality must be mediated or revealed to men through historical ("geschichtlich") events.[44]

Since the first part of this basic assumption is the main point of the investigation, we shall pay the greatest attention to it. But because it is closely connected with the second point we shall also make some comments on it.

1. The answer must contain the acceptance of a transcendent and personal God. Let us then begin with the first part of this basic assumption. It is to some extent identical with what we defined as the religious basic assumption. We shall try to present Heim's view and his arguments in favour of it. He says on a general level:

"Wir brauchen Gott nicht, um unsere Weltanschauung theistisch abzuschliessen. Das wäre nur eine logische oder ästhetische Angelegenheit. Wir brauchen Gott, um von dem verzweifelten Gefühl der Willkürlichkeit unseres Lebens befreit zu werden".[45]

Here the close relation to the notions of relativity and destiny is appearent. What reasons has Heim for mentioning the religious basic assumption in this connection? There seem to be two.

The first starts from a view about what we can call the intellectual needs of men. Heim simply says that it is according to the nature of the human mind to search for a non-contradictory total view of reality.[46] There is something unsatisfactory, or even absurd, to remain in the position that there is no answer to the relativistic paradox and to be satisfied with that.

The second reason consists in a reference to ethical needs of man, or to what, according to Heim, are negative consequences of the absence of an answer to the relativistic paradox.[47] The actions of responsible men must be accompanied by an experience of certainty. Heim even says that there is something abnormal about hesitation in ethical matters,[48] i.e. to be in a situation which calls for an ethical decision without the feeling of such a certianty. This is of course not inconsistent with a rational calculus in some decision-situations. But the rightness or goodness of an action must be apprehended in the same manner as the evidence or certainty of basic distinctions.[49] But he gives no further reasons why the characteristics of right or good actions must be just these ones.

But let us, in spite of these remarks, take his view of the ethical needs of men to be justified and proceed to the more detailed basic assumption concerning the answer, namely that only a transcendent reality, or better the acceptance of such a reality, can remove the paradoxes inherent in the relativity and destiny of man. What are Heim's arguments for this?

This argument starts from the notion of human destiny and it is hypotetically stated.[50] Heim says that if there is to be any explanation at all of human destiny then it must consist in accepting a transcendent reality. This transcendent reality must be a negation of the relativity both within objectifiable and non-objectifiable space. Connected with the concept of relativity is the concept of placing.

And the applying of this concept to human existence can only be justified by saying that human existence, i.e. every individual perspective, is placed by a reality which itself is not placed, i.e. a transcendent reality.[51]

What is then Heim's argument for saying that this transcendent reality also must be personal?

This part of his argument starts from the relativity of personal existence within non-objectifiable space, and it is analogously expressed.[52] It must remove the relativity within the personal non-objectifiable space. And since personal existence is the essence of man's existence then its relativity can only be removed by another personal reality, which does not belong to this space, i.e. it must be transcendent. Only a person can place a person.

2. The transcendent and personal God must be revealed to man through historical events. We shall finally turn to the second feature in this basic assumption, which states that this transcendent and personal God must be revealed to men through historical events. Heim here states that the God, which explains human destiny must be recognizable both within objectifiable space and within non-objectifiable space. It must belong to the realm of past historical events as well to present events.

We shall here only pay attention to the formal content of this assumption, and not to the questions of how these events are discovered or what exactly signifies them.

Now, why must it be historical or belonging to the past? Here Heim's argument runs like this: It must be historical in order to correspond to the twofold nature of the ego. We saw, that the ego had two sides: one turned towards objectifiable and the other turned towards non-objectifiable space. Thus, events revealing the transcendent reality, must on one hand be historical, i.e. belonging to objectifiable space, and on the other non-historical, i.e. belonging to non-objectifiable space. Heim says:

"Kann unser Denken nicht aus den Erfahrungsformen heraustreten, so müssen wir das Ewige in den zeitlichen Erfahrungsformen selbst zum Ausdruck bringen ... So ensteht die Form, die alle Aussagen über ewige Wirklichkeiten in der menschlichen Sprache haben, nämlich die Form des Paradoxons".[53]

And the paradoxical content of these events Heim describes as follows:

"Um uns aus unserer Notlage zu befreien, genügt also weder ein blosses Gegenwartserlebnis, das erst im Werden ist, noch ein Tatbestand, der bloss der Vergangenheit angehört. Es ist vielmehr etwas Drittes notwendig, nämlich ein *vollendeter Tatbes-*

tand, der als solcher zugleich Gegenwartserlebnis ist, also eine Wirklichkeit, die nicht erst im Werden, sondern schon geworden ist, und die doch nicht bloss als Vorstellungsbild, sondern als Wirklichkeit da ist".[54]

But to continue this line of argument would lead us to the more general questions of revelation and Christ. But since those matters are not our main themes, we shall not deal with it any further here.

The problem of rejecting some alternative answers. We said before that the answer to why-questions must be an explanatory answer. We also said that, according to Heim, the only genuine explanation must be to accept the basic assumption that there is a transcendent and personal God. We finally also noticed that Heim said this hypothetically: If there is any answer at all, then it must consist in this acceptance and in no other.

In this connection an important problem appears. Let us for the moment accept that Heim is right when he says that there really exists a transcendent God and that this circumstance also has a genuine explanatory power. But this is of course not a sufficient reason for rejecting some other possible explanatory answer to why-questions. Now, Heim wants to say not only that a transcendent reality is an explanation, but also that it is the only possible genuine explanation. And to show this is the main task of apologetics, according to Heim.

Let us then try to examine Heim's objections to alternative answers to why-questions. Now, these answers, in order to be acceptable, must be answers to (a) the theoretical and (b) the ethical question. They must explain both human destiny and also present a justification for ethical certainty in decision-situations.

But and this is important let us at once rule out some misunderstandings of what is the object for explanation. What is to be explained is not some limited event or change or some part of reality. That causal explanation really applies to objectifiable space, is no problem for Heim. But it is a misleading limitation of the realm of reality to identify objectifiable space with reality. No, what is required is rather on explanation of reality as a whole in a way that also presents an explanation of my personal destiny. And if an explanation cannot satisfy these conditions, then it is not an acceptable explanation.

Now we have two possible ways of presenting Heim.

The first way is to analyse Heim's arguments concerning some rival theories (e.g. causalism or materialism),[55] which claim to present explanatory answers.

The second way is to discover Heim's main criticism of the alternative answers. Since the second way leads us more directly to the critical point, we shall follow it. It seems to be most convenient to do this in the following way. First we shall present some alternative answers,[56] which we, with Heim's words, shall call the positivism-answer, the relativism-answer and the indifference-answer, and then discover in what way they, according to Heim, fail to explain the universe as a whole and the individual destiny.

Let us begin with the positivism answer. To accept this is to accept this kind of reasoning: It is absurd not to accept an ultimate explanatory entity. This is to say that there must be a primus movens[57] or a most perfect being. This is the traditional way of presenting rational proofs for the existence of God[58] and of doing natural theology. This is to say that a causal chain or a scale of perfection must reasonably be concluded.

To this Heim's major objection is that this assumption contradicts the law of polarity,[59] which says that a polar sequence cannot be concluded. Now, on this point there seems to be an obscurity in Heim's argument when he uses the law of polarity as an argument for saying that a causal chain cannot be concluded. The obscurity consists in the law of polarity, which by Heim's own definition, does not signify a causal relation.[60] But this does not rule out that it also is applicable to causal relations, because it signifies polar space as a whole. When Heim says that a polar relation is different from a causal relation he only means that it is not a causal relation, but that it nevertheless belongs to polar space. However, every such position of stating the existence of a first cause or a most perfect being is arbitrary. It is always, from the logical point of view, possible to take a step further, asking for the cause of the first cause.[61] And to stop at one link in a causal chain is simply a kind of "Kreaturvergötterung".[62]

A similar situation arises also concerning the justification of an ethical decision. Say, that a decision is justified by an appeal to a standard. But every standard must then in its turn be justified by an appeal to a higher standard, and so on. To choose one standard as *the* ultimate standard is then also arbitrary.[63]

The next answer we called the relativism-answer. This position is more difficult to explain. Heim says:

"Wir verzichten auf eine erste Ursache und nehmen die Riehe von Ursachen und Wirkungen als eine unabschliessbare Unendlichkeit, die sich selbst schafft und durch sich selbst da ist, also als eine Totalität, aus der alles einzelne wie aus einem allgegenwärtigen Mutterschoss hervorgeht, um dann wieder zu seinem Ursprung zurückzukehren".[64]

"Auch hier (i.e. in ,Weltkonzeption Nietzsches') ist das letzte, hinter das die Warum-Frage nicht zurückgeht, die Totalität der unabschliessbaren Reihe von Ursachen und Wirkungen. Die unendliche Totalität wird als als ein in sich selbst brandendes Meer verabsolutiert".[65]

Now, in order to explain the universe as a whole it may be possible to accept theism. But it must be in a hypothetical manner, because it is impossible to transcend the causal chain. As an example of this position, Heim mentions the "as-if-philosophy" of Vaihinger.[66] To accept theism on these grounds is then only a way of commending a theistic interpretation of the universe. Though it is possible to have good reasons for it, e.g. pragmatic or aesthetic, it has no cognitive content. It cannot be accepted as a true explanation. And besides,

Heim also says that it is an empirical fact that men are unsatisfied with this answer.[67] (We shall not discuss the stronger version of this position: namely that a religious belief is not only a fiction, but really an illusion (e.g. Feuerbach), because the same objections also hold with respect to this version).

This position also corresponds to the attempt to search for a justification for ethical decisions by an appeal to history. i.e. to what in fact have been moral standards during different times. But it is unjustified to accept them only for that reason.

The last answer we called the indifference-answer. To accept this answer is to try to reach the indifferent state of being. In our discussion of the law of polarity, we said that this law could only be conveived against the background of some non-polar state of being. Now, this answer says that it is possible to reach this indifferent state of being by means of certain exercises. Polar relations within the universe can in the last analysis be traced back to energetical transformations in accordance with the principle of the conservation of energy. Thus the answer consists in a reference to this state of being as the source and explanation of polarity.

But this answer suffers from difficulties. As we saw, there were no reasons for stating that this indifferent state of being really exists. And further, it seems strange to point out this reality, if it is a reality, as a kind of source to polar being, since it does not have a causal relationship to polarity. The coincidentia oppositorum does not possess a higher degree of reality. But on this point, Heim seems to be somewhat inconsistent: If he is searching for some kind of non-causal explanation, then he cannot for this reason deny that the indifferent state of being can be a cause. His main argument is rather the hypothetical character and its lack of explanatory power as far as explaining placing, since all placings are in the same degree deducible from the indifferent state of being. And it is irrelevant for the personal aspect of decision.

Therefore either it cannot justify any action at all, or else it justifies them all in the same degree since they are all equally deducible from it.

In conclusion: All these alternative explanatory answers deny the reality of the law of polarity. Therefore they must be rejected.

Another important problem concerning alternative answers. Now, there is also quite another question connected to the problem of rejecting possible alternative answers. It is really necessary to make a supplementary basic assumption that there is a transcendent reality in order to arrive at a true explanation? It is quite possible that there may be hitherto unconsidered answers. It is therefore reasonable to ask Heim for a principal defence of making this supplementary basic assumption.

Let us then present some current arguments against this addition, because it is a principal problem. Now a current objection against this addition is that (1) it is not useful/clarifying or that it lacks explanatory power. This can be developed in a theoretical manner, i.e. religious basic assumptions can be translated into other basic assumptions, not implying the existence of a transcendent God, and thus rationally uninteresting, or in a pragmatic manner, e.g. by demonstrating that they do in fact not have explanatory advantages for a great many reasonable people. (2) It contradicts the principle of Occam's razor which says that one ought not to multiply entities more than necessary. In our context it says that one ought not accept more basic assumptions than necessary.[68] (3) They are for other reasons philosophically unjustified.

To this Heim replies: (1) On the theoretical level it can be shown that it really has explanatory power and advantages, and on the pragmatic level it can be doubted, for sound reasons, whether reasonable people in fact can be satisfied with alternative answers. (2) This principle is not applicable here. (3) The principle of additional basic assumptions can be reasonably defended by showing its logical similarity with noncontroversial additional assumptions.

Chapter 4

The problem of transcendence

In this chapter we shall discuss the problem of transcendence in the thinking of Heim. In order to do this we shall first present a survey of the concept of transcendence (4.1). In connection with this point, we shall also treat two other problems, namely what we shall call Heim's phenomenological reduction and a more accurate definition of objectifiable and non-objectifiable space in the thought of Heim. (4.2) concerns the formulation of the problem of transcendence in the thinking of Heim.

4.1. Different definitions of the concept transcendent / transcencence

As we said, we shall first present a survey of some different meanings of the concept transcendent/transcendence. The first definition, then, we shall describe like this:

Consciousness transcendence (T1). We shall first call transcendent that which is not dependent on the mind or the consciousness.

We shall then say that mental objects are not produced by the mind or the act of consciousness itself, and that their existence is not affected by their being apprehended at a certain time by an individual. In this connection we shall not discuss or settle the difficult epistemological question of whether it is justified to state that there exist transcendent entities in this sense, or the question about what kind of reasonings can answer the question.

The next definition of the concept transcendent/transcendence we shall describe like this:

Sense-transcendence (T2). Transcendent is that which is not accessible to sense experience.

This kind of transcendence we shall call sense-transcendence. It is wellknown fact that for a normal man, sense-transcendent entities exist. We know that there exist entities, e.g. certain vawes of light or sound, which ordinary man can not experience. And it is possible to imagine beings, whose realm of sensual experience is wider than the ordinary human. We also know that some of these wider possibilities are realized by some species of animals.

Thus we can proceed and make this more precise distinction: (We shall have call the sense experiences of a normal man normal sense experiences.)

T2.1 That which in fact is not accessible to ordinary sense experience by a human being, is transcendent and

T2.2 That which in principle is not accessible to ordinary sense experience by a human being, is transcendent.

T2.2 means that it is impossible for logical reasons to have a sense experience of a certain object. The assertion that a certain object is sensually experienced then entails a logical contradiction.

But the concept of transcendent/transcendence can also have this meaning:

Experiental transcendence (T3). That which is not accessible to any form of human experience is transcendent.

This type of transcendence we shall call experiental transcendence. We shall also make here an analogous distinction to the one above, namely:

T3.1 That which in fact is not accessible to normal experience is transcendent. It is not difficult to imagine circumstances in which a certain ordinary experience is possible at time t_1 but impossible at t_2. In this case T3.1 partly coincides with T2.1, with the exception that which is transcendent according to T3.1 covers a narrower scope that that which is transcendent according to T2.1. But they are essentially of the same nature.

But we also get T3.1: That which in principle is not accessible to any form at all of normal human experience is transcendent. By the expression "in principle not accessible" we shall here mean that it is for logical reasons impossible to have an experience of an entity which is transcendent in this case. And what is transcendent in this sense can furthermore be of different kinds. It is, for obvious reasons, logically impossible to have an experience of a square circle. A geometrical figure of that shape does not, and can not, for logical reasons exist.

But there are also other kinds of entities which it seems to be logically impossible to experience. Let us exemplify: A reasonable interpretation of Kant is to say that it is logically impossible to have experiences of a priori (i.e. a priori according to Kant) entities. We can not experience space and time, but only entities which are inserted in a temporal and spatial continuum. Another example we find in a feature in Heim's theory of the ego. The ego seems to be T3.2. It can not be objectively experienced and an objectified ego is an object among other objects. The subject-object-relation then appears as a limit beyond which it is logically impossible to have any experiences at all.[1]

We can thus proceed to the next definition of the concept transcendent/transcendence, which is important here. This definition is of a different kind. We shall describe it like this:

Semantic transcendence (T4). That which is not accessible to any kind of adequate description, is transcendent.

This kind of transcendence we shall call semantic transcendence. And here too we can make analogical distinctions as in the cases T2 and T3. Thus we get:

T4.1 That which in fact is not accessible to adequate description, is transcendent, and

T4.2 That which in principle is not accessible to adequate description, is transcendent.

Now, there may be different reasons why an entity is semantically transcendent. One such reason may e.g. be the structure of different languages. (We shall not discuss this whole complex matter here, which involves e.g. different theories on the question of relations between language, consciousness and reality). But on a general and trivial level we can say that different languages reflect different interpretations of reality. It is also possible to say that what is semantically transcendent in relation to one language may not be so in relation to another language. And it is also possible that the same holds in relation to different times for one and the same individual.

Quite another reason is the logical one. It may be the case that there are entities which can not be otherwise described than by paradoxes or contradictions. We shall call such entities or facts paradoxical. But there need not necessarily be something paradoxical to assert that such entities really exist. It depends on which theory about the relation between language, consciousness and reality one accepts.

Metaphysical transcendence (T5). Finally we shall mention another definition of transcendent/transcendence: Transcendent is that which is supra-mundane.

This meaning of transcendent/transcendence we shall call metaphysical transcendence. It is this definition which is traditionally referred to when talking about transcendence. Then it is asserted that in addition to the ordinary world of experience, there is also another reality, a reality which is in some way (qualitatively) different from the ordinary one. Thus God, for example, according to traditional Christian doctrine, is transcendent in this sense. He has aseity. He does not depend on anything else for his existence, but the world depends for its existence on him. It is also said that God's existence is in some way independent of, or above, time and space. But it is not only traditional Christian theism which accepts a metaphysical transcendent reality. According to the common interpretation of Plato's doctrine of ideas, the world of ideas is transcendent in this metaphysical sense.

Thus we can proceed and make some comments on two important points in Heim's thought.

The phenomenological reduction. The first one concerns the important question of whether transcendent entities according to T1 really exist. We shall not investigate this question in all its aspects. But we shall briefly present Heim's position, because it bears some relation to the question of whether a metaphysically transcendent reality really exists.

Now, Heim says that the question can not be answered from the logical point of view:

"Ich kann zwar bei drei Glockenklängen eines Domgeläutes, die abwechselnd erklingen, von dem Unterscheidungsakt absehen, in dem das Tonintervall hörbar wird. Aber ich kann diesen Akt nicht in Wirklichkeit ausschalten, ohne damit den Klangunterschied selbst aufzuheben. Bei jedem Versuch, das zu tun und das Unterschiedene gegenüber der Unterscheidung zu isolieren, ist der Unterscheidungsakt immer mit dabei. Er ist mir immer auf den Fersen. Er verfolgt mich wie mein Schatten. . .
    Wenn ich also z.B. sage: die Welt ist ,unabhängig von mir' da, so ist dieses ,unabhängig von' eben gerade ein Unterscheidungsverhältnis. Dieses setzt die unterscheidende Funktion immer schon stillschweigend voraus. Es ist nicht da, ohne dass diese Funtion immer irgendwie mit dabei ist".[2]

"Wir mögen uns also drehen und wenden wie wir wollen, wir können nicht aus dem Bann der Unterscheidungsfunktion hinauskommen".[3]

This position can most simply be described as a phenomenological reduction.[4] Heim here says that we must distinguish between what can be abstractly distinguished and what in reality is separated. But an abstract distinction does not say that the distinguished entities really are separated. But we cannot come to a decision about this because such an investigation would presuppose an abstraction of the same kind which is to be investigated, and thus the real coexistence of the act of investigation and the object is asserted again.

This is quite in accordance with the law of polarity, namely that there is an ultimate relation between the object and the subject. It is not possible to conceive a real existing "pure" object and a real existing "pure" subject.

But Heim also says that this circumstance does not affect the theory about the transcendence of God. His argument is that the phenomenological reduction does not affect our interpretation of the kind of limit, which distinguishes "die echte Transzendenz der Ueberwelt" i.e. transcendence T5 from the immanent world. Heim says:

"Wenn wir in den folgenden Abschnitten die Unterscheidungsverhältnisse ins Auge fassen, die unser Weltbild bestimmen, so ist die Aufgabe, die wir uns damit gestellt haben, zunächst noch unabhängig von der Entscheidung der erkenntnistheoretischen Frage nach dem Realitätswert der Welt, in der wir uns vorfinden. Die Frage, ob Raum und Zeit Anschauungsformen des Subjekts sind oder Daseinsformen der Welt, wie sie an sich ist, diese Frage stellen wir hier zurück. Es ist uns hier nur darum zu tun, die Eigenart der Unterscheidungen deutlich zu machen, die uns innerhalb der raumzeitlichen Welt selbst entgegentreten. Die Struktur der Grenzlinie bleibt aber dieselbe, ob wir die raumzeitliche Erfahrungswelt als Erscheinung oder als objektive Wirklichkeit auffassen".[5]

Is the phenomenological reduction justified? Here of course the question of whether the phenomenological reduction can be justified, becomes important. We shall not deal with this whole question here, but shall only restrict ourselves to these remarks, in relation to Heim's position:

The phenomenological reduction may be justified if Heim's single explicit intention is to present a theory of the use of religious language when speaking about the transcendence of God. Thus, in the same way as theory of poetic language, such a theory must not contain an assumption that that which is described in the poetic language does also exist in reality. And the same also holds for a theory of religious language.

But this interpretation can hardly be said to do justice to Heim's intentions, even if it catches a point in this theory. It is obvious that he does not primarily intend to present a theory on religious language only. His main interest is in presenting an ontology.

One way of handling this may be to make a distinction between the use of the phenomenological reduction as (1) a work-hypothesis and (2) a metaphysical theory. Then it is possible to say that Heim intended (1) and left open the question about its metaphysical validity. Is it then justified to use this reduction as a work-hypothesis? From a special point of view it may be so. If one, as a presupposition, accepts that the content of the consciousness is on the same level in relation to a supposed external world, then it is difficult to assert that some of the contents of the consciousness are more real or more true than other contents.[6] And if the concept of transcendence can be put in a systematic and logically coherent relation to other concepts within the consciousness, or can be a part of a system of rules of construction according to which the content of the consciousness can be ordered to a total view of reality, then it may be justified to accept the existence of a metaphysically transcendent reality. Statements about the transcendent then express a certain order of the content of the consciousness which for logical or systematic reasons can not be said to be less acceptable or true than other orders.

The second important point concerns:

The kind of transcendence of objectifiable and non-objectifiable space. We are now in a position to give an accurate description of objectifiable and non-objectifiable space in terms of transcendence.

To objectifiable space belong all entities which are transcendent according to definitions T1 and T2 in some cases, but not according to any other definition.

To non-objectifiable space belong all entities which are transcendent according to the conjunct definitions T1, T2, and T4, but not according to definition T3. It is possible to experience non-objectifiable space, but not in a sensual way. A minor problem here is whether we can properly ascribe this space transcendence according to definition T1. This is not a problem concerning objectifiable space, which contains objects within time and space and objects which are temporally and spatially distant from the subject. The problem appears when we realize that non-objectifiable space does not have an ordinary place within time and space. However, our reason for ascribing it T1, when interpreting Heim, is based on the principle of the preexistence of a higher dimensioned space.[7] The most reasonable interpretation of that principle is that non-objectifiable space is not an invention of the mind, but rather a discovery of something already existing in reality.

Now, we see that T1 is a common property of both spaces. It can thus not help us to distinguish between the spaces. This seems to be pragmatic argument in favour of Heim's opinion that the phenomenological reduction does not affect the question of the real existence of a metaphysically transcendent reality T5.

Finally, the metaphysically transcendent reality T5 (in Heim's terminology: "supra-polar space") is, if existing, also T1 and probably also T4. Here a twofold problem appears:

The first problem is the problem of its being T3. Is the supra-polar space T3? Let us then briefly examine the meaning of T3.

We can then omit the definition T3, at least in its most general and unrestricted form. It is in some way possible to experience supra-polar space. But how can it be experienced? Let us make a distinction between direct and indirect experience. A direct experience is an immediate experience of supra-polar space and an indirect experience of supra-polar space is an immediate experience of a fact, which is a part of the premis in an argument for the existence of supra-polar space. Then supra-polar space is T3 in relation to every direct experience, but not in relation to every indirect experience.

The second problem appears when we compare non-objectifiable and supra-polar space: They are both T1, T2 and T4 but supra-polar space is in addition also T3.2 in an indirect way: in relation to all direct experiences.

This similarity between them makes it plausible to state that it is possible to see the existence of non-objectifiable space as a necessary condition of the existence of supra-polar space, and this is in fact what Heim does. Supra-polar space is as such non-objectifiable. But because this is a main part in our investigation, we shall consider the question on its own.

4.2. The problem of transcendence in the thinking of Heim

Introduction. We can thus proceed to deal with Heim's doctrine on the transcendence of God. We shall do it against the background of the criteria we presented in the preceeding chapter. Heim's doctrine on the transcendence of God then becomes one example—of several—of an object-theory in his thinking. We shall here say that Heim tries to construct this doctrine in such a way that it satisfies the demands of the criterias of an acceptable religious doctrine and belief.

There are several reasons for our choise of his doctrine about the transcendence of God.

1. This doctrine is both interesting and original in Heim.

2. It revals some important features of Heim's apologetics. As we saw it was a basic task for Christian apologetics to present a Christian total view of reality which can also be a reasonable alternative to Non-christian total views of reality.[1] Now, a basic assumption within a Christian total view of reality is that there exists a metaphysically transcendent and personal God. The task of Christian apologetics then becomes to demonstrate that this assumption is reasonable according to the criteria we discussed in the preceeding chapter.

3. Finally, it brings into focus the central and perhaps also the most problematic religious doctrine.

Now Heim seems to maintain that a religion, in order to be acceptable as a religion, must contain the belief in a metaphysically transcendent and personal God. But Heim does not present any arguments for saying that a religion must contain this belief. Reasonably he is of the opinion that it lies in the nature of the matter, in the very definition of a religion.

But we shall mention a line of thought, which perhaps can be interpreted as an indirect argument for this assumption about the content of a genuine religion. In GD Heim makes a distinction between a monistic and a dualistic total view of reality. In this connection the meaning of the word monistic is not the one to which Heim's readers probably were used[2]. Here the word signifies a total view of reality which denies that there is a metaphysically transcendent reality. From a monistic point of view the meaning of the word God is

"... entweder ein anderes Wort für das Weltganze ... oder ein Ausdruck für den Glauben an die Herrlichkeit und den Sieg einer bestimmten Wirklichkeit, die eine Stelle innerhalb der unendlichen Ebene des Weltganzen einnimmt"

and (the word) God then becomes

"... nur ein religiöser Ausdruck für die Gewalt, mit der mich eine Grösse umfängt, die auf der einen allumfassenden Ebene der Wirklickeit liegt ...".[3]

According to Heim a monistic view also has as a natural consequence a theory of religion which says that statements about God can (and perhaps also ought to) be translated into statements about the immanent reality.[4] Here Heim says that there are several religions and interpretations of religion which are monistic in this sense. As examples he mentions different forms of pantheism and mysticism.[5]

Now Heim argues for a dualistic view. A dualistic total view of reality then is a total view of reality which accepts the existence of a metaphysically transcendent reality. We have treated minor parts of Heim's arguments for the acceptance of a transcendent reality before, mainly in the chapter on the existential criterion. There we said that there are some paradoxes which can not be explained unless the existence of a transcendent reality is accepted. And we have also seen that such an acceptance can not be made only on rational grounds. There is always a moment of personal decision in such acceptance. But it is, according to Heim, possible to show that such acceptance can be made reasonable (it can e.g. not be formally distinguished from other types of acceptance).[6]

How Heim presents the problem of metaphysical transcendence. We can then proceed to the question of how Heim treats this problem. He writes:

"Was meint der Glaube, wenn er auch im nachkopernikanischen Zeitalter noch von der Jenseitigkeit Gottes spricht?"[7]

This is Heim's basic question. And as we shall see below it is possible to give his answer to this question different interpretations. Let us therefore continue to quote:

"Was soll das eigentlich jetzt noch heissen, wenn wir nach dem Ueberweltlichen fragen? Was meinen wir mit der Präposition trans, wenn wir vom Transzendenten sprechen und es vom Immanenten unterscheiden?"[8]

"Die zentrale Frage der Gegenwart ist die Frage nach der Möglichkeit der ganzen Unterscheidung zwischen Schöpfer und Geschöpf, die Frage, ob es überhaupt einen Sinn hat, von der immanenten Welt eine transzendente Sphäre abzugrenzen, in der dann Gott oder ein unpersönliches X als Bewohner untergebracht werden kann".[9]

"Warum müssen alle innerweltlichen Transzendenzverhältnisse immer zuletzt versagen und zu vergänglichen Gleichnissen und Symbolen werden, wenn es gilt, die Jenseitigkeit des Schöpfers auszudrücken?"[10]

These passages contain some important thoughts, which need to be somewhat explained.

What are intra-mundane relations of transcendence? The first thought concerns what Heim calls intra-mundane relations of transcendence "innerweltliche Transzendenzverhältnisse". In order to make this concept clearer we shall quote another passage:

"Wir haben die wichtigsten Transzendenzverhältnisse untersucht, die der unzerlegbaren Ich-Du-Es-Welt, in der wir uns vorfinden, das Gepräge geben, die Jenseitigkeit des Gegenstandsraumes für meinen Bewusstseinsraum, die Jenseitigkeit des uns gemeinsamen objektiven Weltraumes für deine und meine Bewusstseinswelt, die Jenseitigkeit, die das unanschauliche Selbst von der Gegenstandswelt scheidet, und die Jenseitigkeit des Du für das Ich. Diese Untersuchung hat zu der zwei Ergebnissen geführt, die für unser Wirklichkeitsverständnis von entscheidender Wichtigkeit sind. . .".[11]

This quotation tells us that the intra-mundane relations of transcendence refer to the system of different spaces, which constitutes Heim's ontology.

98

Every such individual space is now determined by its own rules of construction. These rules we called basic assumptions within a total view of reality. The different spaces with their rules of construction are objectifiable "It-space" and non-objectifiable "Thou-space". We shall treat them more closely in the next chapter.

In what sense are they transcendent? Now, in what sense are the intramundane relations of transcendence transcendent? Let us examine the alternatives. Are they transcendent according to definition T1? The answer to this question is: yes. These rules of construction can not be inferred from some property of the mind or the reason, or from experience alone. This has been stated already in PA[12]. It is this thought that we shall later call the principle of the preexistence of higher dimensioned space.

Are they then transcendent according to definition T2? This question is more difficult to answer. It depends on which spaces are involved, and how exactly the passing from one space to another takes place. They can be indirectly experienced by the senses. But the most plausible answer seems nevertheless to be to ascribe to them also this kind of transcendence. They can not be the objects of sensual experience. On the contrary, they precede every form of sensual experience.

Are they then transcendent according to definition T3? This question is also more difficult to answer. Let us then use our distinctions: Are they transcendent according to definition T3.1? And here the answer is: no. They are not transcendent in this sense. Heim is not the opinion that there are rules of construction which are only present for a certain individual a certain time. But when this has been said, two remarks must be made at once: 1. This assertion is not affected by the fact that it in some cases can be justified, for pragmatic reasons, to disregard certain rules of construction. It can e.g. be a correct methodological rule within empirical science to disregard the rules of construction belonging to supra-polar space.

2. The rules of construction belonging to supra-polar space seem here to be an exception. Heim says if these rules have once been accepted, then they can never again be lost sight of. But we shall return to this later.

And not are they transcendent according to definition T3.2. It is pure speculation to operate with rules of construction which in principle are not accessible to rational knowledge, or which are impossible to apply.

And nor are they transcendent according to definition T4. They can be positively and adequately expressed.

Finally, they are of course not transcendent according to definition T5, they are immanent and have no metaphysically transcendent status.

What is "genuine transcendence"? On the contrary, what "die echte Transzendenz der Ueberwelt" is, can easily be determined. It is supra-polar space, the metaphysically transcendent reality. And this reality is ". . . etwas total anderes. . . als die innerweltliche Transzendenz. . ."[13].

Heim's arguments for the existence of a metaphysically transcendent space. Now we can examine Heim's argument for the existence of a metaphysical transcendent reality. A general formulation of his position is the following: The real existence of non-objectifiable space is a condition for the existence of a metaphysically transcendent reality, supra-polar space. Let us quote:

"Es soll der Nachweis geführt werden, dass die Region des nichtgegenständlichen Gegebenseins wirklich da ist, dass es keine Erfahrung und kein Denken gibt, bei dem diese Region nicht immer schon als gegeben vorausgesetzt ist. Dieser Nachweis ist . . . die Bedingung, unter der allein Glaubensgewissheit möglich ist"[14].

"Da sich das Nichtgegenständliche nur dadurch indirekt manifestiert, dass auf allen Gebieten des Daseins immer Ein Element im Gegensatz zu den andern in den nichtgegenständlichen Zustand aufgenommen wird, so kann ich Gottes nur dadurch innewerden, dass ich auf allen Gebieten zugleich das nichtgegenständliche Element in seinem Gegensatz zur Gegenständlichkeit bejahe. Die indirekte Kundgebung oder ,Offenbarung' Gottes besteht also darin, dass auf allen Gebieten Ein Element in die Sphäre Gottes hinaufgehoben wird"[15].

Three interpretations of his argument. The critical word here is of course the word condition "Bedingung". Now there are several reasonable interpretations of the meaning of the word in this connection.

The first main interpretation we shall call a pedagogical or psychological interpretation. This states that the real existence of non-objectifiable space is a necessary, but not sufficient, condition for the experience of a metaphyscially transcendent reality. Furthermore, an experience of non-objectifiable space must have taken place before an experience of a metaphysical transcendent reality, God, can take place. This seems to be a plausible interpretation of Heim. Sometimes he seems to be anxious to show that everyone, after all, really has a genuine experience of non-objectifiable space. This is then an ordinary human experience and religious experiences only differ from such experiences with regard to their content. Both are "ethical" in character, but the religious experience is different from the non-religious in the way that it is total.[16] But this demand seems to be difficult to justify, before it is known what is in the metaphysically transcendent reality, which makes it not accessible to objectifiable experience. And Heim does not mention such features, but simply refers to the concept of God.

Heim's pedagogical intention can be explained like this: A causal-mechanical world-view has wrongly, according to Heim, made it impossible for modern man to accept the thought of a metaphysically transcendent reality. In order to remove this obstacle it must first be demonstrated that the causal-mechanical world-view can not be defended from the scientific point of view. This is done by showing that there really is a non-objectifiable space. In this sense the real existence of non-objectifiable space can be a condition for the acceptance of a metaphysically transcendent reality.

The second main interpretation is a semantic interpretation, namely that the existence of non-objectifiable space is a necessary, but not sufficient, condition for a meaningful speech about God. Religious language, in order to be meaningful, when used about the transcendence of God, must then in some way refer to non-objectifiable entities, i.e. entities within non-objectifiable space. (In the concluding chapter, we shall try to show that it is possible to read Heim without accepting the real existence of a non-objectifiable space at all.)

But it is also possible that Heim had this intention: Correct and meaningful statements about entities within non-objectifiable space are, eo ipso, also statements about a metaphysically transcendent reality. But, as we have seen before, that which is non-objectifiable is not therefore necessarily something metaphysically transcendent. Thus there is no a priori reason for giving such statements a kind of common and extended reference.

Now we come to the third interpretation: This interpretation states that the existence of non-objectifiable space is a necessary condition for the existence of metaphysical transcendent reality. Beacuse this interpretation seems to be most in accordance with Heim's intention, we shall examine it in more detail.

This position means that the existence of non-objectifiable space is a necessary condition for the real existence of the supra-polar space. If there is no non-objectifiable space, there can be no supra-polar space. We can express this in the following question:

(1) If the predicate transcendence, according to *one* of the definitions T1—T5, is correctly ascribed to an entity, does it then follow that it is also transcendent according to some other of the definitions T1—T5?

When dealing with this question, we shall presuppose that these statements are true: (S1) There are entities, transcendent according to all the definitions T1—T5, and (S2) One and the same entity does not need to be transcendent according to only one of the definitions T1—T5.

Now, an affirmative answer to the question (1) above has another question as a natural consequence:

(2) What kind of justification can then be given for concluding that its being transcendent according to one of the definitions implies that it is transcendent according to another?

Now we can reformulate the question as follows: (T_n and T_m signify transcendent entities according to different definitions).

(1′) Is it possible, from the real existence of a T_n, to conclude that there also is a T_m?

(2′) If so, how can the conclusion be justified?

Now, there is no a priori reason to answer the first question affirmatively. The problematic words here are of course the words "follow" and "conclude". It seems to be possible to give them two different interpretations.

1. The first interpretation we shall call the logical interpretation. Thus the words "follow" and "conclude" signify logical implication. Thus the question (1') can be stated like this:

(1.1) Does the existence of a certain transcendent reality T_n entail that there also is a T_m?

But this is an unsatisfactory way of putting the question, because logical implication only holds between statements. Let us then reformulate the question:

(1.2) Does the (set of) statement(s) properly describing a T_n entail some other (set of) statement(s) properly describing a T_m?

In other words the existence of T_n is a sufficient condition for the existence of T_m. If this logical interpretation of the question is accepted, then the answer to the question (2') consists of a correct use of the logical rules.

2. The second interpetation, which we shall call the metaphysical, is somewhat different. The general metaphysical assumptions, which are (implicitly) made when transcendence is ascribed to an entity, are now required. Then the question (1') becomes something like this:

(1.3) Given that there really exists a transcendent entity T_n, which (set of) metaphysical assumptions must then be made, in order to make it reasonable to ascribe transcendence to it?

In other words, the existence of T_m is a necessary condition for reasonably stating the existence of T_n. If this metaphysical interpretation is accepted, then the answer to the question (2') consists of a kind of a priori argument.

Now we can distinguish between what we shall call a maximal and a minimal version of the metaphysical interpretation.

The minimal version says that it is justified to accept only such assumptions, which are in accordance with the existence of T_n, or which can justify the claim that T_n is transcendent.

The maximal version says that it is justified to accept assumptions which are not only in accordance with the existence of T_n, but which also allow the existence of T_m, i.e. the existence of a T_m does not contradict the assumptions according to T_n.

Remarks on Heim's argument. Finally we can make some remarks on Heim's position. Even if he sometimes seems to accept an affirmative answer to the question (1.2) this can not be a reasonable interpretation of his position. But perhaps there is a weaker version of the question, which is more in accordance with Heim's position. This can be stated as follows:

(1.2') Does the (set of) statements properly describing T_n *and* some other (set of) statements properly describing a fact entail some other (set of) statements properly describing T_m?

But this is still not satisfactory. In order to properly describe Heim's position, we must state the question like this:

(1.2'') Does the (set of) statements properly describing T_n *and* some other (set of) statements properly describing a fact F, in order to explain F, entail some other (set of) statements properly describing T_m?

Here we can for T_n insert statements describing non-objectifiable space i.e. its rules of construction and for F statements describing a paradoxical event or fact, of a kind we presented in the chapter on the existential criterion.

But the metaphysical interpretation of the question (1.3) also seems to describe Heim's intention. Here we can for T_n insert statements describing non-objectifiable space and for T_m statements describing supra-polar space. But Heim seems to confuse the maximal and the minimal versions of the argument. And the argument only holds in its maximal version. Even if non-objectifiable space exists, there are no reasons for making other metaphysical assumptions than those which are in accordance with the existence of non-objectifiable space, i.e. we can be satisfied with accepting non-objectifiable space, but no more. It is not necessary to make assumptions saying that there also exists a metaphysically transcendent space, supra-polar space. But it is also possible that Heim intends to say something like this: For T_n shall be inserted statements describing non-objectifiable space *and* statements describing human destiny. Then the argument perhaps becomes stronger in connection with the accepted view on the concept of explanation. But this raises many questions: Must we accept a supra-polar space as the only explanation, before alternative explanations are investigated? Why can not human existence ultimately be relative and paradoxical? Why must there be an explanation at all? Therefore, if the maximal version shall be accepted, it must be accepted at least partly for personal reasons.

Chapter 5.

Heim's solution of the problem of transcendence: The doctrine about polar and supra-polar space

Introduction. We shall begin this chapter by paying some attention to a little book which appeared at the end of the nineteenth century in England. Its title was "Flatland, a Romance of many Dimensions, by a Square". The author of the book was the theologian Edwin Abbott. At its appearance the book passed rather unnoticed, but it seems later to have played some role for Heim (it appeared in a german translation in 1932) and he refers to it several times.[1] Because it fascinated Heim and because its content is rather original, we shall present its main content as an introduction. This will also reveal some features of Heim's thinking on the concept of space.

The author begins by presentating a being, which we can call a "time-being". This being has no spatial extension, and its only possibility to order, or to structure, its experiences is to order them temporally. We can say that it exists in one dimension or in a one-dimensional space. Now, for this being it is impossible to imagine two experiences as simultaneous. Simultaneity constitutes a paradox for this being, as long as it can only order its experiences temporally. But let us now suppose that its experiential possibilities are suddenly extended. Let us say that it no more exists as a "time-being" but as a "surface-being". Then we can say that it exists in a two-dimensional space. Now the simultaneity of experiences is not a problem. Experiences can be simultaneous with regard to time, but not with regard to space, or the reverse. And now we can easily imagine experiences, which in an analogous manner are paradoxical for the "surface-being", but not for a being which exists in a three-dimensional space. This being we can call a "space-being". And the consciousness of such a being we can imagine as rather similar to ours, and this being orders its experiences in a way rather similar to ours. In addition: Let us imagine a system of coordinates: A time-being can determine its experience by mentioning one coordinate (a), the surface-being by two (a, b) and the space-being by three (a, b, c) in relation to a given system of coordinates.

Now we can also see that it is not necessary to limit the number of dimensions to three. It is also possible to imagine beings, living in a multi-dimensional space, even if we cannot imagine exactly how their experiential world is shaped. But it is quite possible to give such a multidimensional world a mathematical description.

Corrections to Ingemar Holmstrand: Karl Heim on Philo
Science and the Transcendence of God.

Text

page.line	reads	should be
4.3	science	Science
11.4	dialectal	dialectical
14.37	limit[3]	limit[2]
14.38	"Urfaktum"	"Urbeziehung"
15.1	insoluble.[4]	insoluble.[3] This is a said in GD.[4]
29.14	interprete	interpret
21	interpretation	interpretations
34.7	Letzte	letzte
39.55	commonsence-"fact"	commonsense-"fact"
48.15	explicitly	implicitly
59.15	'Standpunkt'	‚Standpunkt'
79.2	views.[1].	views.[1]
92.11&13	experiental	experiential
21	T3.1	T3.2
97.32	Wirklickeit	Wirklichkeit
107.31-32	in-halte	In-halte
111.37	datum	datur
113.15	quesiton	question
115.11	Dritte	Dritten
116.2	"existierend hin-eintreten"	"hineinspringen oder gerufen werden".[41]
129.20	sense-experience.[40]	sense-experience.[41]
131.4	supra-polar space.[52]	supra-polar space.
23	upon further	further upon
24	interpetation	interpretation
135.12	here	there
138.8	cf	cf.
139.5	consistent	inconsistent

Notes

	reads	should be
1.3 n.10	WZ 96ff, 14ff	WZ 96ff, GL 14ff
n.15	e.g. 114f	e.g. 112ff
n.32	JH 136f	JW 136f
1.4 n.14	to be omitted: ...and [2]GD 157f	
n.18	G 154	G 251f, cf. GL 27
n.19	WW 114f	GD 189ff
2.2 n.4	to be omitted: ...JH 56f	
n.19	[2]GD 74, GL 72f	GD 74, GD 72ff

```
      n.24 Cf. GL 17              GL 27ff
3.1 n.1  E.g. in GN 255f          GN 23, cf.255
    n.3  LI 75f, 79f, 96f         LI 75f, 79f, 90f
    n.5  cf.88                     cf.18f
3.2 n.27 Cf. also ²GD 167ff        Cf. also ²GD 172f
3.3 n.20 GD 111                    GD 113f
    n.39 E.G. GL 170, G 188        E.g. GL 170, G 188
    n.56 to be omitted: ... GL 170
3.4 n.16 des Gottlose              der Gottlose
    n.21 WuW 74                    WuW 71
    n.40 Traub 1971, 189          Traub 1917, 189
    n.44 ... Gegenständlichen ... gegenständlichen
    n.46 should be GL 15ff
    n.48       "    GL 29ff
    n.52 to be omitted: LI 54f
    n.2  GN 114f                   111f
    n.3  E.g. ²GD 66₂              Cf. GN 175
1.1 n.9  should be: ²GD 58ff, GD 73f, 141, GN 141f
    n.26 WW 95f                    92f
1.2 n.7  LI 70ff                   LI 76ff
2.1 n.16 JH 173                    Cf. GD 195, 203f
2.2 n.4  JH 176                    Cf. G 168ff, GN 175f
    n.13 GN 207                    GN 203ff
    n.18 Baillie 1964,215         Baillie 1926,246ff
    n.19 GN 154                    Cf. GN 154f
    n.35 GL 343                    JH 62
    n.37 to be omitted: WZ 249
    n.39       "        cf. GN 193, GD 215
    n.55       "        WuW 96
    n.58 GN 59, 73                 GN 59ff
2.3 n.20 on Genesis               in Genesis
         WuW 75ff                 WuW 117f
    n.23 should be: GN 213, WuW 135
    n.24       "   :Cf. WuW 154
    n.30 GN 227                   WuW 131f, 153
1   n.21 ²GD 67                   ²GD 65
2   n.6  to be omitted: GD 75, 253

Literature
176.18 Malevez,              Malevez,L.
176.26 to be inserted after Michalson, C.
       Mitchell, B. 1973: The Justification of
       Religious Belief. Towbridge and London.
```

This little story, which Heim appreciated, also describes two features in Heim's notion of the concept of space:

(1) What seems to be a paradox in one space may not be so in another, and
(2) It is possible to imagine quite different ways of ordering experiences, than ways we are used to.

In this story such concepts as the concepts of "space" and "dimension" are central concepts. They are also central in Heim's theory. But also a reader of Heim, who has Heim's own characteristic of his thinking as "Philosophie der Räume"[2] or as "Denken in Räume"[3] present, must also observe that Heim's terminology is not simple, clarifying or consequent. As well as the concept of space he also uses a number of other concepts in the same or almost the same sense. The most frequent of these other concepts are the concepts of "Dimension" and "Welt". The relation between these concepts, or to be more correct, between Heim's different ways of using them is complicated.

We shall first observe that the concept of space, as we shall meet it in the following quotations, has not only nor principally the ordinary meaning. In the writings of Heim the concept of space is generalized and extended in a way that can be related to philosophical and scientific theory.[4] According to Heim, this is a necessary condition for a reasonable and meaningful talk about the transcendence of God.

A possibility here would perhaps be to analyse Heim's different uses of these concepts and their associates with regard to a supposed similarity between them. There certainly are such similarities. So for example, the use of the concepts space and dimension have several features in common. But apart from the fact that such an investigation would be rather comprehensive, the differences in their various uses would not be especially enlightening for us. And, in addition, Heim also operates with other concepts than those we have mentioned.

We shall instead choose to use the concept of space only in the following ways:

The first definition of the concept space is the definition which is operative in the expression "polares Raum", polar space. Heim also uses the expressions "polares Welt" or "polares Weltform" in the same sense. Now, polar space is the world in which we all live and ordinarily experience. It is the immanent world. Polar space is constituted by the law of polarity. All entities within polar space have polar relations to eachother.

Polar space contains two other spaces, objectifiable and non-objectifiable space. And these constitute our second definition of the concept space. Now, Heim's terminology concerning these spaces is also unclear. The following list of similar concepts does not claim to be complete: "gegenständliches — nichtgegenständliches Raum", "Raum des Gewordenen — Präsenzraum", "Raum der Vergangenheit — Raum der Gegenwart", "Raum des Gewordenen — Raum des Werdens", or "gegenständliches Region", "gegenständliches

105

Welt" on the one hand and "Raum der Begegnungen", "Wir-Raum", "Raum der Unentschiedenen", "nichtgegenständliches Sphäre" or "Gebiet" on the other.

Finally we shall also let the concept space signify the areas of experience, which are contained in objectifiable and non-objectifiable space. Then we shall talk about Ego-, Thou- and It-space.

The next important concept is the concept of "dimension". We shall make some remarks on this concept. Heim's terminology is not entirely clear about this either. Perhaps we can, somewhat briefly, divide Heim's uses of it in the following way.

First he uses it in a proper way; thus, the word "dimension" signifies time and space. This is the usual meaning, as when we say that euclidian plane space has two dimensions. We shall extend this usage, and in the following call the "parts" of a space for its dimensions.

Secondly he uses it in a more analogical way. Then the word "dimension" signifies the different fields of experience of an individual subject. There are three such fields of experience, the experience of an "It", a "Thou" and some aspects of a subject's experience of itself. When this is the case we have already said that we shall use the concept space.

Finally the word "dimension" appears in an even more analogical way, e.g. in expressions like " a new dimension appears", which further is convertible into expressions like "an entirely new possibility arises" or "new light is shed on the matter". In our opinion this use refers to the activity of making a supplementary basic assumption.

We shall set out the following chapter in this way: First we shall treat polar space (5.1.). We have to do this, because Heim, as we shall see, determines supra-polar space in terms of polar space.

This part (5.1.) deals with three points: What is a space? (5.1.1.) How is a new space discovered (5.1.2.) and How are the polar spaces related to each other (5.1.3.). (5.2.) treats supra-polar space and is set out in like manner: What is suprapolar space (5.2.1), How is suprapolar space to be discovered? (5.2.2.) and How is supra-polar space related to polar space? (5.2.3.).

5.1. Polar space

It may be convenient to repeat here what we earlier have said about polar space because Heim defines the concept of supra-polar space in terms of polar space.

Now, polar space is basically and universally signified by the law of polarity. We have earlier discussed this law. Polar space is the immanent world or reality. And a partial space of polar space is of course also polar. Objectifiable and non-objectifiable space as well as It-space, Thou-space and Ego-space are also polar. According to Heim, all entities within these spaces hold a polar relation to eachother.

But in order to investigate the concept of polar space, it is of course necessary not only to treat the concept of polarity, but also the concept of space. We shall do this in the following.

5.1.1. What is a space?

We shall also here proceed in the same way as we have done earlier, namely by quoting some important passages concerning the concept of space. (As before, the roman numbers within brackets refer to the following comments. The italics are ours.)

Heim writes:

"Die letzten Gegebenheiten, auf die wir stossen, sind Räume. Das Wort ‚Raum' muss dabei in einem erweiterten Sinn genommen werden. Ein Raum ist ein *in sich unendliches Kontinuum* (I), in dem nach einem *bestimmten Strukturgesetz* (II) eine Mannigfaltigkeit von Inhalten angeordnet ist...

Das Dasein der einzelnen Räume und ihrer inneren Strukturgesetze bildet also *die Voraussetzung, durch die es erst möglich wird, dass sich Inhalte gegeneinander abgrenzen* (III). Jeder dieser Räume, die das Fundament der Wirklichkeit bilden, *trägt ein eigenes Ordnungsgesetz in sich* (IV), zum Beispiel der Zeitraum mit seinem Nacheinander, der Flächenraum mit seinem Nebeneinander, der dreidimensionale Körperraum, der alle diese Räume in sich schliessende Gegenstandsraum und der unanschauliche Gegenwartsraum, in dem ich und du einander begegnen. Aber so verschiedenartig die Inneneinrichtung der Räume ist, so ist doch ein Grundzug ihnen allem gemeinsam. Jeder Raum ist ein *in sich geschlossenes Kontinuum* (V)".[1]

"Die Mathematik kennt einen ‚Raum', der zwar nicht unendlich, aber unbegrenzt ist, zum Beispiel die Oberfläche einer Kugel, bei der wir nirgends auf eine Grenze stossen, weil sie in sich zurückkehrt. Von da aus entsteht ein neuer Raumbegriff. Wir nennen in diesem Buch ‚Raum' *ein Kontinnum, das unbegrenzt ist und alles Gegebene umfasst* (VI). Das Wesen eines solchen Raumkontinuums besteht lediglich *in seiner Struktur, also in dem Gesetz, nach welchem innerhalb dieser Struktur die Inhalte angeordnet sind* (VII). Das einfachste Beispiel ist der Zeitraum, der dadurch entsteht, dass die inhalte, die er enthält, in zeitlichem Nacheinander angeordnet sind, im Gegensatz zum Körperraum, in dem die Inhalte sich nebeneinander und übereinander befinden."[2]

(Heim has before treated euclidian plane space and proposed the possible existence of "... Räume ... die wir uns zwar nicht anschaulich vorstellen können, deren Struktur sich aber algebraisch ohne weiteres vorstellen lässt". He continues:)

"Wenn wir aber mit *einer Vielheit von Räumen rechnen müssen, in denen der Weltinhalt nach verschiedenen Ordnungsprinzipien und Strukturgesetzen angeordnet sein kann* (VIII), so sind dabei offenbar vier Fälle möglich.
1. Ein Raum kann wie unser *euklidischer Raum der Anschauung und geometrischen Darstellung restlos erschlossen sein* (IX).
2. Es kann sein, dass ein Raum für uns zwar nicht vorstellbar ist, aber dass wir ihn erschliessen können, indem wir die Axiome unseres Anschauungsraumes *so*

verallgemeinern und abwandeln, dass sie in übertragenem Sinn auf einen Raum an-gewandt werden können, der ausserhalb unser Abschauung liegt (X). Diesen Fall haben wir bei den Räumen, mit denen Riemann rechnet.

3. Ein Raum kann eine Struktur haben, die sich überhaupt nicht mehr mathematisch darstellen lässt, weil dieser *Raum vollständig ausserhalb der ganzen Gegenstandswelt liegt* (XI). Dennoch kann es ein Raum im echten Sinne des Wortes sein, weil auch in ihm *eine Mannigfaltigkeit von Gegebenheiten nach einem bestimmten Ordnungsprinzip angeordnet ist* (XII). Dieses Ordnungsprinzip ist uns genau so *unmittelbar bekannt und leuchtet uns als allgemeingültig ein wie die Axiome der euklidische Geometrie. Diesen Fall haben wir beim nichtgegenständlichen Raum¹ der Begegnungen. Ueber diesen weiss jeder von uns unmittelbar Bescheid* (XIII). Das Dasein unseres eigenen nicht-gegenständlichen Ich und das Wesen der unanschaulichen Begegnung mit ein Du ist uns vertrauter als die ganze Gegenstandswelt, die und gegenübersteht. Die Existenzialaussagen, die Heidegger über unser ,Dasein' und ,Mitsein' macht, wollen durchaus nicht bloss als persönliche Erlebnisse eines Einzelmenschen gewertet sein. Sie machen den Anspruch, *allgemeingültige Strukturgesetze und Ordnungsprinzipien zu sein, die jeden einleuchten, der im nichtgegenständlichen Raum steht* (XIV). *Die Allgemeingültigkeit dieser Ordnungsprinzipien unserer Existenz ist unabhängig davon, ob diese Strukturgesetze dir oder mir oder irgendeinem anderem schon zum Bewusstsein gekommen sind oder ob wir noch nie darüber nachgedacht haben* (XV) und erst durch die Existenzialphilosophie darauf aufmerksam gemacht werden müssen. . .

4. *Ein Raum kann aber auch jenseits von allem liegen* (XVI), was wir sehen oder mathematisch erschliessen können, auch jenseits aller Räume, in denen wir existenziell stehen, ohne dass uns das schon zum Bewusstsein gekommen ist . . . Wir müssen also auch für die Möglichkeit von vornherein offenbleiben, dass es Wesen geben könnte, die in einem Raumschema leben, das uns völlig verschlossen ist".³

"Der Körperraum, der gewöhnlich Raum schlechthin genannt wird, ist also nur ein *Spezialfall von Räumlichkeit*, von der sich andere einfachere und kompliziertere Räume unterscheiden lassen (XVII)".⁴

"Gegebenheiten, die sich dimensional zu einander verhalten, haben wir Räume genannt, das Wort Raum in dem allgemeinen Sinne genommen als ein *in sich un-endliches Kontinuum* (XVIII), innerhalb dessen nach einem *in seiner Struktur enthaltenen Ordnungsprinzip Inhalte* (XIX) ihre Stelle finden können. Die Gegenstandswelt, innerhalb deren *Bewusstseinsräume als Teilräume* (XX) aufeinander bezogen sind, haben wir als . . . unanschaulichen Weltraum bezeichnet. Aber er erscheint uns auf den ersten Blick neu und ungewohnt, wenn wir die Seinsregion, der die Gegenstandswelt als Objekt des Erkennens und Wollens gegenübersteht, also die nichtgegenständliche Sphäre, in der wir selbst im Präsenzzustand der Entscheidung stehen, als einen *Bewusstseinsraum* (XXI) bezeichnen. Und doch *müssen wir diesen Schritt tun, wenn wir Ordnung in das Weltbild der Gegenwart hineinbringen wollen* (XXII). Dem Weltraum, in dem das Gegenständliche seinen Ort hat, steht der Raum der Nichtgegenständlichkeit gegenüber, also der Raum des Werdens, dem *ich und du als Teilräume angehören* (XXIII). Wir können ihn darum auch als den Wir-Raum bezeichnen".⁵

"Meine Gegenstandswelt und deine Gegenstandswelt sind nicht zwei Inhalte oder zwei Gegenstände. Sie müssen vielmehr *als Räume in dem . . . definierten Sinn bezeichnet werden* (XXIV). *Jeder von ihnen ist eine in sich unabschliessbare Mannigfaltigkeit, in der nach einem in ihrem Wesen liegenden Ordnungsprinzip Inhalte ihren Ort erhalten können* (XXV). *Zur Struktur eines Bewusstseinsraums gehört vor allem das perspektivische Bezogensein auf eine Mitte* (XXVI). Im übrigen können wir über den Bewusstseinsraum des andern keine allgemeingültige Aussage machen. Er kann eine eindimensionale Strecke sein oder ein Flächenraum oder ein Körperraum. Er kann auch *irgeneine andere, uns völlig unbekannte Struktur haben* (XXVII)".[6]

From these quotations we shall mention some features which, according to Heim, signifies a space. They are

(1) A space is an infinite continuum. (I, VI, XVIII, XXV)

And from this Heim concludes that

(1.1.) A space encompasses reality as a whole[7] (VI).

(2) A space is characterized by having a certain structure or it is ordered according to one (or many) rules of construction (II, VII, VIII, XII, XXV, cf. XXVI). We have already called them basic assumptions.

(2.1.) A rule of construction is immediately apprehended[8] (XIII, XIV).

(2.2.) A rule of construction is in some way inherent in the nature of the space (IV, XIX, XXV).

(2.3.) A rule of construction has an a priori-axiomatic character.[9] (III, XIII, cf. XXII)

Examples of spaces are time (one-dimensional space), a plane (two-dimensional space) and the ordinary three-dimensional space. There are also, from the matemathical or conceptual point of view, more complicated types of space. Further, an individual experiential world i.e. an individual perspective, an Ego-space, as well as non-objectifiable Thou-space and objectifiable It-space, are spaces (IX, X, XIV, XVI, XXI, XXIII, XXIV, XXVII).

(3) The number of possible spaces is infinite (cf. VII, X).

Therefore, according to Heim:

(3.1.) The ordinary three-dimensional space is only one of many possible spaces (XVII, cf. XXVII).

All these properties essentially characterize a space. We shall examine them below under the general heading "what is a space?"

(4) A new space is established by supplying a new dimension to the already existing (or accepted) ones (cf. XXII).

(4.1.) In the discovery of a new space there is an inherent insight that this new space has somehow existed before its discovery and independent of it[10] (XV).

We shall examine this point in 5.1.2. under the heading "How is a new space discovered?"

(5) Different spaces can be conceived as being contained in eachother (XX, XXIV).

We shall examine this point in 5.1.3. under the heading "How are different spaces related to eachother?"

Finally Heim says that

(6) It is possible that a metaphysically transcendent space exists (XVI).[11]

This point is our subject in 5.2. "Supra-polar space".

What is a space? Now we can analyze Heim's concept of space in more detail. We shall start from the points (1–3) above.

A space is an infinite continuum. The first important feature of a space is that it is an infinite and closed continuum and that a space therefore encompasses reality as a whole.

Let us start with the notion of infinity.

It is obvious that Heim does not want to say that a space is infinite in the ordinary, "local" or quantitative, meaning. This is trivial, and it is follows from the fact that there are non-local spaces. Therefore there is no contradiction between the assertions that a space may be limited and that it is infinite. The surface of a sphere is limited, but it is also infinite.[12]

The most plausible meaning of the infinity of a space seems to be this. It is difficult to give it a proper name, but let us call it logical infinity. Now, a space, as we shall see below, can be formally expressed in the form of an either-or-structure. This means i.a. that an entity always has a position P within a space. This means then that every attempt to cease asking for its position in the continuum is impossible. The point where the questioning ceases is always arbitrarily chosen. And within the world which is accessible to us in our experiences, all entities have a position within a certain space. We shall say that the infinity of a space ought to be interpreted in this way, otherwise Heim's theories about a dimensional limit and spatial subordination make no sense. We shall return to them in 5.1.3.

The next part of Heim's description of a space says that it is a closed continuum of contents. We shall make some remarks on this.

The first way of interpreting Heim here is to say that when using the word "content" he means a class of entities, to which one and the same rule of construction is properly applicable. Thus we have many spaces, each one constituted by its own rule of construction. According to this interpetation the world-space, "Welt-raum", can be seen as the sum of all possible entities. And this interpretation is compatible with Heim's description of a space as infinite, because there are no reasons to suppose that the number of entities belonging to a certain class is limited. But then Heim's conclusion that a space encompasses reality as a whole is mistaken. It can only encompass a part of it, namely the entities of a certain class. And it also follows that his theory about a dimensional limit between spaces cannot be defended at least not as a general theory on the relation between spaces. It is quite possible that there are two quite different classes of entities, which cannot be subordinated to the same rule of construction.

The second way of interpreting Heim here is to say that the word content refers to all entities seen from the same perspective centre. Thus a space becomes the same as the content of mind, "Bewusstseinsraum", and the content of such a centre can of course be seen as ordered according to several rules of construction. Then the world-space can be seen as the sum of all the contents of all perspective centers. This interpretation can make sense both of Heim's assertion that a space is infinite and encompasses reality as a whole. This is compatible with all entities within the same class being ordered from the same perspective and that it is infinite in this meaning. It may also possible be the case that there is a perspective centre which possesses all necessary rules of construction for ordering all kinds of facts. And it is also compatible with the circumstance that a human perspective centre for some reason, e.g metaphysical, cannot possess all the necessary rules of construction for ordering all facts. This interpretation also makes sense of Heim's distinction between a limit of dimension and a limit of content. To encompass reality as a whole means to ascribe to reality some property in a collective sense. From a Christian point of view such assertions as that the world has been created or that it has fallen, are examples of this. And as we have seen, Heim's theory of knowledge can be interpreted as a theory according to which it is possible for man to really and properly ascribe to reality as a whole such general properties, to apprehend such rules of constructions, according to which all facts can be ordered. In this sense it can properly be said that a space encompasses reality as a whole. And that ordinary man in fact does not do this is due to the circumstance that there are an enormous number of contents of which man is unaware, and therefore no man, nor all men together, can grasp reality as a whole.

A space is characterized by having a certain structure. The next important property of a space is that it has a certain structure or that it is ordered according to one or many rules of construction. Now Heim says that these rules of construction have a common feature. They all express an exclusive "either-or"-relation:

Jede Dimension muss immer irgendwie durch ein disjunktives Verhältnis ausdrückbar sein, also durch ein Entweder-Oder zwischen zwei Möglichkeiten, die nach dem logischen Gesetz vom ausgeschlossenen Dritten miteinander unvereinbar sind. Daraus folgt weiter: Eine Dimension lässt sich immer auch in Form einer disjunktiven Frage ausdrücken... Jede Mannigfaltigkeit, die in einem disjunktiven Verhältnis ausdrückbar ist, ist eine Dimension...".[13]

"Jede elementare Unterscheidung ... ist nur möglich ... innerhalb einer Mannigfaltigkeit ... innerhalb dessen die Unterscheidung zustande kommt. Eine solche Unterscheidungssphäre nennen wir eine Dimension".[14]

"Im bisher bekannten Raum stehen wir vor dem Entweder-Oder zwischen zwei Möglichkeiten, das unter der strengen Regel steht: ‚Tertium non datum'... Das, was im bisher bekannten Raum das ‚ausgeschlossene Dritte' war, ist im neuen Raum, nicht ausgeschlossen, sondern eingeschlossen in den erweiterten Bereich der dimensionalen Möglichkeiten, die dieser neue Raum in sich enthält".[15]

He says here that a space is characterized by its being ordered according to an exclusive "either-or"-structure. It should be possible to express the essence of an order in a disjunction. This means e.g. within a temporal space that an event takes place at a certain time t or at non-t, or, within a two-dimensional space, that an event must be situated at (a, b) or not, or that an event belongs to my perspective or not. We can say that every continuum, in which an entity can be described by using a system of disjunctions is then a space. Thus we have a temporal space, a plane-space and the ego-space, each one having its own proper rules of construction, i.e. disjunctions in different respects. This is moreover a consequence of the law of polarity, and therefore by definition it holds for polar space as a whole. We shall return to the meaning of this in 5.2.1.

That a space is characterized by having different structures of course means different things. We can distinguish between different rules of construction, determining different spaces.

Concerning objectifiable space they are:

A temporal order

A spatial order

A causal order. Heim says

"Die gegenständliche Erfahrungswelt muss also einen geschlossenen Kausalzusammenhang darstellen".[16]

Finally, Heim sometimes seems to say that different laws of nature, e.g. the law of conservation of energy, are rules of construction for entities within objectifiable space. But his position here is not wholly clear.

Concerning non-objectifiable space they are existential statements, "Existenzialaussagen", in the sense of Heidegger (XIV). But it is not clear exactly what Heim means. The most plausible interpretation is that these statements refer to existentials in the philosophy of Heidegger. In which case they tell us something about the inescapable conditions of human existence. They order non-objectifiable facts. It is also possible that Heim means to say that statements describing human existence such as subjected to "destiny" and "being placed" have their place here.

On the ontological status of the rules of construction. We shall now turn our attention to the question of the ontological status of the rules of construction. This is a problematical question, and we have considered it before. The problem is connected with Heim's opinion that the basic assumptions or the rules of constructions are "immediately apprehended" (XIII), that they "essentially signify the space" (XIX) or have an "apriori-axiomatic character" (III). But as we have seen, the notion of immediate apprehension is unclear in Heims' thinking. It refers both to the apprehension of sense-data and to the apprehension of relations between sense-data. And the rules of construction describe such relations. When Heim justifies this claim, he argues from the basic ability of the mind to distinguish entities from each other. But the problematical point is whether this assumption, even if it is correct, is sufficient to entail that rules of construction are also immediately apprehended.

Let us then consider the question from another point of view and connect it with the phenomenological reduction.[17] We saw that Heim's opinion was that the question of whether the rules of construction have their anchorage in the object or in the subject, was wrongly stated.[18] To put the question in this way is to confuse an abstract distinction with a factual separation.[19] Therefore Heim says:

"Der Raum kann immer nur im Ganzen der Subjekt-Objekt-Beziehung seinen Grund haben".[20]

The correct way to put the question is:

"Welche Bedeutung hat der Raum für das Zustandekommen dieser Beziehung?"[21]

Therefore Heim puts the quesiton about the existence of an independent external world within brackets:

"Wir klammern die Frage ein, ob das Erfahrungsganze, in das wir hinengestellt sind, eine letzte Realität ist oder eine Erscheinungswelt, die die wahre Wirklichkeit wie ein Schleier verhüllt"[22]

It is not easy to determine Heim's position. But a purely subjective interpretation of his position does not seem to be correct. The rules of construction are not simple inventions of the mind. They are somehow anchored in reality. But it is also true that the subject plays a role, in the construction of a total view of reality. But to say this is not the same as to say that it plays this role arbitrarily. Reality is always a corrective. Otherwise, Heim's thesis that a new space is discovered by a paradoxical insight or experience makes no sense.[23]

The number of spaces is infinite. We shall now pay some attention to another feature in Heim's philosophy of spaces. This is a somewhat speculative feature. Heim says that the number of possible spaces is infinite. This does not mean that the number of individual perspectives, or Ego-spaces, is infinite. Perhaps Heim would admit this, but this interpretation has no bearing upon the question of supra-polar space.

From the mathematical point of view it is quite possible to conceive of a multi-dimensional space. Theories about such spaces are well-known within mathematics.

But then it becomes difficult to imagine a being, which can experience such a multi-dimensional space, and to imagine how the experiental world of such a being is shaped. Our experiential world is three-dimensional. This fact is simply part of our destiny.[24] But of course it may be possible that there exist beings which can conceive of other spaces than our three-dimensional one. To disallow this possibility would seem to be a sign of lack of imagination rather than anything else.

But we nevertheless know that all possible spaces must be polar, i.e. that their rules of constructions must have an "either-or"-structure according to the law of polarity. And even if we cannot imagine such a space and its experiential character, we do know that it must be oriented from a perspective centre.[25]

Finally we shall in this connection mention a rather speculative thought which has its proper place here, even if it plays no role in Heim's theory about the transcendence of God. We are still moving within polar space.

Heim says that there is no reason why we should say that only human beings can be perspective centres. This raises the question: Can it be the case that a possible space may also be a real experiential space? And Heim's answer to this question seems to be affirmative. And he develops his answer in an interesting chapter on the question of whether or not the universe as a whole is to some extent animated.[26] This is an interesting proposal, developed in a fascinating way, but to examine it would lead us far away from our theme.

5.1.2. How is a new space discovered?

We have touched upon this important subject several times before. We shall now treat it in more detail.

We saw that a new space appears when a new dimension or a new rule of construction is added to the already existing ones. When this is done, a new and higher dimensioned space is established. It was such an addition we called a supplementary basic assumption. This principle holds generally, from the simplest one-dimensional space to the discovery of supra-polar space.[1]

Here an important question arises: For what reasons, or under what conditions, is it justified to make a supplementary basic assumption? Heim's answer briefly is: It is justified because there are facts or events which are not possible to integrate in a scheme of dimension, i.e. they cannot be ordered according to the accepted rules of construction. We have called such a fact or event a paradox. When a paradox is recognized, then, in order to explain it, it is necessary to supply a new rule of construction to the already accepted ones. And we saw according to Heim that there really are paradoxes, and that they are general in the sense that all men have, or can have, a genuine insight into them.[2]

A plausible interpretation of this is to say that there is always relative to every dimensional scheme at least one paradox which cannot be integrated in that dimensional scheme. And further, because there are insights and experiences, which, when analysed, appear to be inherently paradoxical, even if they are not always prima facie experienced as being paradoxes, as for example the real co-existence of many perspectives, then this according to Heim shows that a supplementary basic assumption is already made, and therefore that there really exists a new and higher dimensioned space, non-objectifiable space, in which the paradox is removed.

This means from the formal point of view that the making of a supplementary basic assumption, and therefore also the acceptance of a new space, brings about the solution of a paradox:

"Das Aufgehen eines neuen, umfassenderen Raums kündigt sich immer dadurch an, dass der Gegensatz zwischen zwei einander ausschliessenden Möglichkeiten, der dem bisherigen Raum sein Gepräge gegeben hatte, durch eine neue dritte Möglichkeit aufgehoben und überbrückt wird. Die beiden Möglichkeiten, in die wir innerhalb des eindimensionalen Zeitraums eingeschlossen waren, standen unter der logischen Grundregel des ‚ausgeschlossenen Dritte'. Mit der Erschliessung der Zweidimensionalen Fläche wird dieses innerhalb des Zeitraums ‚ausgeschlossene Dritte' eine unleugbare Wirklichkeit".

And what before was impossible now becomes possible:

"Wenn sich ein neuer Raum erschliesst, so taucht dabei eine Wirklichkeit auf, die das Entweder-Oder sprengt, auf das die Struktur des bisher bekannten Raums aufgebaut war. Jedesmal tritt eine neue Möglichkeit in Kraft, die innerhalb des bisher bekannten Raums ‚das ausgeschlossene Dritte' gewesen war".[3]

This means that something which earlier appeared as a paradox, in relation to a certain dimensional scheme, now becomes non-paradoxical. It is a paradox which demands a new rule of construction. We have earlier seen examples of this. The most illustrative of these is perhaps the story about the inhabitants of "Flatland".

An interesting point is, according to Heim, that there are not always contental reasons for making a supplementary basic assumption. Heim uses this figure as an illustration. It is ordinarily seen as a cube, i.e. as a three-dimensional body, but this way of seeing it is of course not necessary. It is also quite possible to see it as three to each other limiting square figures on a two-dimensional plane.

This example can also illustrate that it is not possible to present rational and conclusive arguments for establishing a new space. It is not the case that experiences totally determine the dimensional scheme. This means that the rules of construction cannot be derived from experiences alone. On the contrary, the opposite holds. It is the dimensional scheme which determines the interpretation of the experiences:

"Dass ich mich dem Bild gegenüber anders einstelle und es mit andern Augen ansehe, dazu kann ich also nicht durch die Wahrnehmung der Linien und Farben oder durch einen Schluss aus dem Wahrgenommenen geführt worden sein. Das Verhältnis ist vielmehr umgekehrt. Die Zweidimensionalität oder die Dreidimensionalität bestimmt die Art, wie ich das Bild sehe. Das Hineingestelltwerden in einen Raum liegt also noch diesseits der Sinneswahrnehmung. Es muss daher eine andere Art von Innewerden sein als der Sinneseindruck. In Räume kann man nur existierend hineintreten oder existierend drinstehen und dann daraus heraus wahrnehmen und denken"[4].

In this quotation we shall make some remarks on the expression "existierend drinstehe". He also uses the similar expression "existierend hineintreten".[5] When using these expressions Heim refers to the activity of making a supplementary basic assumption and he also says that we have an immediate insight into this assumption and that we also know that this new rule of construction really holds. And this insight is also connected with the insight that this new space thus established, has in some way existed before and independent of its discovery. This "before" cannot of course be understood chronologically. It is this we have called the principle of the preexistence of higher dimensioned space.[6] But what can this preexistence reasonably mean? The most plausible interpretation of Heim is to regard it as a consequence of the theory that the basic assumptions are not inventions of the mind but founded in reality. When facts are recognized as paradoxes, then they are paradoxes in relation to a dimensional scheme, and they have always been so. And it is a mistake to accuse facts of being paradoxical (and perhaps therefore declare them to be illusionary). It is more natural to search for the faults in the applied dimensional scheme. And when a higher dimensioned space is discovered, than it cannot be lost again.[7] This is quite compatible with Heim's assertion that in some cases it can be justified to disregard it.

Finally, a second important question arises: Are there necessary paradoxes, i.e. facts or events, which are paradoxes in relation to every dimensional scheme, based on polarity? We shall return to this question in 5.2.2.

5.1.3. How are different spaces related to eachother?

In this section we shall describe Heim's view on the relation between different spaces and shall discuss the question of how they can be delimited. Heim's problem is: What kind of relation can there be between two infinities? We saw that a space, according to Heim, was infinite. Is it then meaningful at all to talk about a limit between infinities? How can there be a limit between them?

But in order to treat this problem, we first have to deal with another kind of limit than that between spaces. And this kind of limit is important here. This limit is the limit between entities or contents within the same space. Thus we have two different kinds of limit, one between what Heim calls "Sphären oder Mannigfaltigkeiten" (i.e. spaces) and one between entities or contents within the same space.

It may be convenient to threat the latter kind of limit first. Then we only have to draw some conclusions from what we have said earlier in 3.1. There Heim said that the mind has a basic ability to distinguish entities from eachother or to immediately apprehend their difference. This is the ability to make "elementary distinctions" ("elementare Unterscheidung"). When this is done, a limit of content ("inhaltliche Grenze") recognized. In this case, the entities have a polar relation to each other.[1] They have always a temporal or spatial distance from eachother.[2] This case Heim illustrates with a chessboard. The square a1 is limited by the squares a2 and b1. The point is that every entity, which is limited by a limit of content must belong to the same space.[3] The example concerned the two-dimensional plane of a chessboard, but the same holds of course for every space, from one-dimensional time to a multi-dimensioned space.

The other kind of limit is the limit between different spaces. This type of limit Heim calls a limit of dimension ("dimensionale Grenze"). In this case the limit is not constituted by the contents of the spaces involved. Instead it appears to be due to the different rules of construction which constitute the different spaces or orders entities within them.[4]

Now we can more exactly describe Heim's view on the relations between different spaces. There are two types of relations, corresponding to the two types of limits. These types of relation Heim calls dimensional coordination and dimensional subordination. These terms need some consideration.

Let us say that a dimensional coordination is the case when a space is related to another space and both have the same rules of construction but not the same content. This corresponds to the limit of content.

A dimensional subordination is the case when spaces, having different rules of construction and at least one content in common are related to each other. This corresponds to a dimensional limit. A two-dimensional plane is subordinated to a three-dimensional space, *or* that the experiential world of a point-being is subordinated the plane-being in the story of Flatland, the rules of construction of a plane-being allow a more differentiated way of ordering impressions than that of a point-being. This Heim expresses by the term "Teil-Raum", partial space. A two-dimensional plane is a partial space of a three-dimensional space.

We shall in the following, 5.2.3. see that Heim treats polar space as a whole in relation to the supra-polar. A point here is that there is in no way a limit of content between them and that polar space is a partial space of the supra-polar.

5.2. Supra-polar space

5.2.1. What is supra-polar space?

We can now proceed from polar space to supra-polar space. The question of supra-polar space is the central question for Heim. His main interest is not in some periferial or limited theological question, but in the central question of the transcendence of God. Heim says:

"Die zentrale Frage der Gegenwart ist die Frage nach der Möglichkeit der ganzen Unterscheidung zwischen Schöpfer und Geschöpf, die Frage, ob es überhaupt einen Sinn hat, von der immanenten Welt eine transzendente Sphäre abzugrenzen, in der dann Gott oder ein unpersönliches X als Bewohner untergebracht werden kann"[1].

117

And the answer to this question sheds decisive light on the existence of man in the world.

The reasons why this question is central for Heim are of course easy to see. The main reason is the breakdown of the old Aristotelian scientific world-view and the rise of the modern world-view based on the foundations of modern science. This change has made the traditional idea of divine transcendence difficult to justify and to believe. There are both scientific and philosophical reasons against a traditional notion of the transcendence of God.

Heim wants to show that it is still meaningful to talk about and assume the existence of a transcendent reality. This transcendent reality he describes in terms of the theory of spaces which we have described in the preceeding section.

We can describe this transcendent reality, as in the terminology of Heim: supra-polar space. (From now on the predicate transcendent means metaphysically transcendent.)

Supra-polar space is a space in exactly the same sense as polar space.[2] Supra-polar space is also determined by certain rules of construction. Heim says:

"Aber einem Raum kann immer alles, was es gibt, nach einem bestimmten Strukturprinzip eingeordnet sein. Das gilt in ganz besonderem Masse vom überpolaren Raum, der auch alle Räume, von denen bisher gesprochen wurde, in sich fasst. Wenn es also diesen überpolaren Raum gibt, dann sind alle Verhältnisse und alle Beziehungen, in denen wir innerhalb der polaren Welt stehen, immer gleichzeitig im überpolaren Raum aufgehoben. Wenn dieser höhere Raum überhaupt da ist, so tritt er auf der ganzen Linie in Kraft. Die neue Strukturordnung, die im überpolaren Raum gilt, kann dann nicht bloss innerhalb eines abgegrenzten Bezirks der Wirklichkeit zur Geltung kommen, sondern er muss alles umfassen. Dann gibt es überhaupt keine Beziehung, in der das Entweder-Oder, in das diese Beziehung innerhalb der polaren Welt unentrinnbar eingeschlossen ist, nicht in der höheren Synthese aufgehoben und überwunden wäre, die im überpolaren Raum auf der ganzen Linie in Kraft tritt"[3].

This passage contains the main points of Heim's doctrine of supra-polar space. Here we shall only mention two and return to the others later.

First Heim says that an "Entweder-Oder"-relation within polar space, and indeed every such relation, is in an astonishing way "aufgehoben"[4] within supra-polar space. How this more exactly can take place, we shall return to in the part on the relation between polar and supra-polar space.

He also says that supra-polar space, as well as the polar, is determined by certian rules of construction. But as it was the case with polar space, it is difficult to tell exactly what these rules of construction are which shall determine supra-polar space.

One reason for this difficulty is the fact that Heim says that supra-polar space is both a negation of polar space and thus wholly transcends it, and that polar space is contained in the supra-polar.[5] A difficulty then arises when we examine the definition of supra-polar space. In it the exclusivity between en-

tities within polar space is removed. But to apply a rule of construction according to which it is by definition impossible to make distinctions, is meaningless.
There can be nothing to structure. But it will be more meaningful if we could
say that polar space is a partial space of supra-polar space. Then it can
reasonably be said that supra-polar space can give a "new direction" or "a new
and higher order" to polar space as a whole. Heim says:

"Die Wirklichkeit Gottes greift vielmehr in die Struktur aller Beziehungen gleichermassen ein, indem sie eine neue Richtung erschliesst, die jenseits der drei immanenten
Möglichkeiten liegt".[6]

This new direction or "higher order of things" means that the "Entweder-
Oder" which signifies polar space no longer holds.[7] The exclusivity between
entities is simply removed. It is this which Heim means when talking about a
new and higher order. We earlier called this a supplementary basic assumption
which made it possible to establish a complementary total view of reality.

This is very important for Heim. But it is difficult to exactly mention these
new possibilities. But it seems to be important for him to be able to explain
human destiny, to show that there really can be an immediate relation between
God and every part of polar space, that miracles can happen and prayers can
be answered.[8] These are of course all depending on belief, i.e. acceptance of the
religious basic assumptions. This is, according to Heim "... das Sein des
ganzen Mensch in der überpolare Sphäre":

"Wenn ihr Glauben habt, so wird euch nichts unmöglich sein. Denn ihr lebt ja dann
unter völlig anderen Bedingungen und Möglichkeiten. Ihr steht ... in einem völlig
anderen Raum, der eine ganz andere Grundstruktur hat als der polare Raum, in dem
wir zunächst eingeschlossen sind".[9]

But concerning facts which it is claimed are e.g. miracles or answers to
prayers, nothing can be said.[10] The only statement which can be made about
these events is that it must also be possible to order them in terms of the rules
of construction which holds for polar space:

"Dieses Verhältnis, bei dem ein und dieselbe Wirklichkeit unter zwei verschiedenen
Aspekten erscheint, ist aber nicht zwischen Inhalten, sondern nur zwischen zwei
Räumen möglich, in denen derselbe Inhalt verschieden angeordnet ist. Nur so ist die
Haltung verständlich, die die Menschen, von denen schon das Alte Testament erzählt,
immer wieder eingenommen haben".[11]

We have already mentioned that Heim says that supra-polar space is a space
in the same sense as polar space. And we have mentioned some difficulties in
relation to this. We shall treat them later.

Supra-polar space is the space of God. We shall now consider another idea:
Supra-polar space is the space of God. The existence of God is supra-polar.
This identification is for Heim almost a tautology, and he does not present any
arguments for it. Perhaps this was his reasoning. If there is a God, then his ex-

istence must have a supra-polar character. Because it is only supra-polar space which has the character and relation to polar space, such that a supra-polar existence is the only one which can properly be ascribed to God, because it is a God which has these properties, that a believer in fact believes in. Any other kind of God is, from the religious point of view, uninteresting: He is then neither transcendent nor omnipresent. But we have seen that God, according to Heim must be conceived as metaphysically transcendent. Human destiny can only be explained if we accept not only a supra-polar space but also a transcendent and personal God.

Now, the fact that supra-polar space is the space of God means that God is not totally comprehensible. Heim says:

"Wie die Sprache nicht der Inhalt des Buches selbst ist, sondern die Form, in der dieser Inhalt sich einer bestimmten Lesergemeinde kundgibt, so ist auch der überpolare Raum, in dem Gott für uns gegenwärtig ist, nicht die Wirklichkeit Gottes selbst. Diese letzte Wirklichkeit bleibt ‚das ganz andere' und völlig Unfassbare, das dem Zugriff unseres Denkens und unserer Beobachtung völlig entzogen ist . . . Wenn wir vom überpolaren Raum sprechen, kann damit nicht die ewige Wirklichkeit Gottes selbst gemeint sein, sondern nur ein Aspekt, eine uns zugekehrte Seite, von der aus Gott, wenn er sich uns überhaupt erschliessen will, für uns, die wir hier miteinander reden, allein zugänglich sein kann" [12].

Here Heim says that it is not possible to speak objectively about God. It is possible only within a relationship to him.[13] This is due to the fact that our language is determined by polarity.[14] What God is in himself cannot be revealed to us, He infinitely transcends our knowledge. Therefore, contrary to a natural interpretation, the statement that supra-polar space removes the polarity of polar space is inconsistent with the doctrine of analogia entis.[15] Therefore, supra-polar space is something different from the indifferent state of being.[16] God is turned towards polar space, but his supra-polar essence is incomprehensible.[17]

Now this question becomes a problem: How can God, whose existence is supra-polar also be personal? The property of being personal is not a necessary property of supra-polar space, and it does not accord with the definition of supra-polar space. On this question Heim has no positive and conclusive answer, but he argues that supra-polar space must, for some reasons, be conceived as personal.

Instead he answer this question indirectly, by analysing the relative and existential paradoxes. He puts the question something like this: Is it justified to suppose that the God to which a believer pray, is also a personal God? Is it justified to say that supra-polar space, whose existence offers the only possible explanation of the existential and the relative paradoxes, can be conceived as personal? Stated like this, we are able to follow some lines of thought in the writings of Heim, which can be interpreted as answers to these questions.

The first of these answers has as its starting-point the fact that polarity is removed in supra-polar space. This also holds for entities within non-objectifiable Thou-space. Now, the natural antagonism between different individual perspectives cannot be conceived as removed within an indifferent state of being. Personality cannot be thought of as negated in this way. The removing instead demands the assumption of an absolute person, which can consummate the state of being, whose extremes are a solipsism on the one hand and an alienation from the Thou on the other hand. Heim says:

"Ich kann Gott nur finden, indem er mir als mein Du begegnet. Aber dass kann nicht eine Du-Begegnung sein, wie sie im Raum der polaren Du-Begegnungen möglich ist . . . Jeder Verkehr zwischen Mensch und Gott, der dem Verkehr zwischen Mensch und Mensch analog bleibt, steht eben damit auch unter der Schranke, unter der jeder Verkehr zwischen Ich und Du innerhalb des polaren Raums steht . . . Gott ist das überpolare Du, das dieses Entweder-Oder sprengt, dessen Gegenwart uns alle umschliesst . . . Damit tritt ein ganz neues und einzigartiges Verhältnis zwischen Ich und Du in Kraft, das grundlegend verschieden ist sowohl von der Zuschauerhaltung des wissenschaftlichen Beobachters wie von der mystischen Versenkung in mich selbst und von der Du-Begegnung mir einem Mitmenschen . . . Dieses neue und einzigartige Verhältnis ist das Gebet. Im Gebet kommt die Bewegung zur Ruhe, in der ich unablässig mein Du suche, dem ich mich ganz hingeben darf. . .

In Gottes Gegenwart, sind alle Ich mitenhalten, die das Weltall in sich schliesst. Denn alle stehen in seiner Gegenwart; alle leben jeden Augenblick vor ihm. Und doch ist Gottes Gegenwart nicht die Aufhebung aller Ich-Unterschiede . . . Gott ist vielmehr der einzelne, der sich jedem einzelnen von uns in seiner tiefen Einsamkeit als sein Du erschliesst, zu dem er beten darf ,mein Gott' . . ."[18].

This reasoning can hardly be called an argument, but rather a phenomenological analysis of prayer. It is certainly true that a believer recognizes himself in this analysis. That the praying man feels himself to have a close relation to a personal God is certainly a fact. But to say that this is a conclusive argument for a belief in a personal God can still be doubted. And this doubt can never be refuted by any correct phenomenological analysis of prayer.

Let us consider the other answer. Heim's thesis can be stated like this. To explain human destiny demands acceptance of the existence of supra-polar space. But this acceptance also means that man's existence within the world can be described as "placed" by a personal "Ultimate Thou". Heim's reasoning runs like this:

The ego can be conceived as either placed by itself or as not placed by itself. If the former alternative is chosen, then this means to accept positivism. But, as we have seen, this is arbitrary. If instead the latter possibility is chosen, then two new alternatives appear. The ego can be conceived as placed either by some "It" or by a "Thou". If the first of these alternatives is chosen, then we have, according to Heim, also accepted that human existence in the world cannot be explained. Human existence then ultimately appears in the light of "destiny", "accidence" or "arbitrariness". But this view cannot be accepted within a religious belief. There remains one alternative: man can be conceived as placed by a "Thou". But then this "Thou" cannot belong to polar space. If so, the answer is a kind of positivism. But it can also be conceived as a supra-polar Thou. And this corresponds to religious experience. Heim says:

121

"Fassen wir das Gesagte zusammen, um daraus den letzten Schluss zu ziehen: Die Instanz, die mich gesetzt hat, kann nicht ein Es sein. Sie kann auch nicht ich selbst sein. Sie kann auch nicht irgendein Du sein, also ein anderes Ich innerhalb der polaren Ich-Du-Reihe. Aus dem allem ergibt sich der unausweichliche Schluss: Entweder es gibt überhaupt keine Antwort auf die Frage, wo ich herkomme . . . Oder aber die setzende Instanz ist ein Ich. Aber dieses Ich kann nicht unter dem Gesetz der Polarität stehen. Es kann nicht ein Glied der unabschliessbaren polaren Ich-Du-Reihe sein. Es muss überpolar sein" [19].

Also this reasoning contains some difficulties. We have already made some remarks on the meaning of the word "setzen" in this connection. And we do not need to treat this question further here. But it also seems to be the case that this reasoning does not show that God must have a personal character. Perhaps this hypothetical formulation of Heim's position is more reasonable: If it really is the case that man is "placed" by a supra-polar instance, then it is also reasonable to conceive this supra-polar instance as a personal being. And the reasons for this can very well be found in religious experience. An objection to this reasoning would be that it seems to suffer from a kind of circularity: In order to be placed by a personal being, then the personal being must first be recognized.

One would expect that Heim's doctrine about supra-polar space should be quite in accordance with mystical theology and piety. This could be argued from some consequences of (quite apart from the influence of Württemberg Pietism, with its special form of mysticism, an influence of which he was deeply aware) Heim's theory, which states that God is nearer to man than man can ever imagine, that an intuitive "Durchblick durch das Danze" is possible and above all that in the discovery of supra-polar space, "das überpolare Ursein", man breaks through the polar existence of manifold. But on the contrary Heim explicitly rejects mysticism, and his arguments here are more easier to discover. His main argument is that no kind of mysticism—whether Christian or Non-Christian—can escape the polar scheme and thought. It only passes the intra-mundane relations of transcendence. Mystical theology can after all be reduced to a kind of subjectivity. It essentially consists of being lost in the ego, either it consists of "das Ich-Pathos Fichtes" or of buddist mysticism.[20] But it does not really transcend the limits of the ego. And secondly the mystical experience is also "verfügbar", i.e. controllable e.g. by means of different kinds of practice,[21] which according to Heim contradicts the character of a genuine experience of God. But polarity cannot be escaped. Therefore, a mystical experience cannot be interpeted otherwise than as an abstraction from the polarity between a subject and an object.[22] But the reached point of indifference beyond the plurality of polar space is a pure concept without a content.[23] And therefore it cannot, according to Heim, explain human destiny. It has still not been explained and the mystical experience gives no guidance for man's actions.[24]

5.2.2. How is supra-polar space to be discovered?

We shall now see that the same rule holds for the discovery of supra-polar space as for the discovery of polar spaces. From the formal point of view, there is nothing different in the discovery of the supra-polar space compared with the discovery of a polar space:

"... es gilt *auch* von der letzten Dimension, was von allen innerweltlichen Dimensionen gesagt werden musste".[1]

Therefore, it is also the case that the acceptance of supra-polar space solves an "Entweder-Oder"-question with the same formal content as polar spaces:

"Das muss sich darin zeigen, dass kraft dieses neuen Raums (i.e. supra-polar space), der hier entdeckt wird, mit einemmal etwas möglich ist, was innerhalb des polaren Raums ein Widerspruch wäre. In diesem höheren Raum, über den wir nicht selber verfügen können, muss das Entweder-Oder des polaren Raums gesprengt, der Abgrund, der sich im polaren Raum zwischen den beiden Möglichkeiten Relativismus oder Positivismus auftut, muss überbrückt sein. Der Satz muss sich erfüllen ,Tertium datur', ,Es gibt ein Drittes'. Das durch die Struktur des polaren Raums ,ausgeschlossene Dritte' muss in Kraft treten"[2].

But it is not possible, according to Heim, to give some contental criteria for the contents of events or facts, which can reasonably be adduced as arguments for the acceptance of supra-polar space:

"Ein Anlass, durch den in dieser unberechenbaren Weise der Raum der Ewigkeit erschlossen werden kann, kann fast jedes Ereignis sein, das uns bis in die Tiefen unserer Existenz erschüttert"[3].

Now, in supra-polar space it is only possible to "existierend hineintreten", according to the same rule which also holds for polar spaces, and this existential entrance contains also an immediate certainty about the reality of supra-polar space.[4] But there are not any contental reasons, derived e.g. from the content of the experience itself, for the acceptance of supra-polar space. Heim says:

"Wir können die Raumentdeckung weder durch einen kausalen Rückschluss aus der Erfahrungswelt noch durch ein Postulat, weder durch unser Denken noch durch eine Willensanstrengung herbeiführen."[5]

"Wir können von uns aus weder den Ort noch die Zeit noch den Inhalt des Ereignisses selbst bestimmen, durch das wir wie ein Schwimmer in einen Strudel hineingerissen werden, so dass mit einem Schlag unser ganzes Wirklichkeitsbild von Grund aus umgewandelt wird und wir uns selbst und die ganze Welt um uns her plötzlich mit neuen Augen ansehen"[6].

"Dieses Herausgeworfenwerden aus der Sicherheit, mit der wir bis dahin Gott verneint oder vorschnell bejaht haben, kann durch alles ausgelöst werden, was unser Leben mit sich bringt"[7].

These quotations reveal two problems in the thinking of Heim on this matter. We shall deal with them in more detail. The first of them is (1) What events?

and How can the acceptance of supra-polar space be inferred from them? We have treated them before[8] but we shall make some additional remarks here. The second problem concerns the question (2) What experiences is Heim talking about? We shall see that Heim, in spite of his refusal to present some criteria for the content of such experiences, nevertheless stresses a certain kind of experience, which we can call 'encounter' with Jesus.

In spite of his open view concerning those events which can be an argument for accepting supra-polar space, he has more to say about the paradoxes, to which the acceptance of supra-polar space offers a solution. As we have said, these paradoxes are of a certain kind. The most convenient interpretation of them is that they are analogical to the paradoxes demanding the acceptance of a new polar space.

The first kind of paradox we shall call the paradox of total views of reality. Heim says that there are two equally possible total views of reality, based on polarity, namely relativism and positivism. They have an "either-or"-relation:

"Alle Werte, alle Versuche, eine Wertskala, eine Rangordnung der Werte, aufzustellen, alle Normen, alle Rechtsgrundsätze, alle sittlichen Prinzipien stehen unter dem Entweder-Oder zwischen diesen beiden Möglichkeiten. Sie sind entweder Ergebnisse einer geschichtlichen Entwicklung, die im Lauf der Zeit unter mannigfaltigen völkischen und kulturellen Einflüssen zu diesen Werten geführt hat. Sie sind also relative Grössen, die geworden sind und wieder vergehen können. Oder sie sind durch souveräne Entscheidungen von menschlichen Gesetzgebern, Machthabern oder Staatsgründern gesetzt werden. Sie sind also Setzungen (posita)"[9].

The relativistic position means that one gives up the attempt to determine an ultimate entity or value, from which it is possible to order ones thoughts or actions. We have treated this in point 3.4. Such a choice of an ultimate reality cannot be justified. The consequence for the relativist will then be that he, according to Heim will lose

"... den inneren Halt und die Geschlossenheit des sittlichen Standpunktes".[10]

We have already remarked that Heim is mistaken in this.[11]

The positivist then on the contrary arbitrarily chooses some entity or value as the ultimate entity or value. And according to Heim there are of course also theological and religious versions of positivism. A natural theology and a consequent idealistic interpretation of religion are examples of this.[12]

Heim's thesis here is that the only way to solve this paradox is to accept the reality of supra-polar space.[13] Supra-polar space is not subjected to relativism and it is not a "positum" within polar space. But we will be able to return to this below.

But let us now return to the second kind of paradox, which we called the paradox of human destiny. Heim now states that

"Wir können mit unserem Denken und Wollen den Bann der polaren Verhältnisse, in die wir eingeschlossen sind, nicht durchbrechen. Wir können wohl die hohen Worte aussprechen, die den krönenden Abschluss aller menschlichen Philosophie bilden:

,das Absolute', ,das Unbedingte', ,der Ursprung'. Aber diese Worte sind für unser Denken nur Grenzbegriffe oder Symbole für eine ungelöste Frage und ein ungestilltes Bedürfnis, jedoch keine Realitäten, an die wir uns halten können. Von diesen Worten geht darum keine Kraft im Leben und kein Trost im Tode aus"[14].

Heim says that a correct analysis of human existence within polar space, as a polar being, always reveals that man's existence as an I-here-and-now is always arbitrary and conditional. We have treated this before. And from this Heim concludes:

"Denn innerhalb der polaren Welt kann es keine absolute Wahrheit geben, sondern immer nur Standpunkte, Weltaspekte und Einstellungen, die gleichberechtigt nebeneinander stehen und von denen keiner den Anspruch auf ewige Geltung erheben darf"[15].

And there is nothing in my situation as an I-here-and-now which can exhaustively explain my actual situation. From the logical point of view my situation might as well have been quite another. And a conceptual framework based on polarity cannot offer such an explanation, because such a framework entails relativism:

"Ebenso ist mein ganzes Weltbild, die Weltanschauung, von der aus ich alles beurteile, das ganze Schema, in das ich alles einordne, die raumzeitliche Anschauungsform und die logische Verstandeskategorie, in der ich denke, eine ganz zufällige Einstellung, ein perspektivischer Aspekt, von einer Stelle aus aufgenommen, auf die ich hingeworfen bin wie ein Schiffbrüchiger von einer Welle irgendwo an den Strand geworfen wird, und an der ich nun willkürlich mein Leben lang festhalte. Hätte mich der Zufall an eine andere Stelle geschleudert, in ein anderes Jahrtausend, unter einen andern Himmelsstrich, in eine andere Kulturwelt, wäre ich nicht dieser, sondern einer von den unendlich vielen andern, in deren Haut ich ebensogut stecken könnte, so hätte ich ein anderes Grundschema. Ich würde in einem anderen Raum leben".[16]

But it is not only the abstract possibility, which is stated in this quotation, which brings about the insight that the paradox of destiny really is a paradox, but also the fact that the analysis is correct. The impossibility of explaining the here-and-now of a particular individual makes it reasonable to say that its existence suffers from relativity:

"Es ist darum von diesem Schema aus unerklärlich, wie wir dazu kommen, dass wir nicht bloss unter einer bestimmten einzelnen Möglichkeit leiden, unter einem Lebenslos, an das wir auf Grund dieses Schemas jetzt zufällig gerade gefesselt sind, sondern dass wir unter dem ganzen Schema als solchem leiden und es für unerträglich erklären".[17]

Heim's thesis here is that only an acceptance of supra-polar space offers an explanation of the paradox of destiny. By means of the relation to, or better existence in, supra-polar space the individual perspective receives decisive weight, content and direction which nothing can alter. If a higher dimensioned space is once discovered, then it is possible to disregard it occasionally. Now, we shall return to the question about the experiences, which can bring about such an acceptance of supra-polar space. Here we shall only say that a necessary feature of such an experience is that it is un-controllable, "nicht-verfügbar". Here this remark only serves as a background to Heim's criticism of theories of religion, which on the basis of a philosophical argumentation assert the real existence of a transcendent reality, supra-polar space, without regard to the necessity for concrete experience. According to Heim, examples of such theories of religion are a priori theories of religion.

Heim's criticism of a priori theories of religion is mainly directed against R Otto's version of it, but Heim says that it is also relevant to other versions.[18] (In this connection he also mentions R Jelke and E Troeltsch.) The criticism also emphasizes the moment of a concrete experience in the discovery of the reality of supra-polar space. Now, without regard to the exact definition of the religious a priori, it is by definition independent of the factual existence of the individual man. But it is, according to Heim, impossible to give a satisfactory explanation of my here-and-now on the basis of an a priori theory of religion. And if an individual in fact has accepted the reality of supra-polar space, (in Heim's terminology 'has its existence in supra-polar space')[19] then this acceptance is also impossible to justify from an a priori theory of religion. Heim says:

"Denn die eigentümliche Art, wie die Schicksalsfrage entschieden wird, wie aus den vielen a priori gegebenen Möglichkeiten gerade diese eine ausgewählt ist und zur unentrinnbaren Wirklichkeit wird, ist das tiefste Mysterium, das in allen höheren Religionen den numinosen Eindruck erweckt ... Der Mensch stösst auf das letzte Rätsel seiner persönlichen Existenz, auf die irrationale Tatsache, dass er sich nicht selbst hervorgebracht hat, dass sein ganzes Dasein mit allen dunklen Lebensschicksalen, die es in sich trägt, etwas ist, das sich nicht kausal erklären lässt, das aber ebensowenig aus einer menschlichen Willensentscheidung stammt".[20]

And it is not possible, from an a priori interpretation of religion to demonstrate either the absoluteness of Christianity, or its claim of absolute certainty, or to explain the contradictions between the different higher religions.[21] From an a priori point of view all religions (or at least all higher religions) are equal. Therefore a concrete experience must be a necessary condition for a personal acceptance of supra-polar space:

"Dieses dunkle Rätsel ... kommt vom Apriori aus nicht zum Bewusstsein ... Soll dieser persönliche Charakter des Schicksals zum Bewusstsein kommen, so muss zum Apriori noch etwas hinzutreten, etwas, das aus der Richtung der Erfahrungswelt kommt; aber nicht etwa nur der Erfahrungsstoff überhaupt, der dem Apriori eine Fülle von Möglichkeiten darbietet, sich empirisch zu aktualisieren, sondern eine geheimnisvolle Entscheidung, eine Moria, die aus der Fülle der Möglichkeiten mir gerade diese eine für mich bestimmte ‚zuteilt', eine Lachesis, die den Würfel gerade so fallen lässt, wie er fällt".[22]

The experience of a certain fact or event which is imposed on us from outside in this unpredictable way, must from the apriori point of view be wholly accidental. Nobody can command such an experience. And nobody can choose or bring about this experience. It is not possible to predict:

126

"Niemand kann durch ein Wahlverfahren das Ereignis selbst herbeiführen, das für ihn zum religiösen Erlebnis wird. Was wir uns selbst geschaffen und ausgewählt haben, kann uns innerlich nie ganz überwältigen und unbedingt an sich fesseln. Was uns innerlich binden soll, das muss ohne unser Zutun schicksalhaft über uns gekommen sein".[23]

To say this is of course not the same as to say that such experiences have no causes or that they are causally inexplicable. On the contrary, by an analysis of such events in retrospect, it is always possible to discover their causes. So e.g. the action of God, with hindsight always appears as an event within a causal chain and never as a result of a supra-natural intervention in the course of nature. But such an analysis is only possible after the event. The event can in the very moment when it takes place only be experienced immediately.

Now, the demand that there must be an experience as a part of the premise in an argument for the acceptance of supra-polar space is, as we saw, not a condition which holds only for the acceptance of supra-polar space. On the contrary, it holds also for polar spaces. The general rule says that one more dimension must be accepted in order to pass from one space to another:

"Auch das, was wir aus der Richtung der Gegenständlichkeit oder der Du-Beziehung erhalten, ist ja nicht in unserer Gewalt. Es liegt darum auch bei den Sinneseindrücken und bei der Begegnung mit einem andern nicht in unserer Hand, ob wir überhaupt aus diesen Richtungen etwas empfangen . . . Was uns aus der Richtung der letzten Dimension gegeben wird, wenn wir *glauben*, das kann also genau, wie die andern Empfänge, über die wir nicht verfügen, sehr undeutlich, unbestimmt und ungewiss sein".[24]

But in order for this to be possible at all, then this important condition must be acceptable:

"Ein und dasselbe Erfahrungselement muss in zwei entgegengesetzten Dimensionen stehen. Es muss einerseits der relativen Erfahrungswelt angehören. Und es muss andererseits, ohne dass an seinem relativen Charakter das geringste geändert wird, ein Strahl aus der anderen Dimension darauf fallen".[25]

It appeals that, in spite of Heim's open position[26] to the question of what kind of experiences these can be, he nevertheless in this connection emphasises a group of experiences, which he says are important. This group of experiences can be called "encounter with Jesus". Now, the person of Jesus can of course, be conceived from different points of view.[27] That this encounter with Jesus in fact for a great many people has revealed supra-polar space to them is certainly empirically true but trivial. This was appearently the case with the first christans. The most frequent example from the new testament that Heim often refers to is S:t Paul.[28] Now, it is not necessary here to present the whole content in such an encounter or to present a comprehensive account of Heim's christology.[29] The important point in this connection is Heim's opinion that in this encounter an intellectual and moral basis is laid, from which a man's experiences can be ordered in a new way. Relativism and positivism can be defeated. Man's thought and actions get a new and decisive order and direction. But now it is important that

"Diese Erfahrung ist vom polaren Raum aus völlig unverständlich. . . . Jene Erfahrung ist nur verständlich, wenn es einen überpolaren Raum gibt, in dem die Gesamtwirklichkeit, die sich im polaren Raum in unabschliessbare Reihen auflöst, in einer höheren Ordnung als Einheit zusammengeschaut wird. Unter dem Eindruck der Person Jesu erschliesst sich uns dieser ewige Urraum, in dem wir zusammen mit der ganzen Wirklichkeit stehen, für den wir blind waren, solange wir im Bann der polaren Welt gefangen waren".[30]

According to Heim it is certainly the case that it is such experiences which constitute a Christian total view of reality, and it is only on the basis of such experiences that a proper foundation for a Christian theology can be laid.

"Wir können uns auch nicht unabhängig von Jesus ein Bild von der Struktur der menschlichen Existenz machen und von dort seine Weissungen interpretieren".[31]

"Alle Aufschlüsse, die wir über den Sinn der Welt und des Lebens gewinnen können, sind für uns also nicht dadurch erreichbar, dass wir uns eigene Gedanken über das Wesen Gottes und seine Schöpfungsordnungen machen, sondern nur dadurch, dass wir vom Tatbestand der Herrschaft Jesu ausgehen und dann darüber nachdenken, was sich aus diesem Tatbestand für das Verständnis der Welt und des menschlichen Daseins ergibt. Unser Denken kann also immer nur nachzeichnen, was uns durch die Wirklichkeit vorgegeben ist".[32]

We have seen before that a new space cannot be discovered only on rational grounds, and that this hold also for supra-polar space. There are also no contental reasons to choose historical events, whether a temporally limited event, e.g. the life of Jesus,[33] or a wider chain of events, e.g. the history, recorded in the Bible,[34] or a contemporary event, as being a divine revelation.[35] Such an objective choice is simply not possible. Concerning Jesus, his claims, and the importance which Christian belief ascribes to him, there are only two possible attitudes: "Glaube" or "Ärgernis".[36] About such a choise Heim says:

"Ich kann den ‚Sprung ins Jenseits' nur angesichts der lebendigen Wirklichkeit wagen, die mir in der Person Jesu entgegentritt. Ich nehme aber keinerlei wissenschaftlichen Vorzug meiner Position . . . in Anspruch".[37]

Therefore, Heim's criticism of apriori theories of religion can be said to be twofold:

Firstly there are the reasons why we make the person of Jesus so important. This Heim takes to be a consequence of the claim of absoluteness of Christianity. But isn't Heim introducing a new condition here? The claim of the absoluteness of Christianity can only be justified if those experiences, on which this claim is based, are experiences of historical events, past or present.[38] Only events with such a historical anchorage can solve the paradoxes, and the claim of the absoluteness of Christianity depends after all on a personal decision.

Secondly he says that an apriori view cannot explain man's destiny.

Now it is possible to interpret Heim, as we have seen before, as meaning that the arguments for the existence of supra-polar space are independent of belief. But if this is the case, then this argumentation cannot be a criterion for

128

some of the doctrines of Christian religion. A possibility here is that Heim means that only doctrines based on a personal decision or on an experience of encounter with Jesus can make justified claims to possess Christian legitimacy. Only on the basis of such an experience is it possible to present a Christian total view of reality.[39] But this proposal contains further difficulties, e.g. What kind of reasoning, exactly, can be used to justify the inference from a certain experience to the claim that a certain doctrine is Christian? But it is not necessary to go into this problem here.

An important formal criterion for the experiences leading to the discovery of supra-polar space is, as we saw, that they are uncontrollable, "nicht verfügbar". But the meaning of this term is not very clear. Let us examine some possibilities:

The first possibility is that Heim means that uncontrollable experiences are unusual, sudden or surprising.[40] Due to this, they can make a very strong impression on an individual, and therefore can be reasons for the acceptance of supra-polar space. But Heim's own examples show that these events can also be quite ordinary experiences. But because this interpretation is rather trivial, it does not do justice to Heim's intention. Therefore we shall leave it.

The second possibility is that uncontrollable experiences appears "from outside", i.e. they can ultimately be derived from sense-experience.[40] It cannot be derived from the constitution of the subject only nor from the dimensional scheme used for the moment. Such an experience is always paradoxical. This seems to be a reasonable interpretation in accordance with Heim's rejection of an apriori theory of religion. We shall develop this below in connection with the double concepts "actio-passio".

The third possibility is that it means that uncontrollable experiences are non-objectifiable. We shall develop this in connection with the central concept of decision, "Entscheidung".

Now we can examine this in more detail in connection with the concepts of "actio-passio". This distinction is central for Heim (he also uses the equal terms "Tun" and "Leiden"). Our reasoning contains three steps: (1) The meaning of the general distinction between actio and passio, (2) how this is manifest within an I-Thou-relation, (3) a relationship with God shares the characteristics of a Thou-relation.

Let us begin with the general distinction between actio and passio. They are, Heim says, components or moments within every event or change:

Das Geschehen ist entweder ein Tun oder ein Leiden".[42]

Aktion und Passion sind ja zwei Arten, wie das Werden zustande kommt".[43]

In this connection actio is characterized as "überwindung eines Widerstandes",[44] but it is also the case that no event can be characterized as a pure actio or as a pure passio:

"... es gibt kein Leiden, das nicht mit einem, wenn auch noch so schwachen Handeln verbunden ist".[45]

This brief analysis of an event is not an empirical analysis. Heim presents no empirical arguments for this. It is rather a kind of apriori assumption on the content of every event:

"Die Unterscheidung zwischen aktivem und passivem Geschehen ist eine Urunterscheidung. Wir können sie nicht auf etwas anderes zurückführen und sie aus nichts anderem erklären ... Das lässt sich schon daran sehen, dass jede Definition der Worte Tun und Leiden nur eine Umschreibung durch andere Worte ist, die diese Unterscheidung schon voraussetzen und in sich enthalten".[46]

It is rather an intuitive insight which is given at the very moment of the event. But let us proceed. Heim now accepts, as a new apriori assumption, that

"Wie sich Aktion und Passion dabei (i.e. in the event) verteilen, darüber lässt sich apriori nichts sagen".[47]

From this Heim also concludes that a future event is impossible to predict.[48]
    The next step in Heim's reasoning is also a postulate. He says:

"Das Du-Erlebnis ist ... ein Leiden".[49]

Every encounter with a Thou is eo ipso an encounter with another and alien will, and this encounter is characterized by the unity between actio and passio:

"... Also muss auch die Begegnung zwischen Ich und Du ... eine unzerlegbare Einheit sein. Beides steht in einem unzerreissbaren Zusammenhang, meine Begegnung mit dir innerhalb des noch nicht objektivierten Werdeprozesses...".[50]

But there is a connecting link between an I and a Thou. According to Heim this link is the word, "das Wort". The word in this sense belongs to the common and coinstanteous experience.

"Dasselbe, was in meinem Bewusstseinraum eine Passion ist, das ist im Raum des anderen eine Aktion und umgekehrt. Ich höre das Wort, das du sagst. Ich spreche das Wort, das du hörst".[51]

We can then proceed to the third step in Heim's reasoning. He says that this holds, not only in the encounter with another person, a Thou, but he states also that the discovery of supra-polar space shares the same characteristics:

"Ohne dass sich der Inhalt des Geschehens, wie er in der Zuschauerhaltung des Ich-Es-Verhältnisses erscheint, irgendwie verändert, erscheint er letzt im Licht der Du-Beziehung das eine Mal als ein Tun, das andere Mal als ein Leiden. Etwas Ähnliches geschiet, wenn uns die letzte Dimension aufgeht. Es zeigt sich jetzt: unser Handeln und Leiden kann, ohne dass sich inhaltlich etwas daran ändert, sobald es ins Licht der letzten Dimension tritt, einen doppelten Charakter haben".[52]

Here we recognize the principle we have met before, that the same content can be conceived in a double way, or can be ordered according to different rules of construction. And Heim's thesis is that the property of being an actio or a passio is not an objective property, but rather a property, related to the set of applied rules. But the main point here is that this also holds for the acceptance of supra-polar space. In the discovery of it, there is a common content which is the connecting link between my perspective and supra-polar space,[52] a connecting link which is the word of God. And concerning the divine revelation, it is God who talks from outside:

"Sobald ich aus irgendeinem allgemeinen Prinzip, das zu meinem geistigen Besitz gehört, ableiten will, wo und wie Gott gesprochen haben muss, habe ich vergessen, dass ich in dem gottlosen Zustand bin, in dem ich aus mir selbst heraus über die Entscheidungen, die Gott trifft, nichts wissen kann, dass ich also das, was er will, nur erfahren kann, wenn er selbst das Wort ergreift. Es gehört zum Wesen des Wortes, dass der Redende allein der Aktive und Gebende ist, der Hörende aber nur das passive und empfangende Gefäss".[53]

Therefore the only way of interpreting Heim's talk about the uncontrollable is to refer it to the moment of passio, which every event contains. And according to Heim, it is not difficult to do this in terms of personal categories. But to give the criteria for events which can have the function of being God's actio or the word of God, cannot be done. For Heim it is a characteristic of human existence that we

". . . von Natur keinerlei Kriterien in uns tragen, um zu erkennen, ob und wo und wie Gott zu uns geredet hat. Wenn Gott zu uns redet, muss er uns selbst die Augen öffnen, dass wir die Stelle sehen, wo er sich uns erschliesst".[54]

It is not necessary to comment upon further this latter passage.

The second main interpetation of Heim's thesis that events which are the basis for the acceptance of supra-polar space, are uncontrollable says that such experiences are not predictable or that they cannot be brought about by man.

We shall relate this interpretation to the concept of decision. Now the concept of decision is a central concept for Heim and covers a spectrum of meanings. But it is sufficient for our aim here to mention only these three meanings of the word:

The first of these meanings is the common or trivial meaning. Then the word decision means a daily decision.[55] This meaning is not of interest for us here.

The second meaning is more qualified. We can call it the existential meaning. The word decision here refers to an existential decision in an "Entweder-Oder"-situation.[56] In this meaning decision is connected to the subject. It signifies a personal decision, which is not made for contental reasons. Therefore it is uncontrollable. And to accept supra-polar space is an example of such a decision. The important point here is, as we have said, that Heim wants to show that this ultimate decision from the formal point of view is no different from other decisions.[57] On the contrary, every choice of a total view of reality has this personal-existential character. And this holds also for a choice of a total view of reality not containing supra-polar space.

The third meaning is more difficult to name. Here the word decision means a change within reality. The fact that reality has altered between two times is ascribed to the fact that a decision has been made. Here a decision is not ascribed to an individual subject, but the word rather refers to reality as a whole. A problem, which we do not need to examine here, is in what sense it can be reasonable to ascribe to reality as a whole the ability to make decisions and what assumptions must be made in order to make ascription reasonable.[58] Heim rejects the idea that it can be seen as analogous to human acts of will.[59]

"Die Welt, die wir erleben, ist nicht eine ruhende Dauer, sondern eine Aktion, eine einzige, allumfassende Entscheidung, in der die unübersehbare Fülle aller Einzelentscheidungen ... zu einer ungeheuren Gesamtwirkung zusammengefasst ist".[60]

A change within reality contains these possibilities:

"Denn bei allen diesen massiven Granitblöcken oder Gebirgswänden steht immer nur fest, dass sie in dem Augenblick, über den eben entschieden wurde, die Gestalt haben, in der sie jetzt vor mir stehen. Ob sie im nächsten Augenblick noch so bleiben werden, wie sie sind, darüber ist jetzt noch nicht entschieden...".[61]

And this means, as we have seen, that reality is not totally determined.[62] Its state of being in the next moment is not yet decided. Anything can happen. And in this sense reality is uncontrollable. Therefore every event can be conceived of as the word of God and thus a reason to accept the real existence of supra-polar space.

5.2.3. The relation between polar and supra-polar space

We shall set out this concluding section as follows: First we shall make some remarks on (1) polar space as a whole and the relation between polar and supra-polar space. Then we shall (2) investigate the central concept which describes this relation, i.e. that supra-polar space means the "Aufhebung"[1] of polar space. The concept of "Aufhebung" can here be interpreted in two ways, as meaning both a continuity and a discontinuity between polar and supra-polar space. An investigation of the concept "Aufhebung" together with some remarks on the question of God's activity within polar space and on the doctrine of analogia entis, is the main part of this section. Finally (3) because Heim's doctrine of supra-polar space has as a natural consequence that the doctrine of eschatology becomes important, we shall also make some remarks on this matter.

Now, it is important to state that the relation concerns polar space as a whole, i.e. all possible polar spaces, including objectifiable and non-objectifiable space. The relation does not concern some parts of polar space and supra-polar space. The concept of "Aufhebung" refers to polar space as a whole, and not only to some of its parts.

It is also important to state, that, according to Heim, the relation between polar and supra-polar space is in some respects of the same nature as the general relation which holds between different polar spaces. We saw that the passing from one polar space to another takes place in a certain way under certain circumstances, and that this holds also for the passing from polar to supra-polar space.

We also saw that there are two kinds of limits, the limit of content and the limit of dimension. The limit of content distinguishes entities within one and the same space, while the limit of dimension distinguishes spaces from each other. Now, one would expect that the limit between the polar and supra-polar space would be such a dimensional limit.[2] But this is precisely what Heim denies[3]. We shall examine this denial below.

Finally we saw that the supplying of a new dimension to already existing ones, which means he discovery of a new space, is a necessary condition for an explanation of a paradox. It is this meaning of explanation which Heim designates with the term "Aufhebung". This holds for the discovery of a new polar space, and, as we saw, also for the discovery of supra-polar space.

But let us now quote some central passages on supra-polar space. Heim says:

"In Gottes Sein ist das ganze Strukturgesetz *aufgehoben* (I), auf dem die Unendlichkeit von Zeit und Raum beruht. Wenn Gott ist, ist die ganze Zeitform und Raumform, die den Charakter der Unendlichkeit hat, nicht ein Letztes, sondern etwas Vorletztes".[4]

"Wenn Gott ist, so hat alles, was ist, Ich und Du alle Wesen und alles, was gegenständlich um uns her ist, sofern es in Gott ist, göttliches Wesen, also ein überpolares Ursein, denn Gott ist ja das Sein, das *durch sich selbst ist* (II), das *allumfassende* (III) Sein, ausserhalb dessen nichts sein kann. Alles, was in Gott ist, muss *teilhaben* (IV) an seinem Wesen. Den gäbe es ein anderes, nichtgöttliches Sein, das ausserhalb des göttlichen Seins stände, so wäre dieses ein Gegenpol zum göttlichen Sein. Dadurch würde das göttliche Sein selbst polar. Es hätte ein Korrelat, durch das es in seinem Dasein und Sosein mitbedingt wäre".[5]

"Wir müssen uns das Entweder-Oder zum Bewusstsein bringen, das allem Sein, das wir kennen, die gemeinsame Grundform gibt, und dann müssen wir *diese Grundform verneinen* (V). Damit haben wir das jenseitige Ursein nur *negativ ausgedrückt* (VI). Wir haben nur *indirekt davon gesprochen* (VII). Wir haben uns nur die Grenze zum Bewusstsein gebracht, die unser Sein von jenem Sein scheidet. Aber diese Negation oder Grenzziehung ist die *einzige Form* (VIII), in der wir vom Ursein sprechen können".[6]

"Jene Erfahrung ist nur verständlich, wenn es einen *überpolaren Raum gibt, in dem die Gesamtwirklichkeit, die sich im polaren Raum in unabschliessbare Reihen auflöst, in einer höheren Ordnung* (IX) als Einheit zusammengeschaut wird".[7]

"Er (i.e. der Auftrag auf den der Akzent der Ewigkeit fällt) kann nur aus einem Raum kommen, dessen *Struktur der Anschauungswelt entegegensetzt ist* (X) und der dennoch die ganze Wirklichkeit *in sich schliesst* (XI)".[8]

"Aber einem Raum kann immer alles, was es gibt, nach einem bestimmten Strukturprinzip eingeordnet sein. *Das gilt in ganz besonderem Masse vom überpolaren Raum,
der auch alle Räume, . . . in sich fasst* (XII) . . . Die neue Strukturordnung, die im überpolaren Raum gilt, kann dann nicht bloss innerhalb eines abgegrenzten Bezirks der
Wirklichkeit zur Geltung kommen, sondern er muss *alles umfassen* (XIII). Dann gibt
es überhaupt keine Beziehung, in der das Entweder-Oder . . . nicht in der *höheren
Synthese aufgehoben und überwunden wäre* (XIV), die im überpolaren Raum auf der
ganzen Linie in Kraft tritt (XV)".[9]

"Die Jenseitigkeit, die der Schöpferglaube meint, wenn er von einer transzendenten
Macht spricht, durch die alles *gesetzt* (XVI) ist, muss etwas *total anderes* (XVII) sein
als die innerweltliche Transzendenz, . . . wenn Gott der Schöpfer ist, sind *alle innerweltlichen Räume jeden Augenblick durch ihn gesetzt* (XVIII)."[10]

"Gottes Allgegenwart ist der alles erfüllende Raum, in den auch die relativen
Räume dieser Welt *hineingenommen sind* (IXX). Es kann darum auch kein Widerstreit entstehen zwischen dem Walten Gottes und irgendwelchen Naturgesetzen,
die wir durch *Beobachtung feststellen können* (XX) . . . Die Ordnungen der Welt sind
also nicht Naturnotwendigkeiten, die sich aus dem *reinen Kausalzusammenhang
erklären lassen* (XXI), sondern persönliche *Festsetzungen* (XXII) des allmächtigen
Willens, eine Bundesschliessung Gottes mit den Mächten, die die Natur durchwalten,
die dem Bund gleichgestellt werden, den Gott mit dem Volk einging. . .".[11]

"Das Ursein ist nicht polar. In ihm ist das *Grundgesetz aufgehoben* (XXIII), unter
dem alle innerweltlichen Unterschiede zwischen Inhalten und Räumen gleichermassen
stehen und das dem Dasein in allen diesen Räumen den Charakter einer ruhelosen
Bewegung gibt (XXIV). Wenn das Ursein ausserhalb der Polarität steht, kann die
polare Welt, *deren Teil wir sind* (XXV), nicht neben oder ausser ihm sein".[12]

The first thing which these quotations show is that there are two interpretations
of the concept "Aufhebung" (I, XIV, XXIII) as describing the relation
between polar and supra-polar space.

The first of them states that there is discontinuity between them (I, V, X,
XVII, XXIII) and the second that there is a continuity (III, IV, XI, XII, XIII,
XIX, XXV).

Let us begin with the discontinuity interpretation. This aspect, illustrated by
statements saying that supra-polar space is something "total anderes" (XVII)
or that it represents a "höhere Synthese" (IX) of reality, says that there is a gulf
between polar and supra-polar space, and that that gulf can not be bridged
from the side of polar space. According to this interpretation supra-polar space
is metaphysically transcendent. This is what expressions like (II) mean. The
basic rule of construction for polar space, the law of polarity, does not hold
within supra-polar space. Consequently, there is no accurate description of
supra-polar space, since human language is ultimately determined and shaped
by polarity (cf. V, VI, VII) and can not escape from this dependence.[13] There
only remain negative or indirect ways of speaking about supra-polar space.

This means that the reality of supra-polar space (and consequently the existence of God) is impossible to explain, but that it is the ultimate condition for
an explanation of polar space as a whole and for facts within it. When the

limits for explanation by using the conceptual frameworks of polar space are recognized, then another kind of explanation is needed. This seems to be Heim's intention when he uses expressions like (IX, XXI, XXIII).

When Heim maintains the interpretation of discontinuity between polar and supra-polar space he is anxious to protect and do justice to a traditional doctrine within a religious total view of reality, namely that God is a metaphysically transcendent being which can not in any respect be compared with the world. His being is really "totally otherwise", and can only be expressed as a negation of the being of the universe. Therefore, in this interpretation, Heim's doctrine of supra-polar space presents an either-or relation between the world and God, and there is no inter-change between them.

According to the second interpretation it is said that here is also a continuity between polar and supra-polar space. Polar space is in some sense said to be contained in supra-polar space. The most reasonable interpretation of this, expressed e.g. in (III, IV, XI, XII, XIII, XXV), is that polar space as a whole, and thus also all spaces contained in it, is a partial space of supra-polar space. Then supra-polar space contains polar space, but they cannot be identified, in the same way as ordinary three-dimensional space can be said to contain a two-dimensional plane, but these latter spaces are not identical. But to say this is to say that the content of polar space is also the content of the supra-polar.

This aspect of the relation between the spaces of course expresses the thought that God is immanent in the world but still can not be identified with it and that he also is omnipresent in it.[14] This is a necessary condition for a reasonable general theory of God's activity within polar space, containing i.a. a theory about divine miracles and answers to prayers.

The focus of this contradictory combination of the aspects of continuity and discontinuity in the relation between polar and supra-polar space can be found in the theory about the limit of dimension. We saw that this kind of limit holds between spaces.[15] Now, since a space is an ordered and infinite set of entities, it follows that two or more spaces can have a common entity. That is the point of common reference (XX). And we saw that there is no contradiction in ascribing one and the same entity a place within two of more different ordered spaces. This means that it is possible to give them different and complementary explanations. Different spaces have their own proper explanations. An entity may then belong to one or more polar spaces, but it may also belong to supra-polar space and can be ordered according to its rules of construction. But the problem is that Heim explicitly denies that there is a limit of dimension here. This assertion is quite in accordance with the discontinuity-interpretation, but hardly with the continuity-interpretation. Otherwise the talk about activities of God within polar space is nonsensical.

Now we shall try to show that this may clarify the understanding of Heim's theory of the activity of God within polar space. The key to this theory lies in the combination of the theories that polar space is a partial space of supra-polar space and that we, according to the continuity interpretation, assume that there is a limit of dimension between them.

If a space presents reality as a whole as having a certain order, then it is also possible that it may present an ordered universe as being the place of the activity of God (cf. IX, XVII, XXII). But if polar space is a partial space of supra-polar space, it follows according to Heim, that the activity of God cannot be seen as contradicting the rules of construction of its partial space. This means e.g. that God's activity within objectifiable space must not consist in breaking causal laws (cf. XX)[16], or that his activity within non-objectifiable space must not contradict the assertion of the existence of a connecting link between different spaces.

There is also an interesting point in Heim's theory of the activity of God within polar space. This point is its connection with Heim's dynamic interpretation of reality.[17] This seems to imply the following position. The activity of God cannot take place contrary to changes within reality, and it cannot consist in events which really contradict the laws of nature. But since polar space is a partial space of supra-polar space, it follows that the activity of God within polar space also can take place within objectifiable space and even physical objects. Now Heim describes reality as dynamically and constantly changing. And he also describes the changes in personal categories, e.g. in terms of will and decision.[18] This can perhaps be confusing and bring about some kind of an animistic interpretation of physical nature. But this is not necessarily so. It is not necessary to infer the existence of some universal mind as the subject behind personally described changes. It is plausible that it is only an analogous way of speaking. But the important point is that the alternative static way of describing nature seems to exclude a theory about the activity of God within the universe. This becomes clear in Heim's criticism of the doctrine of analogia entis.

An important feature in Heim's theory about supra-polar space is his conviction that it entails the denial of the traditional doctrine of analogia entis, and that the philosophy of spaces must not be interpreted as a kind of natural theology. But what does Heim exactly mean when maintaining this position? He writes:

"Der überpolare Raum ist ja ... der Raum, in dem Gott für uns gegenwärtig ist. Wenn der Raum Gottes mit dem Raum dieser Welt unter einen gemeinsamen Nenner gebracht wird, ist das nicht der titanische Versuch des menschlichen Denkens, sich Gottes zu bemächtigen und ihn, der doch ‚das ganz andere' ist, in das Netz unserer menschlichen Begriffe und Kategorien einzufangen? Führt uns das nicht auf die apologetische Methode, die aus dem Prinzip der ‚analogia entis' entstanden ist, das heisst aus dem Gedanken: Gott ist, und die Welt ist auch, also fallen beide unter denselben Begriff des Seins; folglich können wir aus dem Sein der geschaffenen Welt, die ja ein Spiegelbild des Schöpfers ist, auf das Sein des Schöpfers schliessen?

Auf diesen Einwand muss geantwortet werden: Gerade das Gegenteil ist der Fall. Der Gedanke, dass Gott im überpolaren Raum für uns gegenwärtig ist, ist gerade die Aufhebung des Satzes von der analogia entis. Ja, er ist der einzig wirksame Schutzwall, der imstande ist, die Gefahr abzuwehren, die unser religiöses Leben von dem verführerischen und auf den ersten Blick so ausserordentlich einleuchtenden Satz von der analogia entis her bedroht".[19]

Here Heim seems to say two things. First he wants to say that the doctrine of analogia entis contradicts the philosophy of spaces. This is the meaning of his assertion that God is present for us in supra-polar space which is the "Aufhebung" of analogia entis. This can further mean either that the philosophy of spaces says something more, which the analogia entis does not say, or that the doctrines really are logically incompatible. But both these possibilities seems to be invalid. What is this 'more' in the first case? Heim does not tell us. Is it perhaps the assertion that God is omnipresent? But it is not the case that this feature contradicts the analogia entis or is incompatible with it. And concerning the second possibility, it is doubtful whether the philosophy of spaces really is incompatible with the doctrine of analogia entis. On the contrary, there even seems to be a similarity between the theory of the analogia entis and the theory of polar space as a partial space of supra-polar space.

The second idea in the quotation is that the doctrine of analogia entis states that there is a predicate, existence, which is prior to God and independent of him, and which in the same manner, but not in the same degree, can be applicable to all existent entities. Maybe there is a point in this argument. The doctrine of analogia entis can perhaps not do justice to the aspect of discontinuity between God and the world in the same extension as Heim's philosophy of spaces can. And this seems to be Heim's decisive argument.

Now, the doctrine of supra-polar space has, together with the dynamic view of reality, an important consequence: The doctrine of eschatology becomes important. Let us briefly sketch the reasons why this is the case.

Heim seems to accept the following reasoning from the law of polarity in connection with the dynamic view of nature. The reasoning is not a strict argument, but it is in some way natural here. It runs something like this.

1. There is something abnormal about the world's state of polar existence, which implies relativity and destiny both with regard to creation as a whole and human existence within it. When Heim interprets this in theological terms he says that polarity expresses the Christian doctrine of a fall, both of creation as a whole and of man.[20]

2. This means that man suffers from an inescapable guilt and ignorance of God.

These points in the reasoning correspond to existential needs of man. It is unsatisfactory, and in the long run absurd, to accept that there is no explanation according to a conceptual framework, based on polarity. And further; the relativity of a decision-situation contains the problem of ethical certainty, and consequently, as long as this problem is not solved, it reveals the metaphysically based guilt of man. Therefore, in the polar conditions of man's existence, there is an inherent demand for deliverence from the polar state of being[21] and a need for higher order of things.

Now, we saw that in the doctrine of supra-polar space, there is a real possibility of an "Aufhebung" of polar space.[22] But the interesting point in Heim's way of stating the doctrine of eschatology is that it differs from a traditional presentation of it within protestant theology, when Heim maintains the possibility of an apokatastasis panton. Why is it so?

Heim first expresses his position in terms of negation of the concept to place ("setzen"). This concept refers both to creation and to God's present relation to the creation (cf XVIII, XXIII). The ultimate future must then be conceived as a kind of withdrawal, a "Zurückgenommenwerden",[23] or even a "Heimnehmung",[24] of polar space as a whole into supra-polar space, resulting in a final end of all change.

There is of course a connection between the doctrines of creation and eschatology. We shall not treat the doctrine of creation in detail, but only point out that the creation also is seen in categories of a divine "Setzen". And this primary placing is a free and sovereign decision of God. "Setzen" means the appearance of polarity out of nothing, ex nihilo.[25] Ex nihilo means that the creation as a whole cannot be causally explained. Therefore the doctrine of the creation ex nihilo is a supra-empirical assertion and falls outside the range of scientific discourse.[26]

The interesting point here is that the doctrine of eschatology does not mean a restauration of the creation into its primary state[27] and that therefore the state of polarity only was a disturbing episode in the "eternal" harmony. Heim's arguments for this are based on a linear notion of time[28] and the actual existence of anti-divine powers.[29] Thus the final passing of polar space into the supra-polar can not take place as a restoration, but rather as a judge and a new creation. And consequently, this is also a supra-empirical assertion.[30] But this, in Heim's opinion, does not exclude the possibility of apokatastasis panton.[31]

Concluding remarks. We shall conclude this chapter by making some remarks on the interpretation of Heim's theory of supra-polar space as a whole. We saw that it stated that there is a dual relation between polar and supra-polar space. It presented both a discontinuity and a continuity between them. But there is something unsatisfactory about leaving the matter like this, as a kind of ultimate complementary religious total views of reality. We shall therefore ask if it nevertheless can not be argued that one of the aspects ought to be preferred as the most plausible interpretation of Heim's position.

This aspect is the aspect of continuity.

This having been said, then two counter-arguments, both having good support from Heim appear.

The first of these arguments is that if the continuity-aspect is accentuated, then the transcendence of supra-polar space is not a real or genuine transcendence. Support for this can be found e.g. in Heim's sayings on the incomprehensibility of God. We quoted it in 5.1.1. But a reply to this argument then is: Is it really the case that God is transcendent only if his essence is wholly incomprehensible? This is certainly a difficult question, which involves considerations on epistemological and ontological questions, but perhaps it is too hasty to answer it affirmatively.

The next argument is that to accept the continuity-interpretation is consistent with Heim's rejection of the doctrine about analogia entis. But this needs not necessarily be the case. It can be doubted if the discontinuity-interpretation excludes analogia entis. But perhaps this argument against our interpretation is worth some consideration. But to decide this involves a closer investigation of the doctrine of analogia entis.

However, even if these arguments deserve some consideration, they seem nevertheless to be decisive.

On the contrary, not to prefer the continuity-interpretation would mean to create even more problems. We shall mention some of them below, after having presented another argument for our interpretation.

This argument is that it is very plausible and natural to assume that there is a continuity between polar and supra-polar space. This follows naturally from Heim's theory that there is a hierarchy between different spaces which are subordinated to each other and delimited from each other by a limit of dimension. It is natural because it is not reasonable to exclude supra-polar space from the hierarchy. And furthermore, as we saw, supra-polar space is a space in the same sense as other spaces: it is discovered in the same way as polar spaces, and it has its rules of construction as well as polar spaces have.

Now, an obvious objection to this argument is that Heim himself explicitly denies that there is a limit of dimension between polar and supra-polar space. But is this limit not a limit of dimension, what is it then? Of course, it can not be a limit of content. Is it then the case that Heim, when treating the relation between polar and supra-polar space, operates with a third notion of limit? This possibility cannot a priori be excluded. Perhaps the concept of "Aufhebung" refers to such a third sense of limit. But even if this is the case, then it does not mean that our problem is solved, because the relation of "Aufhebung" also holds between spaces within polar space. Thus the same problem appears again. And then, what is the point in Heim's comprehensive analysis of immanent relations of transcendence? If their only function, when talking about the transcendence of God, is to be denied, then the theory about a spatial hierarchy or the view about the discovery of a new space has no bearing at all on supra-polar space.[32] And it is not plausible that this is Heim's intentions.

Our next main argument for preferring the continuity-interpretation says that if it not is preferred, even more serious inconsistencies within Heim's view will appear, than those we mentioned above. We shall only mention two examples.

The first example is that if the continuity-interpretation is not preferred, then

Heim's theological program as a whole becomes rather unnecessary and his apologetics unreasonable, at least concerning the problem of God's transcendence. Why devote so much work to the relation between philosophy, science and religion if they after all have no bearings upon eachother? But if the continuity-interpretation is accepted, then Heim's theological program becomes very natural.

We shall take our second example from Heim's view on the activity of God within polar space. His view on this subject also becomes very strange if we do not accept the continuity-interpretation. If there really is no relation at all between polar and supra-polar space, how can we then reasonable speak about divine activities within polar space? This is only reasonable if there is a continiuity between the spaces, i.e. if polar space is contained in supra-polar space. And furthermore, how can there be a connecting link, a "word", between God and man, i.e. between supra-polar space and ego-space, if they cannot have a common content? And how can a fact within polar space be a fact, revealing supra-polar space to man, if a continuity between the spaces is not supposed? It is difficult to answer such questions if the continuity-interpretation not is accepted.

These remarks are not meant to present an exhaustive interpretation of Heim's philosophy of spaces, with regard to the relation between polar and supra-polar space. But if the one main alternative—to be satisfied with the contradiction of discontinuity and continuity—is rejected, then the other main alternative means a decision. And in this case, according to our opinion, the continuity-interpretation ought to be preferred, because it presents a more coherent view of Heim's theory about polar and supra-polar space.

Chapter 6
Discussion of some features of Heim's theology

Introduction. In this concluding chapter we shall first pay attention to some similarities and differences between some features in Heim's interpretation of religion and recent discussions of religion, exemplified by Kuhn's theory of paradigm (applied to religion) and Torrence's theory of multilevelled knowledge (6.1.). The aim of this part is to show that Heim has anticipated important points in this discussion. Then (6.2.) we shall make some remarks on other features of Heim's theology, and discuss the place of non-objectifiable space in Heim's argument for the existence of supra-polar space and the question of whether Heim can be said to be a rationalist within theology.

6.1. Heim, Kuhn and Torrance

Heim and Kuhn's theory of paradigm. In this section we shall compare some features in Heim's general view of a religious total view of reality with Kuhn's famous theory of scientific paradigms, presented in "The Structure of Scientific Revolutions", 1962. We shall make this comparison as follows: First we shall present some main points in Kuhn's notion of a scientific paradigm. Then we shall see that important points in Heim's philosophy of spaces, and therefore also a religious total view of reality are very similar to characteristics of a scientific paradigm. The aim of this comparison is to connect Heim's interpretation of a religious total view of reality with the discussion about paradigms.[1]

But let us first present the basic ideas of Kuhn's theory of scientific paradigms. Unfortunately, his notion of a paradigm suffers from some vagueness, which Kuhn admits.[2] One of his critics has found twentytwo more or less different meanings.[3] But that vagueness is not of a kind that will affect our reasonings here. Kuhn's general ideas are clear enough for our purposes.

Let us begin by getting an idea of what a paradigm is. Kuhn develops this idea within the context of the history of science, and almost all his examples are from it.

Perhaps it may be convenient to give some examples of scientific paradigms. A good example is Ptolemaic astronomy.[4] This presented a geocentric universe where the planets moved around the earth in a complicated system of compound circles. However, predictions made on the basis of Ptolemy's system never wholly conformed with observations.

These obstacles could be removed by making minor corrections in the system. But this would only do to some extent. And in the long run, these corrections did not make the system into a better scientific tool, but rather created new problems. Copernicus' assumption of a heliocentric universe removed these difficulties. Another example is the Aristotelian theory of movement. A body moves, naturally, from a higher position to a lower position of natural rest.

In these examples the paradigms are the assumptions that the planets move in epicycles around the earth and that a body naturally strives to reach its state of natural rest.

Now, on a general level Kuhn says about a scientific paradigm:

"These (i.e. the scientific paradigms) I take to be universally recognized scientific achievements that for a time provide model problems and solutions to a community of practitioners".[5]

"Paradigms gain their status because they are more successful than their competitors in solving a few problems that the group of practitioners has come to recognize as acute".[6]

(In the following presentation we shall not pay attention to the sociological aspect [the reference to a group of practitioners] of the theory.) Now a scientific paradigm has two characteristics:

"Their achievement was sufficiently unprecedented to attract an enduring group of adherents away from competing modes of scientific activity. Simultaneously, it was sufficiently open-ended to leave all sorts of problems for the redefined group of practitioners to resolve".[7]

An accepted scientific paradigm therefore is (1) the most reasonable or preferable among a set of competing paradigms, and (2) the paradigm defines new problems and offer means for their solution. Thus, generally speaking, a scientific paradigm consists of (1) a set of scientific theories and hypothesis, and (2) some rules for their application.[8] But it seems to be a limitation of the content of a paradigm to say that it contains only scientific theories and rules for their application. Sometimes they also seem to contain something more, namely a set of metaphysical beliefs, which are (implicitly) presupposed together with the scientific theories and hypothesis. Thus a scientific paradigm, due to its metaphysical presuppositions, determines not only the way of doing science,[9] but also what kind of problems are real problems, open for scientific investigation and solution. The metaphysical presuppositions of a paradigm can then also eliminate some problems as pseudo-problems. However, there is no necessary connection between paradigms and the rules for their application. Scientists can agree about a scientific paradigm, but disagree about its application, and vice versa.[10]

Now we shall look at some particular features in the notion of a scientific paradigm.

The first one concerns the nature of a scientific problem. A paradigm must explain and describe a fact, i.e. it must be demonstrated that a fact is compatible with the paradigm. This demonstration Kuhn calls puzzlesolving. A scientific problem can, generally speaking, be regarded as a puzzle. And the scientist, when facing a puzzle, is lead by the conviction that there really is a solution to it, provided that he is careful enough and applies the paradigm correctly. And science is the art of finding good solutions to puzzles.[11]

Connected with a generally accepted paradigm is the notion of "normal science".[12] As long as a paradigm works well and can explain all the facts and offer acceptable solutions to acute problems, its corresponding science can be regarded as well-established and can operate in a considerably quiet atmosphere. Ordinary scientific work consists in puzzlesolving. The result of this is an increase in knowledge, when facts are explained according to he paradigm.

Now, no paradigm is complete. This means that there always remain problems, for which the paradigm cannot offer a solution. This seems to be a presupposition in Kuhn's thinking, for which he has no arguments. This means that there are some facts which cannot be explained by the paradigm.[13] But it is a prejudice to judge such a case as a falsification of the paradigm.[14] Generally Kuhn says: "Discoveries predicted by theory in advance are parts of normal science and result in no *new sort* of fact".[15] Increasing knowledge is quite a normal state of affairs.

However, it sometimes happens that discoveries are not exactly the ones which were antecipated by the speculative and tentative hypothesis.[16] Such new facts Kuhn calls anomalies. They appear only against the background of a given paradigm.[17] Anomalies therefore bring about a change of "paradigm categories and procedures",[18] a process which is often accompanied by some resistance and rejection of the new ideas from the adherents of normal science.[19] This then results in a new way of doing science according to a new paradigm. Then science enters into a revolutionary state, which after some time brings about a new normal science according to the new paradigm.

A second feature of a paradigm is that a new paradigm is not accepted on the basis of empirical evidence only.[20] This is an important point. What is taking place when a new paradigm is accepted? A common and plausible view is that the scientist has changed his interpretation of a set of neutral data. But this is to simplify problem, because to accept the "neutral-data-view" is precisely to accept a paradigm.[21] The paradigm determines the notion of data.

Now, the appearance of anomalies is a prerequisite for the acceptance of a new paradigm. And this is due to a kind of knowing, which Kuhn describes as a kind of intuition: ". . . the choice between competing paradigms regularly raises questions that cannot be resolved by the criteria of normal science".[22] This means that a paradigm is not accepted on the basis of empircal evidence. The appearance of a new paradigm depends on "flashes of intuition"[23] or on the "genius" of the individual scientist.

How is a paradigm shift to be interpreted? Kuhn says that the switch of a visual gestalt is a parallel as the example of the duck-rabbit shows.[24] To accept a new paradigm then means to recognize the new paradigm in familiar facts. However, the parallel can be misleading. It is not the case that there is a set of neutral facts, which can be seen as this or as that: "... the scientist does not preserve the gestalt subject's freedom to switch back and forth between ways of seeing".[25] On the contrary the process is irreversible. For these reasons Kuhn has been accused of being an irrationalist.[26] But this is not correct. On the contrary he sketches, perhaps vaguely, some rational criteria for deciding between paradigms. The first one (1) we can call the criterion of fitness. It means that the new paradigm must really solve the puzzles, which the old paradigm failed to solve. It must eliminate the anomalies.[27] But this ability cannot be completely known before the acceptance of the new paradigm. Thus, the acceptance of a new paradigm is connected with an act of faith: The scientist must

"have faith that the new paradigm will succed with the many large problems that confront it, knowing *only* that the older paradigm has failed with a few. A decision of that kind can only be made on faith".[28]

And of course it is wrong to state that a paradigm, which is accepted on such belief-grounds is mistaken simply for that reason. Besides there is also another criterion (2) which may be called an "aesthetic criterion" which says that a paradigm, to be preferred, ought to be "neater", "more suitable" or "simpler".[29] To this criterion belong the demand that a paradigm ought to be self-consistent and plausible.[30]

A third feature we shall mention is that a new paradigm is some sense contains the old. This is an interesting point, which it is possible to interpret in a double way.

On the one hand they are mutually incompatible and exclusive. This is not to be confused with the course of increasing knowledge within normal science:

"The transition from a paradigm in crisis to a new one from which a new tradition of normal science can emerge is far from a cumulative process, one achieved by an articulation or extension of the old paradigm. Rather it is a reconstruction of the field from new fundamentals, a reconstruction that changes some of the field's most elementary theoretical generalizations as well as many of its paradigm methods and applications. During the transition period there will be a large but never complete overlap between the problems that can be solved by the old and by the new paradigm".[31]

Most of the new knowledge is of course not anomalous. In order to bring about a new paradigm, an anomaly must be shown to be not only a more complex version of a puzzle[32] but also really unsolvable within paradigms of normal science.

But the relation seems on the other hand to be that of an overlapping. There is a kind of coexistence between the old and the new paradigm, at least for some time. A new paradigm does not destroy earlier paradigms,[33] but rather transforms them.[34] Kuhn says:

"Whatever he may then see, the scientist after a revolution is still looking at the same world . . . As a result, postrevolutionary science invariably includes many of the same manipulations, performed with the same instruments and described in the same terms, as its prerevolutionary predecessor".[35]

Older scientific methods can, mutatis mutandis, survive in the environment of a new paradigm.[36] They can be interpreted as approximations of the new paradigm. Normal science can therefore not correct a revolutionary science, but rather the reverse.[37]

We shall now proceed and show that these features in Kuhn's view on a scientific paradigm have counterparts in Heim's interpretation of religion. Our general thesis is that Heim's philosophy of spaces can be seen as a theory of paradigm. Then we shall say that the rules of constructions, signifying different spaces are descriptions of paradigms. This is a plausible interpretation of e.g. the passages from GN quoted in 2.1. There e.g. the world-view of "secularism" is a paradigm and theism and atheism are also paradigms. Here the notion of paradigm is generalized.

We shall also make some remarks on the paradigmatic character of a religious total view of reality, which contains the rules of construction according to supra-polar space. A religious total view of reality determines a view of reality and also which problems really are problems. Heim's conviction is that the traditional religious paradigm is a paradigm in crisis, due to its lacking relation to contemporary revolutionary science. Thus the task of theology is to propose a new religious paradigm, which takes account of the new scientific paradigm.

The first point of similarity between Heim and Kuhn concerns the notion of anomaly. According to Kuhn, one important reason for accepting a new paradigm is its power to offer solutions to anomalies, which the old paradigm failed to solve.

This argument can be find in Heim's thinking. There the anomalies are the paradoxes of human destiny and of relativism contra positivism and of the manifold of perspectives.[38] They cannot be explained by means of the paradigm according to objectifiable space. To explain them must mean to acccept supra-polar space.

But there is also a difference in the nature of the anomalies involved. For Kuhn they mainly seem to consist in a failure to fit a prediction from an accepted paradigm, but for Heim they consist in an (implicit) logical contradiction, which appears when a paradigm fails to explain a fact.

The next point of similarity concerns the view that a new paradigm is not accepted on the basis of empirical evidence only. The same position can be found in the thinking of Heim. He clearly distinguishes between knowledge, inferred from empirical evidence and knowledge, gained from what he called "existential entrance".[39] The former knowledge simply means a quantitative extension of knowledge, but the latter means to accept a new space. And this is another kind of knowledge, different from empirical knowledge. But, and this is also the case in Kuhn, this does not entail some kind of irrationalism. We have treated the criteria and the conditions for accepting a new space before. They are also similar to Kuhn's ideas on the same subject.

When Kuhn says that a new paradigm contains the old, this has also a counterpart in the thinking of Heim. We shall examine this more clearly. We saw in Kuhn's theory that paradigms, or at least parts of them, connected with methodological rules, could be assimilated with a new paradigm, and that it in transition-periods could be a co-existence between paradigms.

This has some parallels in Heim's thinking. His aim is not, as we have seen, to totally destroy well-established scientific paradigms, but rather to incorporate them into a wider paradigm, namely that of a religious total view of reality.

Here an important question arises: Can a co-existence of paradigms be accepted? And if so, on what conditions? It is difficult to determine Kuhn's position, depending on the vagueness of the notion of a paradigm. However, he seems to accept some kind of co-existence. This is a natural consequence from his assumption that no paradigm is complete, which is the main factor in the scientific development.

But Heim seems to deny that there really could be a coexistence of different paradigms. And it is true that, sometimes, it may be justified to use different paradigms in scientific work. But in reality there can be only one paradigm. But this is of course an assumption, for which no rational reasons can be given.

The last point of similarity between Heim and Kuhn concerns the question of how to choose between different and conflicting paradigms or total views of reality.

We saw that, according to Kuhn, it was an act of "faith" to make such a decision. However, it seems here to be a question of rational faith. Kuhn's assertion of the criterion of fitness, which includes a criterion of coherence, indicates this. The scientist in order to decide, must have some rational reasons to believe that the new paradigm will fit the facts and remove the anomalies. And the aesthetic criterion cannot be an argument for accepting every simple or elegant paradigm. This moment seems to be a secondary criterion, but not the main one.

Concerning Heim, we have seen that the ultimate question ("die letzte Frage") cannot be decided on rational grounds only. However, this question seems to be somewhat more complicated for Heim.

On the one hand he says[40] that the alternatives of the ultimate question (theism and atheism) are, from the scientific point of view, equal. This seems to indicate that scientific reasoning would support equally these two total views of reality. But it is not Heim's intention to state this. The most reasonable interpretation of his view is that scientific reasoning is not applicable to this question at all, and that this decision-situation is hypothetical: If scientific reasonings were applicable, then the alternatives would be equal. But when Heim on the other hand says that this decision involves personal reasons he is not an irrationalist, but the rationality is perhaps more difficult to discover. The criterion of coherence here has its counterpart in Heim's intention to describe the ultimate structure of reality by means of one basic assumption: the law of polarity. And this intention also satisfies the aesthetic criterion. However, the rationality is indirectly stated, by demonstrating that the only paradigm which really can explain the destiny paradox is a religious paradigm, which includes acceptance of a metaphysically transcendent reality.

But finally there is an important point on which Heim and Kuhn seems to differ. This is the question: Is there after all a unifying paradigm? Or better and more properly: Is there after all an ultimate paradigm, which unifies everything that exists and eliminates every possible anomaly? And to this question Heim's clear answer is: There certainly is such a paradigm: The religious paradigm, the paradigm of supra-polar space, the paradigm of the living and personal God.

Such questions do not seem to affect Kuhn very much. He would probably reject the claim that a paradigm can be definitive or ultimate. The arguments can be developed from his treatment of the development of science. There is no reason to suppose that there exists such an ultimate paradigm on the principle that every paradigm is incomplete. There is at least one anomaly left. And to show that the ultimate paradigm does in fact not solve a special anomaly may be done by setting forth a counter-example of an unsolvable anomaly. This can perhaps easily be done concerning empirically founded paradigms, but not concerning those otherwise founded. And the religious paradigm of supra-polar space certainly belongs to this latter group.

Heim and Torrance's theory of a multilevelled knowledge. We shall now direct our attention to some similarities between some points in Heim's thinking and some points in the writings of T.F. Torrance.[41] We shall not present Torrance's comprehensive view on the relation between science and theology,[42] but only consider some main points in it.

A suitable starting-point then from which to describe the relevant points in Torrance's view, is his assertion that man's knowledge of reality is what he calls multilevelled. He says that

" . . . the various sciences themselves, ranging from physics and chemistry to the humanities and theology can be regarded as constituting a hierarchical structure of levels of inquiry which are open upwards into wider and more comprehensive systems of knowledge but are not reducible downwards".[43]

This passage contains two ideas of interest here: The first one is the notion of "science" (science here obviously means individual science) or level of inquiry, and the second one is the idea that there is a "hierarchical" relation between the sciences.

Concerning the first idea Torrance says that every science, operating with a conceptual framework, is ultimately based on a set of axiomatical assumptions, which are impossible to verify within the conceptual framework of the science in question. Torrance says (and here he argues from Gödel):

"What we are concerned with here is the proper circularity inherent in any coherent system operating with ultimate axioms or beliefs which cannot be derived or justified from any other ground than that which they themselves constitute".[44]

Therefore, the acceptance of such a system ultimately depends on

"... the question whether we are prepared to commit ourselves to belief in the ultimates which are constitutive of the system".[45]

We shall not consider all Torrance's arguments for this position. His most important here is the argument from Gödel. Now there is a general problem in the interpretation of these passages, namely whether there are sciences on the same level of inquiry, but operating with indifferent conceptual frameworks. Probably Torrance would admit this possibility. But this problem does not affect his theory on the hierarchical structure of different sciences.

Concerning the second idea, about the hierarchical structure of different sciences, or levels of inquiry, with their respective conceptual frameworks, Torrance says, still arguing from Gödel when Gödel says that the ultimate axioms are only provable by reference to a higher conceptual framework:

"There are then in our various levels of inquiry or layers of knowledge certain 'boundary conditions' (to use Einstein's expression) where each one is coordinated with a higher system, in terms of which it becomes explicable and intelligible... While such a science on a higher level relies on the laws governing the science on a lower level, without infringing them, for the fulfilment of its own operations, these operations are not explainable in terms of the laws governing the science on the lower level".[46]

This means that a science with a lower hierarchical position becomes explained in a higher science, but also that laws or operations of the higher science do not affect laws or operations of the lower science. Each law has its universal application within its own realm. This also means that laws and operations of the lower science cannot be an instance of verification for laws and operations of the higher science. Scientific laws and operations of a lower science become meaningful only from the point of view of a higher science.

Now, this offers some problems: The first one is that the notion of a hierarchical relation between sciences seems to be what we shall call a relative hierarchical structure: A science S_1 can very well be a lower science in relation to another science S_2, but a higher science in relation to S_3. But perhaps the science S_3, from another point of view can be a higher science in relation to S_1. And how to decide the starting-point-science in a case like this seems to be a somewhat arbitrary task. The hierarchy then cannot be a hierarchy of science and auxiliary science.

148

The next problem arises, and this problem is not affected by the first one; it is namely whether there is a highest science in hierarchy of sciences. It seems to be the most plausible interpretation of Torrance to say that it is not a certain given science, but rather a kind of metaphysical conceptual framework, which can explain the laws and operations of all sciences. Thus the hierarchy is constituted by the more or less wider scope of the science and with the widest-scope-science at the top of the hierarchy.

This can perhaps be made clearer if we investigate the notions of "openness" or "open concepts". Torrance said in our first quotation that the levels of inquiry were "open upwards but not reducible downwards". Now, in order to understand the notion of openness, it is essential to be acquainted with another idea, namely the idea that knowledge is achieved through a dialectic process between the subject and the object. Therefore, according to Torrance, there is no objective knowledge. All knowledge, he says, is given within a relation between the subject and the object.

"We do not describe the realities we know as they are merely in themselves, for we cannot separate them entirely by themselves apart from the processes in our knowing of them. . .".[47]

Therefore, the proper way to acquire knowledge is within a question-answer-process. Torrance describes it like this:

"It is through questioning that we set out to explore entirely new territory".[48]

"This means further that although it is we who have to frame the questions and the answers to them, so far as the words or symbols are concerned, nevertheless it is not we ourselves who are finally determinative but the object itself, for all what we do presupposes that it is so constituted that we can think it, that it is what it is and not another thing and that it shows itself as it is and therefore as it must be in our conceiving of it and acting toward it".[49]

This passage contains two point of interest to us. The first one is that Torrance stresses the importance or the primacy of the object in the process of acquiring knowledge. There seems to be a natural link or correspondence between objects and our concepts of them. Our concepts are not arbitrarily given. But we shall not investigate his complex view on this matter, but only say that this idea seems to be a kind of ultimate assumption concerning our acquiring of knowledge.

The second, and more important, point concerns his notion of concepts used in the process of acquiring knowledge. Torrance says that it is generally possible to operate with two different kinds of conceptual tools. He calls them open and closed concepts. He describes the difference between them like this:

" 'Closed concepts' are of the kind that we can reduce to clipped propositional ideas, whereas 'open concepts' are of the kind which by their very nature resist being put into a strait-jacket, for the reality conceived keeps on disclosing itself to us in such a way that it continually overflows all our statements about it. Closed concepts are rigid and easily manipulable but open concepts are elastic because they operate on the boundary between the already known and the new".[50]

Here the notion of an open concept is of interest. What is then an open concept? Sometimes Torrance seems to say that an open concept is the same as a "flexible" or "symbolic" or inadequate concept.[51] This needs some explanation. Obviously an open concept cannot be the same as a mythology or poetic language only. It sometimes has connections with this kind of speech, but they are not important. They are rather concepts, which point beyond themselves in a certain way, namely that they reveal new aspects of reality. And this is due partly to the nature of the process of acquiring knowledge and partly to the nature of reality. There are entities within reality which simply cannot be exhaustively described by means of closed concepts. And this seems to be the point of Torrance's view: Reality is so constituted that we simply have to use open concepts. It is difficult to characterize this position. Perhaps we can say that it is an ultimate assumption of the relation between reality and our concepts of it. A plausible interpretation of the notion of open concepts is to say that they are concepts whose use cannot be justified within the conceptual framework in which they occur. Open concepts are then explained and receive their meaning from a higher level of inquiry.

Not we can state some points of similarity between the views of Heim and Torrance.

The main one is obvious. It is that Torrance's notion of "level of inquiry" is similar to Heim's notion of space. We shall develop this point a little more.

A level of inquiry, according to Torrance, and the concept of space, according to Heim, are both a conceptual framework according to which reality is ordered. This is certainly what Torrance means, and we have interpreted Heim in the same way. But there is also an important difference. According to Torrance it is natural to operate with open concepts, and this is the only proper way of doing science, because open concepts correspond to reality. Only when they are used, can the essential nature of reality be disclosed and a new and more adequate knowledge brought about. According to Torrance, it therefore seems to be a kind of continuity between the different levels of inquiry. Open concepts naturally point beyond themselves to this higher level of inquiry. This does not contradict the claim that there is a real difference between different levels of inquiry, and that a higher level cannot be reduced to a lower.

But, according to Heim, there is no such continuity. There is a decisive step from one space to another. And the point in Heim's theory, which makes this clear, is his view on the role of a paradox. It is the appearance of a paradox which makes it necessary to infer a new level of inquiry, i.e. a new space.

But, perhaps the role of the paradox has a counterpart in the view of Torrance, which is at least implicitly stated in the argument from Gödel. But is this really a sufficient argument for operating with open concepts? It may very well be the case that a certain level of inquiry is incomplete, in the sense that at least one of its basic assertions cannot be justified within the system itself. But this fact alone does not mean that it therefore is necessary to operate with open concepts. Also the reverse relation does not seem to be necessary: The use of an open conceptual framework does not entail a higher conceptual framework. And to use a higher level of inquiry as an instance of verification for a lower level is not always the same as saying that the higher level also reveals more of reality. If this is Torrance's position, he seems to be mistaken. Logical dependence is not the same as having an inferior ability to disclose new aspects of reality. Perhaps this thought is confused with a kind of hidden presupposition, which we touched upon above: Reality is inexhaustible in the sense that we can never achieve a complete knowledge of it. But to accept this is to make a metaphysical assumption for which no conclusive arguments can be given.

Now, Heim's position seems to resist his criticism better. When Heim says that reality is inherently paradoxical, he bases this assertion on an analysis of reality in relation to the rules of construction according to a certain space, or level of inquiry, and this analysis reveals that reality is contradictory. But a logical contradiction does not point beyond itself in the same sense as Torrance's notion of an open concept does. It is quite possible to accept the fact that reality is ultimately contradictory. And to make a supplementary basic assumption means to accept a new space, or a higher level of inquiry.

6.2 Concluding remarks

In this part we shall discuss two subjects. We shall make some comments (1) on the role of non-objectifiable space in Heim's argument for the existence of supra-polar space, and (2) on the question of whether Heim can reasonably be said to be a rationalist within theology.

On the role of non-objectifiable space. We shall now return to our previous proposal concerning an alternative interpretation of Heim's ontology. This proposal is based on the elementary notion of change, as an alternative way of describing reality. We saw that Heim's main argument for stating that there is a non-objectifiable space within reality was based on the fact that there was a necessary co-existence of both an "either-or"-relation and a "both-and"-relation between time-instants. We also saw, in addition, that the notion of the non-objectifiable ego was important in two respects, (1) the ego is essentially non-objectifiable, and (2) that the existence of non-objectifiable space is a necessary condition for the truth of the religious basic assumption that there exists a metaphysically transcendent reality, supra-polar space. We shall see below, that this alternative proposal has a general and serious consequence for Heim's argument for the existence of non-objectifiable space: this argument is not valid. Then also the reasons for stating the existence of supra-polar space vanishes. However, we shall argue that the disappearance of non-objectifiable space is an advantage, since the very notion of a non-objectifiable space is problematic.

We shall proceed in the examination as follows: (1) First, we shall undertake a new investigation of the notion of non-objectifiable space. Then (2) we shall ask if the notion of change can reasonably be said to be non-objectifiable. (3) Granted that the ontology of changes is accepted, we shall ask which entities (if any) we still can ascribe non-objectifiability. Finally (4) we shall ask if Heim's argument can still be used and if so, in what form.

(1) Let us begin with the question of non-objectifiable space. For what reasons, if any, can an entity be said to be non-objectifiable? A suitable starting point would be to ask for the conditions under which an entity can be said to be objectifiable, and then assume non-objectifiability to entities which do not fulfill these conditions.[1] We follow the analysis of Forell. The conditions for objectifiability are (1) the condition of intentionality. It says that there must be an intention directed towards the object (which of course must not be a physical object, but also e.g. concepts or experiences), and (2) the condition of non-identity. It says that the intention must not be identical with the intended object.

Objects which do not fulfil one or both of these conditions are then regarded as non-objectifiable.

Now there can be different reasons why an entity is non-objectifiable. One such reason is that the entity is non-objectifiable for psychological reasons. Then the argument consists in a reference to a psychological theory, which entails that an entity is non-objectifiable. This definition can of course be time- and person-related: It may be the case that an entity is objectifiable at time t_1 for a person P but not at time t_2, or that it is objectifiable for person P_1 at time t, but not for P_2 at time t. Another reason is that an entity is non-objectifiable for logical reasons. This is the case when the claim that an entity is objecetified entails a logical contradiction.

Let us now turn to the entities which Heim claims to be non-objectifiable, and start with the notion of the ego.[2]

Heim's main argument for ascribing the ego non-objectifiability seems to be that it cannot satisfy the criterion (2) above. But it is difficult to decide if it is so for logical or psychological reasons. However, it seems to be more plausible to say that it is non-objectifiable for logical reasons. Heim argues that the claim that the ego is objectified entails a logical contradiction.

The next point concerns non-objectifiable space as such. According to Heim, this space is also non-objectifiable for logical reasons. Every attempt to objectify it invariably means a contradiction.[3]

Finally, concerning the question of supra-polar space, the same difficulties arise. But it is most plausible to say that it is non-objectifiable for logical reasons. It manifests both a continuity and a discontinuity to polar space.

Now Heim argues that we have a real and valid knowledge of non-objectifiable space and consequently of supra-polar space.[4] It is obvious that the claim for knowledge of entities within objectifiable space is not problematical. But concerning entities within non-objectifiable space the matter is more difficult. Heim's general position is that apart from objective knowledge there is another way of getting knowledge, the immediate way. Heim seems therefore to deny that condition (1), the condition of intentionality, is a necessary condition for having knowledge. This position presupposes a theory of non-intended acts.[5] Now it is possible to interpret Heim's theory of immediate knowledge in this way. We saw that he simply stated that it is valid.[6]

(2) We can now return to the question of whether the notion of change can be said to be non-objectifiable. We saw that an important feature of Heim's description of reality was that reality is continuously changing. Let us develop this view.

Heim seems to presuppose a way of describing reality according to which the description of reality is always a description of its state at a certain time-instant, and that complex descriptions can be resolved in single statements. Now we saw that every entity within the universe is in a state of continuous change.[7] It also seems to be possible to describe the entities within the universe with respect to this. They are either in a state of change or are static (= not-changing). Let us further assume that this predicate is irreducible and impossible to rediscribe or translate into other concepts.[8]

(3) If we adopt this view, then it also has some consequences: It is still possible to completely describe changing or static states within objectifiable space, i.e. past events, but, and this is important, it is no longer difficult to describe states within non-objectifiable space, i.e. present events. If this holds, then Heim's argument for the existences of non-objectifiable space, namely that a description of it entails a logical contradiction, does not hold. But, and this is also important, it affects only non-objectifiability for logical reasons. It is still possible to argue that the ego is non-objectifiable for psychological reasons, granted that this claim is based on a psychological theory, for which there are other good reasons. But it is no longer possible to state that there really exists a non-objectifiable space in Heim's sense. If this is true, then it also has consequences for the question of the existence of supra-polar space. We saw that the existence of non-objectifiable space was a necessary but not a sufficient condition for the existence of supra-polar space. But if the necessary condition vanishes, then it is impossible to state that supra-polar space exists. And the remaining psychological non-objectifiability of the ego cannot alone be a premise in the argument for the existence of a non-objectifiable space and thus for supra-polar space.

(4) But the important point here is that Heim's theory does not lose its interest for that reason. Even if the basic assumption that there is a non-objectifiable space is mistaken this does not mean that Heim's argument as a

whole fails. Heim's argument seems to be worth consideration without using the assumption that there is a non-objectifiable space. We shall therefore sketch a new version of it. We shall then presuppose (a) that Heim's view on the acceptance of a transcendent reality, supra-polar space, can be interpreted as a paradigm shift, according to Kuhn, or as a higher level of inquiry according to Torrance, and (b) that a basic description of reality in terms of changes and stasis holds. This outline is then based on the premise that:

There is no non-objectifiable space within reality (except the ego, which for logical reasons not can be objectified). This assertion has the consequence that Heim's argument that the existence of a non-objectifiable space together with some experiences, paradoxical or anomalous, made it reasonable to infer the existence of supra-polar space,[9] must be replaced by a new version, namely that objectifiable space together with some experiences makes it reasonable to infer the existence of supra-polar space.

It is necessary to determine the content of experience here. It may contain e.g. both philosophical insights (e.g. concerning human destiny) or personal experiences.[10] This seems to presuppose that Heim and Kuhn operate with somewhat different notions of anomalies. According to Heim anomalies are logical contradictions in relation to the applied paradigm. According to Kuhn anomalies are not logical contradictions but rather inexplicable events in relation to the applied paradigm.

Now it is essential to state that recognizing an event as anomalous presupposes that the applied paradigm is objectifiable. If this condition is not fulfilled, then it is impossible to distinguish anomalous events from non-anomalous ones. An anomalous event can appear only against the background of a distinct paradigm. And this seems to be the weakness of the first version of Heim's argument. A paradigm which includes e.g. the existence of a non-objectifiable space cannot be distinct, and consequently, if such a paradigm is applied, there are no certain anomalies.

However, the second version of the argument escapes this difficulty. This version seems also to be in accordance with Heim's intentions, but it obviously means a reinterpretation of Heim, namely that the religious basic assumptions are accepted on the basis of objective paradigms and experiences together.

Now, the disappearence of non-objectifiable space does not affect Heim's theory that the only way to explain destiny is to accept supra-polar space. The explanatory power of supra-polar space has not vanished with the disappearence of non-objectifiable space.

And this proposal does not affect a theory, which generally says that there are non-objectifiable entities within reality. But it does affect theories which say that the existence of a non-objectifiable *space* is a necessary condition for a belief in a transcendent God.

Is Heim a theological rationalist? We shall finally treat an important question concerning the general interpretation of Heim's theology. The question is: Can Heim reasonably be called a rationalist within theology? And if this is the case, in what and why? The previous investigation may have given the impression that Heim has a quite rationalistic approach towards religion. In this approach great importance is given to the questions of religious belief and rationality, of the relation between a religious belief and commonly accepted philosophical insights and scientific theories and results. And these latter things are indeed matters of rationality. And we have seen that Heim gives them great importance within a religious total view of reality. The provide certain basic assumptions, which, in a generalized version, must be taken account of by theology. An acceptable religious belief must at least not contradict basic assumptions within those realms.

Now the question about rationalism within theology can mean different things. It can mean that a religious total view of reality (or a theology) is rationally constructed, e.g. as a deductive system on the basis of certain theological presuppositions. In this sense Heim is not a theological rationalist. The application of religious basic assumptions is not rationally done.[11]

But nevertheless, it can still be argued that Heim is a theological rationalist for the reasons mentioned above. We shall therefore distinguish three questions which are important to Heim. These questions are: (1) Are there rational criteria for the ultimate choice? (2) Are there rational criteria for the content of an acceptable religious total view of reality? and (3) Is a rational defence of an accepted religious total view of reality possible and desirable?

The first question, concerning the role of rational criteria in the ultimate choice between theism and atheism, is rather easy to answer. Heim is not a rationalist on this point. And as we have seen, from the rational point of view, the ultimate question cannot be answered conclusively.[12] The ultimate choice is a personal decision, in its taking account of personal experiences, and this area is not accessible to objective or rational discourse. The very moment of decision is not accessible to rational considerations.

The second question, of whether there are rational criteria for the content of an acceptable religious total view of reality, ought, according to Heim be answered affirmatively. It can rationally be claimed that a religious total view of reality in order to be acceptable must i.a. explain human destiny, and thus also every individual destiny. But according to Heim, an affirmative answer means not only the acceptance of a metaphysically transcendent reality, but also the claim that this reality is conceived as a personal God. But it must be mentioned again that Heim does not argue that it is possible to give rational proof of the existence of supra-polar space and that it must be conceived as a personal God. But if human destiny is to be explained at all, then it must be explained by making the religious basic assumptions. Otherwise man is left, not with a religious conviction, but with an ultimate despair.

155

The third question, of whether a rational defence of a religious total view of reality is possible and desirable, must also reasonably be answered in the affirmative. According to Heim, this is possible in two ways. First it is rationally possible to demonstrate that alternative explanations of human destiny do not really explain it. This is the case with relativism, positivism and also mysticism. They cannot provide genuine explanations of human destiny, because they do not transcend polarity. And then it is possible to rationally demonstrate that a metaphysically transcendent reality possibly exists. This demonstration Heim develops in the context of his philosophy of spaces. And further, it is, according to Heim, also possible to show that the acceptance of the religious basic assumptions do not contradict other basic assumptions. Thus it is rationally demonstrated that there is one version of the doctrine of the transcendence of God which is acceptable both from the rational and religious points of view.

But even if it is possible to give a rational defence of a religious total view of reality, it does not of course follow that it is also desirable. But it is obviously the case that Heim says that it is desirable. Otherwise his authorship as a whole becomes very strange, and his out-spoken apologetic intentions even more peculiar.

Therefore, if Heim's approach to theology, including his view on the role of reason, is even sympathetically rejected as being a mistake from the very beginning, then his critics ought to present an alternative basis for theological work. But there are, as Heim remarks,[13] some people, for whom questions about the rational content of a religious belief are always existential problems. Because it cannot be denied, as Heim also remarks,[14] that a religious total view of reality also contains (implicitly) some metaphysical beliefs. And if their questions and needs are taken seriously, then a theology, similar to Heim's cannot reasonably do any harm to people who neither ask nor are troubled by those questions. And if Heim's approach to theological work is rejected, then the problems of such people become the problem of Heim's critics.

Finally, there are some boundary lines within theology. The first one is that between theology which denies that any kind of rationality i.e. the use of some kind of criteria similar to those of Heim, ought to be used within the theological work. But Heim rejects such a theology. And there is also another boundary line. It can namely be argued that rationality has a proper place within the theological work, but it is not a task for rationality to consider the fundamentals of a religious total view of reality, the religious basic assumptions. But this restriction Heim also denies. If rationality is to be allowed here, then it must also consider the very heart of a religious belief: God Transcendent.

Notes

* The quotation is from a letter by Heim 1907. It is quoted from Köberle 1959, 147.

Chapter 1. Introduction

1.1 Biographical remarks

[1] This is related in the article "Die Reise..." in GL 688ff.

[2] On the relation to Einstein cf. Timm 1968, 41ff, 65ff and Köberle 1979, 60ff.

[3] Heim's own presentation of the circumstances differs in some respects from that of Nygren 1934, 60 ff. But it is not our task to investigate Heim's attitude to nazism. Some remarks on the matter are given by Köberle 1979, 41ff. Cf. also VZ 262ff.

1.3 Heim's background and its influence on his ideas

[1] On the rise of this spiritual tradition, cf Brattgård 1955, 35ff.

[2] Timm 1968, 16ff, Köberle 1974, 16ff. Cf. also Spemann 1932, 34ff.

[3] Cf. e.g. VZ 26, 67, 274. Cf. also Köberle 1974, 16 ff.

[4] On Heim's relation to Bengel, cf. Köberle 1974, 17f and to Oetinger Köberle 1974, 20. On the general influence of Oetinger on Württemberg Pietism cf. Brattgård 1955, 71ff. Heim's father was a disciple of Beck, VZ 26.

An important term in Heim's thought is "Zentralblick". It signifies the intuitive certainty of a religious belief. (We shall make some remarks on this in 3.1.) Heim is aware that the term is borrowed from Böhme, cf. e.g. JW 188 and GN 197. This term seems to be a kind of terminus technicus within Württemberg Pietism, cf. Nigg 1959, 151f., and Martensen 1881, 15f concerning Böhme and Nigg 1959, 399 concerning Hahn. The same thought can also be found in the theology of Beck, e.g. Beck 1876, 33. It would be an interesting task to follow the transformation of this concept within Württemberg Pietism.

It is also plausible that the basic assumption of the law of polarity bears some resemblence to the thought of Böhme, cf. Hirsch 1951, 216.

[5] Köberle 1974, 18.

[6] On this idea concerning Bengel, cf. Brattgård 1955, 56 and concerning Beck, cf. Hägglund 1966, 344f.

[7] Cf. GL 484. Cf. also Hofmann 1922, 267.

[8] Concerning Böhme cf. Martensen 1881, 28f, 35f.

[9] On the background cf. Brattgård 1955, 71 and Köberle 1974, 23.

[10] GN 165, WZ 96ff., 14ff.

[11] E.g. WZ 98f, G 172, GD 171ff. We shall treat the matter more in 3.3.

[12] VZ 46ff, 92f.

[13] Some of them are collected in GL under the general heading "Jugendbewegung, Kirche und Mission".

[14] E.g. Timm 1968, 23f.

[15] For a general survey of the influences on Heim cf. Cullberg 1933, 141ff, Timm 1968, 74 and all the writings of Köberle. Heim himself treats the matter several times. Most information is to be found in GL and VZ. The influence of Buber is recently noted by Gollwitzer 1976, 68ff.

The influence of Heidegger is most clear in ²GD, cf. e.g.p. 114f, where Heim says that the philosophy of Heidegger is "lebenswahr", p. 122. The influence of Rickert is obvious in G 63ff. The passage concerns different meanings of a subject. Of course, the influence of Kant is great. But to investigate this matter throughly would lead us far beyond the limits of our task.

[16] Timm 1968, 65ff; Gilch 1975, 107. The relation of Heim to the thought of Teilhard de Chardin is noted by Daecke 1967, 222ff.

[17] Concerning Heim's relation to contemporary theology cf. e.g. Michalson 1953, 373 and Köberle 1979, 119ff. Cf. also Holmer 1954, 207.

[18] This Heim himself admits, GL 29. By the expression "dialectical theology" we shall mean the theology, influenced by Barth in the twenties and thirties. For a general presentation of it, cf. e.g. Zahrnt 1972, chap. 1—4.

[19] We shall return to the subject in 3.1.

[20] E.g. in VZ 58.

[21] We shall return to it in 5.2.3.

[22] GN 243ff, WW 17f.

[23] GD 15f.

[24] ²GD 15ff.

[25] ²GD 409ff.

[26] We shall treat this in 2.2 and 3.4.

[27] GL 32, 34f, cf. G 274.

[28] Cf. 3.4.

[29] Cf. ²GD 17f, GN 34.

[30] Timm 1968, 20ff.

[31] GL 561ff.

[32] JH 136f.

[33] Timm 1968, 13f,47, Barbour 1956, 237.

[34] GN 29.

[35] We shall treat this in 6.2.

[36] Reported by Köberle in "Karl-Heim-Gesellschaft Rundbrief" 2/1979.

[37] Cf. Zahrnt 1972, 268.

[38] This feature signifies WZ.

[39] Cf. e.g. Schmithals 1966, 201ff; Malevez 1958, 81.

[40] We shall return to this in 3.4.

[41] Good surveys are given by Ruttenbeck 1925 and Michalson 1953.

[42] Timm 1968, 45, cf. also Köberle 1979, 114ff.

[43] A 387. This paper is a comment on WZ. Cf. also GL 39f and GD 44.

[44] WZ 239ff.

[45] We shall make some more remarks on this in 3.1.

[46] A 386, cf. GN 26.

[47] GN 32.

[48] Cf. Timm 1968, 44.

[49] Heim can be critizised on this point. There is a difference if, in the inference from sience to religion, science is a necessary or a sufficient condition for the inferred rligious belief to be acceptable. Heim's position is valid only if science is a necessary condition.

[50] LI 72f.

[51] GL 58f presents several examples. Cf. also WW chap. 12—16, 20—21.

[52] A 388. Cf. Timm 1968, 44ff.

[53] A 387f, LI 89. Cf. WZ 258f.

[54] In 3.3.

[55] ²GD 21f. Cf. Timm 1968, 32ff and Michalson 1953, 367f. Heim's position has some similarities to Torrance's, Torrance 1978, 113f.

[56] For a god presentation of this feature in Heim's thought, cf. Holmer 1954. Cf. also 3.1.
[57] ^{2}GD 21.

1.4 On the continuity of Heim's thought

[1] This seems to be the general position of phenomenology, and the term is here applied to Heim in this general sense. Cf. v Peursen 1972, 26ff (esp 41f) and Føllesdal 1972, 424. We shall treat the matter more in detail in 4.2.

[2] PA 61f, WZ 11f.

[3] LI 15, G 226f, cf. GL 140f.

[4] ^{2}GD 125, GD 48.

[5] WW 64f.

[6] Cf. GL 15.

[7] PA 69ff, WZ 35f cf. also 98f, 119.

[8] GN 158, JH 22.

[9] WZ 35f, 109f.

[10] WZ 98.

[11] WZ 133.

[12] Cf. 3.2.

[13] G 185ff, cf. 180.

[14] GD 171f, cf. also GN 59ff, 69f and ^{2}GD 157f.

[15] WW chapters 12—15. The most important of them is of course Heisenberg's principle of indeterminancy, ibid 138ff.

[16] Cf. further 3.4. However there is an important distinction between relativity and relativism. The former consists in philosophical analysis and scientific theory and the latter is a kind of worldview. Now a popular (and mistaken) assumption is that relativity in some manner entails relativism, especially concerning questions of ethics. (Cf. the following quotations from Heim in 2.2 and the remarks on the subject in 3.4.)

[17] PA 114, WZ 94, 107.

[18] G 154.

[19] WW 114f.

[20] GD 184ff, GN 156ff.

[21] LII contents and 8, cf. also VZ 111.

[22] G 262ff, cf. GL 28f.

[23] JH 74f, Künneth 1954, 22f and Allen 1950, 28. Cf. also 3.2 note 54.

1.5 An outline of Heim's theory

[1] This attitude is strikingly described by Horton 1938, 128: "Karl Heim has never allowed his message to grow 'irrelevant by anachronism'. No new tendency in modern thought has developed in the last thirty-five years but that he has rushed at once to the spot, entered sympathetically into it, and then proceeded to show, by merciless analysis, how with all its merits it has failed to solve the ultimate human problem, to which only Christ has the answer".

[2] We have touched upon this in Heim's criticism of Bultmann.

[3] We shall treat this concept more in detail in 2.2 and 5.

[4] We shall describe this in 5.1.2.

Chapter 2. Analytical Concepts

2.1. Basic concepts within the analysis

[1] Jeffner 1973, 22f.

[2] Jeffner 1973, 26f.

[3] For a discussion of this cf. Jeffner 1973, 15f, 18f.

[4] This of course depends on what constitutes a correct philosophy. But if a philosophy, which says that philosophical basic assumptions are not intersubjectively testable by rational arguments is accepted, then this claim must be rationally defended.

[5] E.g. Barbour 1974, 77. There he says concerning models, that they, in order to be complementary must (1) refer to the same entity, and (2) be of the same logical type. Heim's view, if interpreted as a model as we shall see, fulfills these demands.

[6] Barbour 1974, 75ff.

[7] On this cf. e.g. Barbour 1974, 71.

[8] This example is from Heim, JW 188. Cf. further Allen 1950, 36f.

[9] E.g. Jeffner 1967, 73f. Cf. also GN 21ff, 180ff.

[10] Cf. our presentation of Kuhn in 6.1. Heim treats the subject in WW 70ff.

[11] Cf. GN 21ff, 180ff.

[12] Bråkenhielm 1975, 187f.

[13] Bråkenhielm 1975, 188f.

[14] This Heim admits, cf. further 3.1. This is a boundary line within theology. But if this assertion is accepted, then the final view depends on how the religious basic assumptions really operate. Here are two basic interpretations: (1) They operate in exactly the same manner as other basic assumptions, but their difference consist in their respective scopes. (2) They operate in an analogical manner, and this analogy can further be conceived in different ways. But we shall not discuss it more here. Cf. further Hof 1967, 206ff.

2.2. What do the analytical concepts reveal when applied to Heim?

[1] GN 180ff.

[2] GN 21ff.

[3] Cf. 3.3. ^{2}GD 182, WW 124ff, 146, 239ff.

[4] Heim treats evolutionism i.a. in WuW 36f, 60f, 67f, JH 56f, GL 351ff, mainly concerning the ascent of man. Cf. also Altner 1965, 42f, Hübner 1966, 169ff, and Beck 1979, 57.

[5] GL 490, cf. WW 64f.

[6] ^{2}GD 118f.

[7] Such arguments can be found in G 140ff concerning the non-objectifiable nature of the ego. We shall return to this subject in 3.2.

[8] E.g. GD 41f, 130f, ^{2}GD 64.

[9] Examples of this are the religious basic assumptions.

[10] In 3.1.

[11] WW 64f, cf. G 149, 176.

[12] G 66.

[13] ^{2}GD 47.

[14] ^{2}GD 65. The same idea appears already in WZ 5.

[15] ^{3}GD 77, cf. ^{2}GD 141.

[16] We shall treat this assumption in 3.3.

[17] Cf. 3.3.

[18] We shall present the argument for this in 3.2. It is based on the distinction between objectifiable and non-objectifiable space.

[19] ^{2}GD 74, GL 72f.

[20] In 3.1.
[21] GN 178.
[22] Cf.GN 153f, GD 210f.
[23] They can of course not be made by non-believers.
[24] Cf. GL 17, GD 16, 218ff, G 252f, 273f. Cf also the similarity to the thought of Whitehead on the question, Torrance 1978, 82.
[25] In 5.2.
[26] I.e. the existence of supra-polar space must be a rational possibility.
[27] In 3.4.
[28] GL 14f.
[29] We shall examine it in 3.2.
[30] Cf. 3.4. There Heim argues that only a religious total view of reality can present a non-contradictory total view of reality.
[31] WZ 249, cf. 241.
[32] WZ 239, cf. 253.
[33] ^{2}GD 295ff. GD 213ff.
[34] Cf. ^{2}G 188f and further 3.3. and 3.4.
[35] G 250.
[36] GN 178ff, cf. G 191f.
[37] GL 399, cf. LI 12, 44. Cf. also Kalweit 1921, 99f and Allen 1950, 21, 32f.
[38] GD 223, cf. WW 122.

Chapter 3. Four criteria concerning an acceptable religious belief.

3.1. The criterion of universality

[1] E.g. in GN 255f.
[2] Cf. the long passage from GN 180ff, quoted in 2.1.
[3] LI 75f, 79f, 96f. Thus they do not satisfy (2) in our description of a total view of reality in 2.1. Cf. also Kalweit 1921, 94ff.
[4] WZ 239f, 254, G 47f, GL 488f, Gp 367ff. Cf. also Vollrath 1920, 407f and Köberle 1979, 114f. Our presentation here contradicts that of Traub 1917, 171f. He proposes there an interpretation of Heim according to the Kant-Schleiermacher line, p. 190f. But from another point of view this interpretation can be defended. There is certainly a similarity between Heim's understanding of the believer's relation to God and Schleiermacher's description of it as "absolute dependence". This can be argued from Heim's description of the believer's conviction to have been "placed" (on this cf. 3.4) by God.
[5] ^{2}GD 421ff, cf. 88, GL 29f.
[6] GN 26, cf. GN 180ff again.
[7] We shall not investigate Heim's view on the use of religious language. The point of common reference does not exhaust Heim's position. Perhaps it can be developed in a way similar to Torrance. Cf. Torrance 1978, 177.
[8] GN 255f.
[9] In 3.4 and 5.2.2.
[10] G 32.
[11] G 38, LI 12.
[12] G 31.
[13] JW 188f.
[14] Jeffner 1966, 164.

[14b] G 38.
[15] G 24.
[16] LI 12f.
[17] G 10.
[18] LI 37. Cf. ²GD 168ff.
[19] ²GD 43f.
[20] ²GD 43.
[21] ²GD 44, cf. 45, 47f.
[22] Cf. ²GD 74. Cf. further 5.1.2.
[23] LI 14, G 32. Cf. ²GD 293.
[24] GD 171, cf. 110f, LI 32ff, G 246f, GN 153.

3.2. The criterion of philosophy

[1] See 1.3 note 15.
[2] JH 20f, cf. WuW 175f.
[3] GN 161.
[4] GN 158, cf. GD 195f, ²GD 70.
[5] JH 22f (the italics are ours).
[6] E.g. GN 162, GD 186.
[7] JH 28f, GN 162.
[8] GD 188f.
[9] GN 158.
[10] JH 20.
[11] JH 36.
[12] E.g. JH 19, GN 164.
[13] JH 20f.
[14] JH 22, cf. 28, G 115.
[15] ²GD 48.
[16] ²GD 49.
[17] JH 30f, cf. WW 14.
[18] E.g. G 79ff.
[19] ²GD 279, cf. 151f, GN 35ff.
[20] G 226f, cf. GL 168f.
[21] G 79f. Schneider 1951, 130f 151n says that the indirect way of demonstrating the existance of non-objectifiable space contradicts the assertion that objectifiable and non-objectifiable spaces are equally real.
[22] G 77.
[23] GD 123f.
[24] G 76ff.
[25] On Heim's criticism of empiricism, cf. Kalweit 1921, 97f.
[26] G 82.
[27] G 90, 95. Cf. also ²GD 167ff.
[28] G 86.
[29] G 116. On Heim's analysis of time see the criticism of Schmidt 1927, 197ff and Traub 1921, 410f. Due to the division of time into these instants, Heim cannot then recombine them in a satisfactory way. The solution of Traub and Schmidt is: Accept time as a sui generis phenomenon of continuity. Cf. further Schneider 1950, 168f. We shall return to this idea in chapter 6.2.
[30] Cf. G 154.
[31] G 179.
[32] G 148, cf. GD 117.

[33] ^{2}GD 150f, cf. G 80, 147.

[34] G 226.

[35] GD 101.

[36] GD 105f, cf. ^{2}GD 147, GN 152.

[37] GD 110f, cf. GN 127.

[38] G 80.

[39] WZ 252ff, cf. GN 238, 254f.

[40] G 227. Emmet 1966, 208 translates the term "perspektivische Mitte" by the expression "percipient centre". But because this term seems to involve a psychologistic interpretation of the perspective centre, which says that the perspective depends on human psychology, it is avoided here. The best presentation of Heim's perspective thinking is Thust 1925.

[41] G 141.

[42] G 129f.

[43] GD 83f, cf. GL 141.

[44] GN 100f, cf. further 5.1.1.

[45] GN 138.

[46] ^{2}GD 96.

[47] G 144, cf. 227.

[48] G 147.

[49] ^{2}GD 264.

[50] ^{2}GD 100f, cf. GN 37ff, 44f, Cf. also e.g. Allen 1950, 17f.

[51] E.g. ^{2}G 173 ff, G 169ff, GN 60f.

[52] GL 483.

[53] GL 28f, cf. G 262. Cf. also Eisenhuth 1928, 69.

[54] On the christocentric character of Heim's theology, cf.Traub 1918, 229, Thust 1925, 647f, Bohlin 1926, 47f, Allen 1950, 31ff, Künneth 1954, 22f, Eisenhuth 1958, 659 and Baillie 1968, 98ff.

[55] In 5.2.2.

3.3. The criterion of science

[1] WW 22f.

[2] Cf. WW 27.

[3] WW 25.

[4] Cf. Jeffner 1967, 19ff for a description of the position of an empirical theist.

[5] Because Heim says that the premise for a scientific approach is the abstraction from the subject-object relation. An example of that is Heim's examination of causality. Cf. also LI 80f.

[6] WW 52f.

[7] GD 109f.

[8] ^{2}GD 151.

[9] E.g. ^{2}GD 140. We shall mention some equivalent concepts in 5.

[10] ^{2}GD 128.

[11] ^{2}GD 166.

[12] GN 109.

[13] GN 152f.

[14] ^{2}GD 143f, cf. 136f.

[15] ^{2}GD 162.

[16] ^{2}GD 144f.

[17] GN 153.

[18] An example of such a criticism is, with some hesitation, given by Traub 1932, 78f and 1935, 232f. Schwarz 1966, 60ff correctly refutes it.

[19] ^{2}GD 146.

[20] GD 111. Jørgensen 1955, 76 correctly maintains this feature.

[21] Cf. M 355f. This idea Aukrust 1956, 191f briefly mentions, but he does not develop it. Aukrust's approach seems to be the most worthy of consideration when to defend Heim's rejection of mysticism. (The rejection of mysticism seem to bee common feature in contemporary german protestant theology, cf. Jeffner 1976, 69f). Cf. also GL 412 for an account of Indian mysticism. Heim had in other respects a positive attitude towards Buddhism, cf. Köberle 1979, 113f. We shall make some remarks on the subject in 5.2.2.

[22] GD 113f.

[23] G 177f.

[24] G 178.

[25] G 95.

[26] G 101f.

[27] G 104.

[28] G 105.

[29] G 108.

[30] G 112.

[31] G 99.

[32] G 96.

[33] G 97f.

[34] G 101f.

[35] ²GD 54.

[36] ²GD 57.

[37] ²GD 62.

[38] ²GD 173.

[39] E.G. GL 170, G 188.

[40] The examples from Hospers 1973, 291f are here slightly altered.

[41] G 184.

[42] Heim wholly accepts Hume's analysis of causality, WW 130.

[43] G 184, cf. GL 172ff.

[44] G 185, cf. LI 23f, ²GD 183, E 70f.

[45] G 187, cf. 191 and LI 82f. A background to Heim's reception of the principle of the constancy of energy is given by Timm 1968, 62ff.

[46] G 188f. Similar reasoning appears in ²GD 182f.

[47] G 191.

[48] ²GD 174.

[49] ²GD 174.

[50] ²GD 177f.

[51] ²GD 180.

[52] Taylor 1967, 361.

[53] GD 116. The idea appears already in WZ 98f, 133, cf. 138.

[54] GD 127.

[55] Maxwell 1974, 150.

[56] WW 138ff. Cf. also GL 170.

[57] GD 174, cf. GL 172.

[58] The term is borrowed from Schwarz 1966, 16.

[59] GD 34, cf. G 186, ²GD 147.

3.4. The existential criterion

[1] Cf. e.g. Hospers 1973, 240ff, Nordenfelt 1974, 37ff or Halldén 1967, 54ff for a brief survey.

[2] On the concept of understanding cf. e.g. von Wright 1971, 5f, 30f.

[3] This position has some connections with Tillich's wellknown method of correlation. Heim also states that the answer must be independent of the question, JH 50. Similar ideas can also be found in the theology of B F Westcott, Olofsson 1979, 53, 58ff, 289.

[4] LI 2, cf. ²GD 174ff, ²G 189.

[5] LI 4, cf. ²GD 31ff. Cf. also on the religious version of the question as a question of meaning, ²GD 320 which is asked concerning reality as a whole, ²G 186. Cf. also Cullberg 1933, 143.Bonhoeffer 1960, 139f, 157 says in his critisism of Heim that Heim is mistaken on this point from the very beginning.

[6] JH 18, cf. 14, GD 184ff, 190, 197f. The close connection between religion and morality is stated in LI 59ff.

[7] This corresponds to Heim's distinction "Denken-Handeln".

[8] E 54ff, ²GD 295.

[9] Cf. e.g. Halldén 1967, 9ff, Furberg 1975, 17ff.

[10] So also Bonhoeffer 1960, 148, 157.

[11] Cf. 3.2 and 3.3.

[12] Bonhoeffer says in his criticism of Heim that they are in fact identical 1960, 148, 158.

[13] Cf. GN 84ff which concerns the question of whether or not the universe as a whole is animated. Cf. also GL 172f.

[14] GD 185ff.

[15] Heim's notion of the perspective center is perhaps an example of this.

[16] On this subject, cf. Eisenhuth 1928, 43, 50 and Michalson 1953, 371f. Eisenhuth says that in WZ and ¹G the concept of decision is the central concept, which, under the influence of Spengler and Einstein, in ²G has been replaced by the concept of destiny, which further, under the influence of Rickert, in ³G is transformed to the concept of non-objectifiable space. However, this development does not affect our reasonings here. Cf. also GL 26ff.

Heim himself is clearly aware of his dependence of both Spengler (GL 389), Einstein (GL 131f, G 146f) and Rickert (G 62ff) (Traub 1933, 89 says that Heim has misinterpreted Rickert's notion of relativity).

We shall also in this connection comment on a minor debate between Heim and Vollrath concerning the use of non-theological concepts within theology. The concept under consideration here was the notion of destiny. (The matter is also noted by Eisenhuth 1928, 47). Though Vollrath 1921, 330ff does not explicitly accuse Heim of using "unterchristliches" concepts, which Eisenhuth ascribes to Vollrath, he is critical. Heim replies very significantly in G 248 that he, in spite of the criticism ". . . das Wort Schicksal zum Ausgangspunkt für das Verständnis der Gottesglaubens nehme. Gerade weil auch des Gottlose das Schicksal kennt und bekennt. Es gilt den Punkt genau festzustellen, bis zu dem wir mit dem Gottlosen zusammengehen können. Dann wird um so klarer, wo die Wege sich trennen und auf der einen Seite die Schicksalsanbetung steht, auf der andern Seite Vertrauen und Gemeinschaft. . .". Cf. also G iv.

A similar ciriticism concerning the notion of supra-polar space is correctly rejected by Schwarz 1966. Cf. also Bonhoeffer 1960, 143, 150f.

[17] E.g. GL 142. WW 115f. The importance and the reception of the theory of relativity in Heim's thought is treated by Timm 1968, 65ff, cf. also 41 where Timm reports, without mentioning his source, a remarkable utterance of Einstein's who said that Heim was one of the very few who had really understood the theory of relativity in all its consequences. Köberle 1979 also touches upon the matter also without any information concerning the source.

[18] Cf. e.g. Schwarz 1966, 21f.

[19] This is Heim's position e.g. in GL 406ff, ²G 173, G 169.

[20] [2]G 175.

[21] WuW 74.

[22] G 170.

[23] G 171.

[24] [2]G 180.

[25] [2]G 178. But Traub 1921, 397 objects that the concept is not wholly neutral.

[26] Schott 1931, 65 is therefore not right when he says: "Das Schicksal ist bei ihm (i.e. Heim) wesentlich der Kausalzusammenhang, in dem ich stehe". And the minor modifications Schott makes in the following cannot remove this judgement.

[27] G 240.

[28] GL 378.

[29] [2]GD 307.

[30] [2]GD 306, 317. It is not our task to examine the influence of Kierkegaard on Heim. But there seems to be some similarity between them on this point, e.g. on the relation between despair, sin and guilt. On these concepts in Heim, cf. e.g. JH 129ff and JW 23ff and concerning Kierkegaard Lindström 1943, 88f, 212. But when Bohlin 1926, 46 says that Heim is "strongly influenced" by Kierkegaard then this seems to be an exaggeration. Aulén 1925, 25 judges more correctly: "The contemporary 'irrationalism', including Heim's, is different from that of Kierkegaard". Cf. also Ruttenbeck 1926, 51.

[31] LI 2, G 242ff, WW 115ff. Causality cannot explain my destiny. Cf. also Traub 1921,397.

[32] GL 392.

[33] [2]G 178.

[34] [2]G 179. A comment on this is given by Traub 1921, 396.

[35] [2]GD 330. But the concepts of placing and destiny do not in themselves imply contradictions, Traub 1921, 398 correctly notes.

[36] G 252, 244f.

[37] E 72f.

[38] E 42.

[39] E 57ff.

[40] JH 31, cf. Traub 1971, 189.

[41] Cf. 1.4 note 16.

[42] Cf. E 54 concerning the foundations of Christian ethics.

[43] That reality is, of course, for Heim, God.

[44] We shall not discuss the distinction between "historisch" and "geschichtlich" here. Heim, as well as Torrance 1969, 63, 72 wants to overcome it because it is misleading. The real distinction is rather between polar and supra-polar space, and God's revelation takes place within polar space, and thus it must be both "historisch" and "geschichtlich". An event which is a revelation of God cannot be explained by the framework of objectifiable space. They are "... notwendig im Widerstreit mit der Gegenständlichen ... Erkenntnis ..." LI, 19. But on the other hand they must consist in some "greifbaren Tatbestand", LI 38. This latter property is another point of common reference. Cf. also Traub 1917, 191f. Cf. also LII 7f, G 244f, JH 52, 176, GN 230.

[45] [2]GD 7f.

[46] [2]GD 319ff, cf. 330, LI 8f, JH 31.

[47] Cf. the presentation of Heim's ethical theory above.

[48] In [2]GD 101f, Heim gives some examples of this. Cf. also JH 83f.

[49] [2]GD 199.

[50] Cf. our considerations of the rejection of alternative answers below.

[51] [2]GD 315f. This can be interpreted as a kind of analogy to other placings, Traub 1918, 228f.

[52] LI 54f, GN 215.

[53] LI 32, cf. 14, 28f.

166

[54] LI 41. Cf. also Kalweit 1921, 108f. Allen 1950, 26 and note 44 above.

[55] E.g. LI 79f.

[56] The following presentation is mainly based on GD 189ff, but cf. also JH 31f.

[57] GD 215.

[58] Cf. LII 25ff.

[59] Cf. LI, 20, 3.2.

[60] Cf. GN 204.

[61] GD 191.

[62] Ibid.

[63] GD 197ff.

[64] GD 193.

[65] GD 195.

[66] GD 194f. Heim gives some early comments on Vaihinger in GL 69ff.

[67] LI 10.

[68] On the use of this principle in a context similar to ours, cf. Jeffner 1966, 253f, 1967, 77 and 1972, 130. He argues that Occam's razor is useful methodological rule within science, but that it can reasonably be asked whether it can be applied to decisions between different total views of reality. Bråkenhielm 1975, 188 treats it as a preference criterion.

Chapter 4. The problem of transcendence

4.1. Different definitions of the concept transcendent/transcendence

[1] GD 100f, 109, G 148f.

[2] ²GD 82.

[3] ²GD 85, cf. 80.

[4] On the terminology cf. 1.4 note 1.

[5] GD 46f, cf. G 174, GN 136.

[6] On the dream argument cf. 3.2.

[7] Cf. GN 175.

4.2. The problem of transcendence in the thinking of Heim

[1] Cf. GN 25ff and the comprehensive presentation given by Daecke 1967, 225f.

[2] Cf. Timm 1968, 54ff for some comments on monism.

[3] GD 13.

[4] Cf. GD 43.

[5] GD 204ff. On Heim's attitude to mysticism, cf. 3.2 note 20 and 5.2.2.

[6] Cf. G 27.

[7] GD 225.

[8] GD 35f.

[9] GD 41.

[10] GD 75.

[11] GD 165.

[12] PA 73f.

[13] GD 75.

[14] G 79f.

[15] G 246f.

[16] Cf. G 31f.

Chapter 5. Heim's solution of the problem of transcendence: The doctrine about polar and supra-polar space.

[1] E.g. GN 134, 141, GD 29, cf. WW 106f and WuW 158f.

[2] GD 31. A historical survey of the philosophy of spaces according to Heim can be found in GN 114ff.

[3] E.g. [2]GD 66.

[4] So Forell 1964, 64 and Gilch 1973, 114f. Cf. GN 167f, 179f.

5.1.1. What is a space?

[1] GD 183f.

[2] WuW 174f.

[3] GN 144f.

[4] GD 60.

[5] GD 118.

[6] GD 87.

[7] GD 63.

[8] WuW 175, GN 111, 145, [2]GD 74f.

[9] [2]GD 58ff, GD 71, 141, GN 143.

[10] GN 175, cf. 145, 253.

[11] WuW 176.

[12] GN 142.

[13] [2]GD 56f, cf. 167ff.

[14] [2]GD 55f.

[15] GN 155, cf. GD 53ff.

[16] G 188.

[17] On this cf. 1.4.

[18] GN 136f, cf. GD 34.

[19] G 71f.

[20] GN 137, cf. 140. Cf. also Schwarz 1966, 24ff.

[21] Ibid., cf. WW 60.

[22] GD 49, cf. ZThK 1928, 418.

[23] In 5.1.2.

[24] GN 192.

[25] G 147. There Heim says, influenced by Einstein, that this is not a psychological law, but an "apriorische Form der ganzen Wirklichkeit" and a "Grundform des jeden möglichen Erfahrung".

[26] GN 145f, cf. 87ff, 118f, WW 95f.

5.1.2. How is a new space discovered?

[1] Cf. GN 151.

[2] In 3.4.

[3] GN 149ff.

[4] GD 72.

[5] GD 73.

[6] GN 175f, 253.

[7] JH 176. Cf. also Schjelderup 1921, 87ff, when he interprets what he calls Heim's "five-step-doctrine", derived from LI 70ff.

5.1.3. How are different spaces related to eachother?

[1] Cf. ²GD 166 and concerning the law of polarity in 3.2.
[2] Cf. GD 54ff.
[3] GD 50f, 57.
[4] GD 51, 57. We have remarked on this in 5.1.1.

5.2.1. What is supra-polar space?

[1] GD 41.
[2] E.g. GN 171, 180.
[3] GN 212.
[3] We shall examine this concept in 5.2.3.
[5] We shall examine this more in detail in 5.2.3.
[6] GD 218.
[7] GN 183, 192ff. Cf. also Forell 1964, 64.
[8] E.g. WW 154ff. Concerning Heim on prayer cf. Alhonsaari 1973, 101ff and on miracles Forell 1967, 204ff, 346ff and Schwarz 1966, 128ff, 153ff, 165ff.
[9] WW 171, GN 178f.
[10] GN 250.
[11] GN 178f, cf. GD 34.
[12] GN 169.
[13] JH 45.
[14] JH 155.
[15] Cf. further 5.2.3.
[16] JH 173.
[17] JH 167. God is non-objectifiable, G 245f, ²GD 318. Cf. also Jørgensen 1955, 81.
[18] GN 218ff, cf. JH 38ff.
[19] GN 215.
[20] Cf. GN 217f, ²GD 263, GL 159.
[21] Cf. GL 454, JH 152.
[22] GD 206f.
[23] GD 195f, JH 22, cf. ²GD 47 and JH 47f.
[24] GD 203.

5.2.2. How is supra-polar space to be discovered?

[1] ²GD 334 (italics ours), cf. also GN 183, G 251f.
[2] GN 192f.
[3] GN 250. This is stated already in WZ 237f.
[4] JH 176.
[5] GN 246f.
[6] GN 176f.
[7] JH 51.
[8] In 3.4 and 4.2.
[9] GN 192, cf. LI 14, GD 193, WW 154.
[10] GN 194.
[11] In 3.4.
[12] In 3.4.
[13] GN 207.
[14] JH 151f.
[15] GN 246.

[16] ^{2}GD 304, cf. 37.

[17] ^{2}GD 306.

[18] Cf. also GL 497ff, WZ 289f. Otherwise there are similarities between Heim and Otto, cf. Baillie 1964, 215 where a presentation of Otto's theory also is given. We shall not discuss the correctness of Heim's criticism.

[19] GN 154.

[20] GL 337. The thought is already stated in WZ 260ff.

[21] GL 498, cf. 343f, 468f, 475, WZ 253ff.

[22] GL 338.

[23] GL 343, GD 210, cf. LI 11.

[24] ^{2}GD 390f, cf. LII 5, GN 176.

[25] ^{2}GD 421. Cf. also WZ 236, LI 34, WW 194f.

[26] JH 184. Cf. Traub 1918, 230.

[27] ^{2}GD 415.

[28] JH 59, 73, 156, G 258f, GL 348, LII 4f.

[29] Cf. Aukrust 1956, 192f and 3.2 note 54.

[30] GN 198, cf. ^{2}GD 363, 388 where Jesus is stated to be the centre of meaning. Cf. also WZ 196.

[31] JH 61f. The same is already stated in WZ 196.

[32] JH 75, cf. ^{2}GD 288, GL 485.

[33] G 264f. Cf. Kalweit 1921, 99f.

[34] ^{2}GD 363f.

[35] GL 343.

[36] G 263. Cf. also Allen 1950, 28.

[37] ZThK 1928, 430f, cf. JH 23, LI 42ff, GL 506, WW 122, WZ 249. No arguments from the content of experience can be given.

[38] LI 36ff.

[39] JH 61, GL 484f, cf. GN 193, GD 215.

[40] Cf. ^{2}GD 380, LI 6.

[41] LI 37.

[42] ^{2}GD 215.

[43] GD 157, cf. ^{2}GD 322.

[44] ^{2}GD 215.

[45] GD 157.

[46] Ibid.

[47] ^{2}GD 234.

[48] Cf. JH 87f.

[49] ^{2}GD 219.

[50] GD 161.

[51] GD 162, cf. JH 163f.

[52] ^{2}GD 321.

[53] JH 178.

[54] JH 184, cf. WuW 96.

[55] Cf. JH 123, GN 185, WuW 96.

[56] GN 239, WW 122, LI 12.

[57] G 31ff, 253.

[58] GN 59, 73. Cf. Schwarz 1966, 31ff for the best presentation.

[59] GD 173.

[60] GD 172f.

[61] GD 172.

[62] In 3.3.

5.2.3. The relation between polar and supra-polar space

[1] It is difficult to translate the term "Aufhebung". The proposals elimination or removing all suffer from some inadequacy. Perhaps the meaning of the word is somewhat explained by the saying that supra-polar space transforms polar space without abrogating it. Cf. also the meaning of the term in Hegel's philosophy, e.g. Taylor 1965, 119. Heim's use of the term is similar to Hegel's.

[2] GN 174, GD 179f.

[3] The notion of "Aufhebung" is not the same as being dimensionally delimited.

[4] GD 212, cf. WB 91.

[5] JH 35.

[6] GD 182f, cf. 12.

[7] GN 198, cf. WW 171.

[8] GN 208.

[9] GN 212.

[10] GD 75.

[11] WW 168.

[12] GD 209.

[13] E.g. WB 47.

[14] WuW 72, GD 180, 208f.

[15] This contains two difficulties, mentioned by Traub 1934, 242f, 245ff. He says there (1) that the very notion of a limit of dimension is ambiguous, p. 243. He is right in this but has not realized that this is the very point in Heim's theory. Traub also says (2) that for this reason it can not be applied to the transcendence of God, and also that even if it could be applied, it would have been inadequate, because it refers only to the one side of the relation between God and the world. But Heim does not explicitly apply it.

[16] Cf. Forell 1973, 36 for a general description of the position. Cf. also Barbour 1972, 436f and Daecke 1967, 230.

[17] E.g. GL 64ff, WuW 72, GN 177. Some comments on this theme can be found in Schwarz, 1966, 177ff. Cf. also Torrance 1978, 83 and Barbour's interesting comment on process philosophy and the dynamic view of reality, Barbour 1956, 234. It would be interesting to treat this matter more.

[18] Cf. GN 72ff.

[19] GN 168f.

[20] Heim interprets the doctrine of the fall as a fall into the state of polarity, e.g. WB 46f. This fall is, however, not a "historisch" event, and the story on Genesis 3 must not be literally understood. The fall takes place ". . . jenseits des Gesichtskreis aller Naturwissenschaft und Geschichtsforschungen. . .". The matter is more in detail treated in WuW 75ff. Heim's interpretation of the doctrine of the fall is called "gnostic" by Althaus 1966, 419.

[21] WuW 136.

[22] Cf. WuW 167f.

[23] WuW 157, cf. WB 87.

[24] GD 212, WuW 135.

[25] WuW 73. Cf. also Altner 1965, 40 ff.

[26] WB 46, cf. 22ff, LII, 37f.

[27] WB 87f, JW 148ff, 209, LII 84ff.

[28] WuW 139, WB 87f.

[29] On this cf. Schwarz 1966, 131f, 162f, 174ff.

[30] GN 227.

[31] LII 88, JW 213.

[32] Cf. Bonhoeffer 1960, 151.

Chapter 6. Discussion of some features in Heim's theology.

6.1. Heim, Kuhn and Torrance

[1] E.g. Barbour 1974, 92ff and on religion p. 119ff, Mitchell 64ff.

[2] Kuhn 1970, 175.

[3] Masterman 1978, 61ff.

[4] Kuhn 1970, 67. Cf. also the quotations given by Mitchell 1973, 64.

[5] Kuhn 1970, viii.

[6] Kuhn 1970, 23.

[7] Kuhn 1970, 10.

[8] Kuhn 1970, 31.

[9] Kuhn 1970, 37, 46f, 103, 184, cf. Barbour 1974, 116.

[10] Kuhn 1970, 43f.

[11] Kuhn 1970, 36ff.

[12] Kuhn 1970, 11.

[13] Kuhn 1970, 97.

[14] Kuhn 1970, 146.

[15] Kuhn 1970, 61.

[16] Kuhn 1970, 61.

[17] Kuhn 1970, 65.

[18] Kuhn 1970, 42.

[19] Kuhn 1970, 77f.

[20] Barbour 1974, 93, 105.

[21] Kuhn 1970, 121f, cf. 129f. This is exactly Heim's view, ²GD 67.

[22] Kuhn 1970, 109, cf. Mitchell 1973, 75ff.

[23] Kuhn 1970, 123.

[24] Kuhn 1970, 111, cf. Mitchell 1973, 65f.

[25] Kuhn 1970, 85, 114.

[26] On this cf. Mitchell 1973, 80f, Barbour 1974, 110f.

[27] Kuhn 1970, 153, Barbour 1974, 105 on paradigm-dependence of criterias.

[28] Kuhn 1970, 158 (italics ours). Cf. also Barbour 1974, 143ff for some comments.

[29] Kuhn 1970, 155.

[30] Kuhn 1970, 185.

[31] Kuhn 1970, 84f, cf. 66, 94, 144.

[32] Kuhn 1970, 82.

[33] Kuhn 1970, 169.

[34] Kuhn 1970, 141.

[35] Kuhn 1970, 129f.

[36] Kuhn 1970, 149.

[37] Kuhn 1970, 122.

[38] Cf. 3.4, 3.2.

[39] Cf. 5.1.2.

[40] ²GD 309ff, G 249ff, ZThK 1928, 429ff.

[41] Torrance is acquainted with Heim's thought but he does not mention Heim in connection with the ideas we shall present in the following.

[42] However it can certainly be argued that Torrance shares Heim's general approach to the relation between science and religion, and it is probably also possible to discover some kind of criterias similar to those of Heim, underlying Torrance's general approach, cf. 1978, 288 and 1976, 180. Concerning the point of interest here they are at least partly influenced by the same sources, e.g. Einstein. Another similarity is the dynamic view of reality. Torrance e.g. 1976, 184 presupposes such a view influenced i.a. by Einstein and Polanyi. There is an appearent similari-

ty between Torrance's interpretation of space and time as relational concepts, 1976, 186f, 1978, 22, 44f, 47f, and the view of the early Heim in PA and WZ. Cf. on this Ruttenbeck 1925, 4ff, 11f, and Eisenhuth 1928, 2f, 9f. However, connected with Torrance's view are some other epistemological and metaphysical presuppositions which we shall not deal with here.

[43] Torrance 1976, 188. The argument from Gödel can be found in e.g. 1978, 259ff and 1976, 180.

[44] Torrance 1976, 15.

[45] Torrance 1976, 15. This acceptance is a kind of personal acceptance, "not made by formal arguments between the two alternatives", 1976, 16. Torrance's idea is that the incarnation and resurrection of Christ are such ultimate facts determining Christian theology.

[46] Torrance 1976, 189, cf. again 1978, 259ff. The relation is a kind of logical relation, but it is also "different levels of inquiry", 1976, 191. This corresponds exactly to Heim.

[47] Torrance 1978, 296, cf. 1976, 120f.

[48] Torrance 1978, 228.

[49] Torrance 1978, 229, cf. 260f.

[50] Torrance 1978, 15.

[51] Torrance 1976, 231.

6.2. Concluding remarks

[1] The presentation is based on Forell 1967, 332f.

[2] Cf. 3.2.

[3] This differs from Forell 1967, 347.

[4] These spaces are discovered in the same way, cf. 5.1.2, 5.2.2.

[5] Forell 1967, 347.

[6] E.g. G 78ff, ²GD 42ff, GD 121, 75, 253, GL 172f, GN 141.

[7] This Heim stated already in WZ 98f, 133. On the dynamic view and its connections to process philosophy, cf. Barbour 1965, 234. Cf. also 6.1. note 42 above.

[8] Maxwell 1974 gives an outline of such an ontology. Nordenfelt 1976, 43ff gives a presentation of basic concepts with respect to such an ontology.

[9] In 4.2.

[10] In 2.1.

[11] In 3.1.

[12] ZThK 1928, 418ff.

[13] G 52f.

[14] GL 488f.

Literature

Adam, K. 1936: Karl Heim und das Wesen der Katholizismus: Gesammelte Aufsätze. Augsburg.

Alhonsaari, A. 1973: Prayer. An Analysis of Theological Terminology. Helsingfors.

Allen, E.L. 1950: Jesus our Leader. London.

Altner, G. 1965: Schöpfungsglaube und Entwicklungsgeschichte in der protestantischen Theologie zwischen Ernst Haeckel und Teilhard de Chardin. Zürich.

Althaus, P. 1966: Die christliche Wahrheit (6th ed.). Gütersloh.

Aukrust, T. 1956. Forkyndelse og historie. Bergen.

Aulén, G. 1921: I vilken riktning går nutidens teologiska tänkande? Sveriges kristliga studentrörelses skriftserie 133. Stockholm.

Beck, H.W. 1979: Biologie und Weltanschauung. Neuhausen-Stuttgart.

Beck, J.T. 1870: Einleitung in das System der Christlichen Lehre oder Propädeutische Entwicklung der Christlichen Lehrwissenschaft. (2nd enl. ed.). Stuttgart.

Baillie D.M. 1968: God was in Christ (3rd ed.). London.

Baillie, J. 1929: The Interpretation of Religion. Edinburgh.

Barbour, I.G. 1956: Karl Heim on Christian Faith and Natural Science. The Christian Scholar Vol. 39, 229–237.

– 1972: Issues in Science and Religion (3rd ed.) Trowbridge.

– 1974: Myths, Models and Paradigms. The Nature of Scientific and Religious Language. Chatham.

Bohlin, T. 1926: Tro och uppenbarelse. Stockholm.

Bonhoeffer, D. 1960: Karl Heim: Glaube und Denken. Gesammelte Schriften III, 138–159. München.

Brattgård, H. 1955: Bibeln och människan i M.F. Roos teologi. Lund.

Bråkenhielm, C.R. 1975: How Philosophy shapes Theories of Religion. Nyköping.

Cullberg, J. 1933: Das Du und die Wirklichkeit. Uppsala.

Daecke, S.M. 1967: Teilhard de Chardin und die evangelische Theologie. Die Weltlichkeit Gottes und die Weltlichkeit der Welt. Göttingen.

Eisenhuth, H.E. 1928: Das Problem der Glaubensgewissheit bei Karl Heim. Studien zur systematischen Theologie I. Göttingen.

– 1958: Im Gedenken Karl Heims. Theologische Literaturzeitung Vol. 83, 657–662.

Emmet, D. 1966: The Nature of Metaphysical Thinking. Edinburgh.

Forell, U. 1964: Gud och Rummet. Vår Lösen Vol. 55, 64-71.

– 1967: Wunderbegriffe und logische Analyse. Lund.

– 1970: Begreppet Guds verksamhet i ljuset av naturvetenskapliga förklaringstyper. Forell-Lyttkens, Religion, erfarenhet, verifikation. Lund.

Furberg, M. 1975: Allting en trasa? Lund.

Føllesdahl, D. 1972: An Introduction to Phenomenology for analytical Philosophers: Olson, R.E. and Paul, A.M. (Eds.) Contemporary Philosophy in Scandinavia, 417-429. Baltimore.

Gilch, G. 1973: Die Theologie Karl Heims heute. Zum 100 Geburtstag von Karl Heim am 20 Januar 1974. Luther, Zeitschrift der Luthergesellschaft 1973.

Gollwitzer, H. 1978: Martin Bubers Bedeutung für die protestantische Theologie. Leben als Begegnung. Ein Jahrhundert Martin Buber (1878–1978). Vorträge und

Aufsätze. Veröffentlichungen aus dem Institut Kirche und Judentum bei der kirchliche Hochschule. Berlin.

Halldén, S. 1967: Universum, döden och den logiska analysen. (2nd ed.). Uddevalla.

Heim, K. 1902: Psychologismus oder Antipsychologismus? Entwurf einer erkenntnistheoretischen Fundamentierung der modernen Energetik. Berlin. (PA)

— 1904: Das Weltbild der Zukunft. Eine Auseinandersetzung zwischen Philosophie, Naturwissenschaft und Theologie. Berlin. (WZ)

— 1906: Eine neue Apologetik. Die Reformation. Deutsche evangelische Kirchenzeitung für die Gemeinde Vol. 5, 386–389. (A)

— 1911: Das Gewissheitsproblem in der Systematischen Theologie bis zu Schleiermacher. Leipzig. (Gp)

— 1916: Glaubensgewissheit. Zur Lebensfrage der Religion. Leipzig. (^{1}G)

— 1920: Glaubensgewissheit. Eine Untersuchung über die Lebensfrage der Religion. (2nd ed). Leipzig (^{2}G).

— 1923: Leitfaden der Dogmatik I. (3rd ed.). Halle a d Saale. (LI)

— 1925: Leitfaden der Dogmatik II. (3rd ed.). Halle a d Saale. (LII)

— 1926: Der protestantische Mensch: Der Protestantismus der Gegenwart. Stuttgart (M)

— 1928: Glaube und Leben. Gesammelte Aufsätze und Vorträge. (3rd ed.) (GL)

— 1928: Zur Frage der Glaubensgewissheit. Zeitschrift für Theologie und Kirche. Vol. 9 N.S., 417–431. (ZThK 1928)

— 1931: Die Weltanschauung der Bibel. (6th–8th ed.) Leipzig. (WB)

— 1931: Glaube und Denken. Philosophische Grundlegung einer christlichen Lebensanschauung. (2nd ed.). München. (^{2}GD)

— 1949: Glaubensgewissheit. Eine Untersuchung über die Lebensfrage der Religion. (4th ed.). Leipzig. (G)

— 1952: Weltschöpfung und Weltende. Glückstadt. (WuW)

— 1952: Jesus der Weltvolländer. (3rd. ed.). Glückstadt. (JW)

— 1953: Die christliche Gottesglaube und die Naturwissenschaft. (2nd ed.). Glückstadt. (GN)

— 1954: Die Wandlung im naturwissenschaftlichen Weltbild. (3rd ed.). Glückstadt. (WW)

— 1955: Die christliche Ethik. (Ed. by W. Kreutzberg). Regensburg. (E)

— 1955: Jesus der Herr (4th ed.). Glückstadt. (JH)

— 1957: Glaube und Denken. Philosophische Grundlegung einer christlichen Lebensanschauung (5th ed.). Glückstadt. (GD)

— 1957: Ich gedenke der vorigen Zeiten. Glückstadt. (VZ)

Hirsch, E. 1951: Geschichte der neueren evangelischen Theologie II. Gütersloh.

Hof, H. 1967: Att säga det outsägliga. Myt och symbol, 143–215. Stockholm.

Hofmann, O. 1922: Die Eigenart der religiösen Gewissheit. Theologische Studien und Kritiken Vol. 94, 253–306.

Holmer, P.L. 1954: Karl Heim and the Sacrifice of Intellect. Lutheran Quarterly Vol. 6, 207–219.

Horton, W.M. 1938: Contemporary Continental Theology. New York and London.

Hospers, J. 1973: An Introduction to Philosophical Analysis. (2nd rev. ed.). Surrey.

Hübner, J. 1966: Theologie und biologische Entwicklungslehre. München.

Hägglund, B. 1966: Teologins historia. (3rd ed.). Lund.

Jeffner, A. 1966: Butler and Hume on Religion. A comparative Analysis. Stockholm.

— 1967: Filosofisk religionsdebatt. Stockholm.

— 1972: The Study of Religious Language. Bristol.

— 1973: Livsåskådningsforskning. Uppsala.

— 1976: Kriterien christliche Glaubenslehre. Eine prinzipielle Untersuchung heutiger protestantischer Dogmatik im deutscher Sprachbereich. Uppsala.

Jørgensen, P.H. 1967: Die Bedeutung des Subjekts-Objektsverhältnisses für die Theologie. Vinderup.

Kalweit, P.: 1921: Einführung in die Religionsphilosophie. (2nd ed.). Leipzig.

Kuhn, Th. 1970: The Structure of Scientific Revolutions. (2nd ed.) Chicago.

Künneth, W. 1954: Karl Heims systematisches Lebenswerk. Zum 80. Geburtstag: Evangelische-Lutherisches Kirchenzeitung Vol. 8, 20—23.

Köberle, A. 1959: Theologie der Kontakte. Gedenkenrede für Professor D Dr Karl Heim DD. Theologische Literaturzeitung Vol. 84, 147—152.

— 1964: Gottesglaube und moderne Naturwissenschaft in der Theologie Karl Heims. Neue Zeitschrift für systematische Theologie Vol. 6, 115—125.

— 1974: Die schwäbische-spekulative Erbe in der Theologie Karl Heims. Theologische Beiträge Vol. 5, 14—24.

— 1978: Karl-Heim-Gesellschaft Rundbrief 2/1978.

— 1979: Karl Heim. Leben und Denken. Sindelfingen.

Lindström, V. 1943: Stadiernas teologi. En Kierkegaard-studie. Lund.

Malevez, 1958: The Christian Message & Myth. London.

Martensen, H. 1881: Jacob Bøhme. Theosophiske Studier. Köpenhamn.

Masterman, M. 1978: The Nature of a Paradigm. Criticism and the Growth of Knowledge, ed. by J. Latakos & A. Musgrave. New York.

Maxwell, N. 1974: Can there be Necessary Connections between Succesive Events? The Justification of Induction, ed. R. Swinburne. Oxford.

Michalson, C. 1953: The Task of Apologetics in the Future. Scottish Journal of Theology Vol. 6, 362—379.

Nigg, W. 1959: Heimliche Weisheit. Bem-Bümpliz.

Nordenfelt, L. 1974: Explanation of human actions. Uppsala.

— 1977: Events, actions and ordinary language. Lund.

Nygren, A. 1934: Den tyska kyrkostriden. Den evangeliska kyrkans ställning i det "tredje riket". Malmö.

Olofsson, F. 1979: Christus Redemptor and Consummator. A study in the theology of B.F. Westcott. Skara.

v Peursen, C.A. 1972: Phenomenology and Reality. Pittsburgh.

Ruttenbeck, W.: 1925. Die apologetisch-theologische Methode Karl Heims. Leipzig.

Schjelderup, K.V.K. 1921: Positivistisk filosofi og kristelig apologetik. Norsk teologisk tidskrift Vol. 10 N.S., 56—91.

Schmidt, W. 1927: Zeit und Ewigkeit. Gütersloh.

Schmithals, W. 1966: Die Theologie Rudolf Bultmanns. Tübingen.

Schneider, Fr. 1950: Erkenntnistheorie und Theologie. Gütersloh.

Schott, E. 1931: Das Problem der Glaubensgewissheit. Greifswald.

Schwarz, H. 1966: Das Verständnis des Wunders bei Heim und Bultmann. Stuttgart.

Spemann, F. 1932: Karl Heim und die Theologie seiner Zeit. Tübingen.

Taylor, C. 1975: Hegel. London.

Taylor, R. 1967: Art. "Determinism". Encyclopedia of Philosophy 2, 359—373.

Thust, M. 1925: Das perspektivische Weltbild Karl Hems. Zeitwende Vol.1, 634—652.

Timm, H. 1968: Glaube und Naturwissenschaft in der Theologie Karl Heims. Witten-Annen.

Torrance, Th. F. 1976: Space, Time and Resurrection.

— 1978: Theological Science. New York.

Traub, F. 1917: Ueber Karl Heims Art der Glaubensbegründung. Theologische Studien und Kritiken Vol. 89, 168—197.

— 1918: Zur Dogmatik. Monatschrift für Pastoraltheologie Vol. 14, 226—241.

– 1921: Das Irrationale. Zeitschrift für Theologie und Kirche Vol. 2. N.S., 391–424.
– 1933: Erkenntnistheoretische Fragen zu Karl Heims ‚Glaube und Denken'. Zeitschrift für systematische Theologie Vol. 10, 62–93.
– 1935: Die neue Fassung von Karl Heims ‚Glaube und Denken'. Zeitschrift für systematische Theologie Vol. 12, 219–254.
Vollrath, P. 1920: Zum Verständnis der Theologie Karl Heims. Neue Kirchliche Zeitschrift Vol. 31, 401–432.
– 1921: Religionsphilosophie und Gewissenstheologie. Neue Kirchliche Zeitschrift Vol. 32, 317–336.
v Wright G.H. 1971: Explanation and Understanding. London.
Zahrnt, H. 1972: Die Sache mit Gott. Nördlingen.